Revie's unsung Heroes

Away from the headline makers, 11 players recall the Revie Revolution

David Saffer

Vertical Editions
www.verticaleditions.com

First published in the United Kingdom in 2017 by Vertical Editions, Unit 4a, Snaygill Industrial Estate, Skipton, North Yorkshire BD23 2QR

www.verticaleditions.com

ISBN 978-1-904091-98-1

A CIP catalogue record for this book is available from the British Library

Cover design by HBA, York

Printed and bound by Jellyfish Solutions, Swanmore, Hants

Contents

Acknowledgements 5
Foreword 7
Introduction 8
1   Peter McConnell 10
2   John Hawksby 26
3   Ian Lawson 38
4   Rod Johnson 61
5   Barrie Wright 82
6   Nigel Davey 96
7   Dennis Hawkins 114
8   James 'Sean' O'Neill 137
9   Chris Galvin 153
10 Roy Ellam 173
11 Glan Letheren 193
Leeds United Roll of Honour 1961 to 1974 210
Player Records 211
Bibliography 215
About the Author 216

Acknowledgements

I would initially like to thank Peter McConnell, John Hawksby, Ian Lawson, Rod Johnson, Barrie Wright, Nigel Davey, Dennis Hawkins, Sean O'Neill, Chris Galvin, Roy Ellam and Glan Letheren for reminiscing about their Leeds United careers in *Revie's unsung Heroes*. Spending time with each former player was informative, thought provoking and a privilege.

I'd like to also thank John Wray for providing the foreword to this book. An esteemed journalist for five decades, most recently with Gosney's Sports Agency, I've been fortunate to know John a number of years and he is among a handful of writers to have had a unique insight into the Revie era having reported on the club extensively during this period.

Background information is essential and I'm indebted to Phil Goldstone once again for allowing me access to his library of football books. Further statistical information and advice was provided by Gary Shepherd, Vanessa Harrison, staff at the English Schools' Football Association together with club historians Garry Bray (Rotherham United), Gwyn Rees (Swansea City), Ian Rigby (Preston North End) and John Vickers (Lincoln City).

At this juncture, I'd would like to point out that every effort has been made by myself and the publisher to attribute the journalist and periodical for 'match report' clippings noted in this book. This has not been possible in a number of cases, as material used for illustrative purposes did not have original source detail.

Last, but by no means least, a huge thanks to Karl Waddicor of Vertical Editions for publishing this book.

Foreword

Their names may not trip off the tongue like Billy Bremner, Bobby Collins and the like, but Don Revie's unsung Leeds United heroes still had a part to play in the club's rise from relative obscurity to immense prominence at home and abroad.

Many of them have been forgotten, even by long-term supporters, so author David Saffer has produced an intriguing memory-jogger for those of us old enough to remember just some of the names from an era long gone.

They trained with the big names, knowing they had little or no hope of becoming first team regulars as Revie understandably stood by the players whose exploits had brought such glory to Elland Road.

The most successful manager in the club's history was criticised in some circles for failing to break up the Super Leeds side he had built so impressively, and inevitably that policy meant frustration for players who found themselves on the outside looking in.

Some felt they could have been handed more opportunities to break into the first team, while others were realistic enough to accept the inevitable. More were just pleased to play even a small part in the wider picture.

This is their story.

John Wray, Football Journalist and Leeds United Correspondent, 1964 to 2016

Introduction

LEEDS United was a struggling Second Division club when Don Revie began his tenure as player-manager in March 1961. Since United's formation in 1919, no major honours had been won, but that historical fact would change dramatically during a 13-year period with Revie at the helm. Equally adept at battling to victory or putting on the style with free-flowing football, after gaining promotion to the top flight in 1964, Revie led Leeds to the First Division Championship and Inter-Cities Fairs Cup twice, the FA Cup, League Cup and Charity Shield. One of British and European football's most feared outfits, under Revie, United were also First Division runners-up on five occasions, FA Cup finalists three times, Fairs Cup finalists and Cup Winners' Cup finalists.

When football historians look back on this era they often cite Revie's legendary XI – Gary Sprake, Paul Reaney, Terry Cooper, Billy Bremner, Jack Charlton, Norman Hunter, Peter Lorimer, Allan Clarke, Mick Jones, Johnny Giles and Eddie Gray – even though this United team only played one game, versus Mansfield Town in an FA Cup third round tie in 1970. A bizarre fact, but true, because Paul Madeley was always in the side!

Historians also note the endeavours of Bobby Collins, Albert Johannesson, Willie Bell and Alan Peacock as legends whilst United became a force in the game. Other heroes include Jimmy Greenhoff, Rod Belfitt, Mike O'Grady, Mick Bates, Terry Hibbitt, David Harvey, Terry Yorath, Joe Jordan, Trevor Cherry and Gordon McQueen as they were members of trophy winning squads.

It is at this juncture that *Revie's unsung Heroes* begins, because Don selected 75 players to play for Leeds United during his time as manager.

And for every 'first teamer', there were a plethora of footballers where fate, injury, timing, ability or lady luck came between them and an extended first team run.

There are books aplenty about the Revie era packed with stories about famous players, notable matches and achievements, but none from the perspective of players on the 'periphery'. So this was my starting point and it was essential to find a group of former United players that spanned the period from Revie's announcement as 'gaffer' through to the First Division title race of 1973/74.

Peter McConnell, John Hawksby, Ian Lawson, Rod Johnson, Barrie Wright, Nigel Davey, Dennis Hawkins, James 'Sean' O'Neill, Chris Galvin, Roy Ellam and Glan Letheren all played under Don at various times during this timeframe, and I'm indebted to them all for agreeing to tell their stories. Each has a unique tale to tell in terms of how they joined the club and then fared.

I've intertwined their reminiscenes with archival material, in many cases from the players themselves, and press publications of the day to illustrate how their individual journey was reported at the time. Among numerous anecdotes it was a privilege hearing first hand about Revie's first game as manager, Don's initial victory at a fog-bound Old Trafford, apprentice capers, famous triumphs, infamous defeats, injury nightmares, 'offside' goals, first team 'reserve' line-ups, glory goals, Wembley heartache and practice match shenanigans.

This group of footballers trained, travelled and played alongside Bremner and co during a time ensconsed in club folklore. Their stories are enlightening, engaging and noteworthy. Most importantly, they are representative of former Leeds United players often forgotten in the history of time.

This book is dedicated to all of Revie's unsung heroes.

David Saffer

1

Peter McConnell

PETER McConnell witnessed the dawn of a new era when Don Revie took the helm at Leeds United. Major honours had eluded the club since its formation in 1919 but that would change following Revie's appointment as player-manager in March 1961.

McConnell made his first team debut against Bolton Wanderers shortly after Revie's £12,000 transfer from Sunderland and impressed United's new signing with his never-say-die attitude. Indeed, when Revie was set to apply for the vacant manager's job at Bournemouth, he sounded out McConnell about joining him at the south coast club. However, 24 hours later, club director Harry Reynolds announced Revie as United's boss.

The Bournemouth discussion never came up again, and when McConnell played in Revie's first match as manager against Portsmouth, his place in club folklore was assured.

Born in Reddish on the outskirts of Stockport in March 1937, Peter attended North Reddish Primary and Mile End Secondary Schools. Clarence and Dorothy McConnell believed in a hard working ethic and, although a bright pupil, football dominated their elder son's formative years.

McConnell recalled:

Dad was a centre half for Droyslden in the Cheshire League and guested for Manchester City during the war, which really meant a lot to him. He was a useful player but had a fiery reputation that got him sent off on numerous occasions. His name though didn't help if a ref booked him because they thought he was taking the mick when he said it was Clarence McConnell, so after a warning he'd get his marching orders. In the end, dad would sigh and tell them it was Charlie McConnell!

Dad was a real character and so was my mam who would watch his games. And she was one person not to get into an argument with because mam would always win. Fans having a go at my dad would soon know about it as mam would think nothing of giving them a thwack on the back of their head with her handbag!

Kids of my generation played football on the cobbled streets at every opportunity. We were also spoilt in terms of watching top class football because Manchester City and Manchester United played at Maine Road for a number of years after Old Trafford was bombed during the Manchester blitz in March 1941 (Old Trafford reopened in 1949).

My brother, Barry, and I were Reds and one of my earliest recollections was meeting United stars Johnny Carey, Jack Rowley and Henry Cockburn when they visited North Reddish Primary School. That was really memorable for an 11-year-old kid and all three played against Blackpool in the FA Cup Final at Wembley in 1948.

The Cup Final was the big game every season and Blackpool had the great Stanley Matthews in their side. There was huge anticipation from everyone at home and United won 4-2 to lift the Cup.

McConnell won his first honour at 13 years of age when he helped The Brigadoons defeat Bredbury United 2-1 in the Kerbside Cup Final at Stockport United's Edgley Park ground. Seventy one teams took part in the local competition with the Final attracting an attendance of 5,000, a third more than Stockport's clash with Rotherham at the preceding home game.

Representative football followed for Stockport Boys, then Cheshire Boys, which in turn brought the attention of Football League clubs including Leeds United.

McConnell recalled:

Winning meant everything to me, so beating Bredbury was a good start to my football career. As I progressed, I knew scouts had been to games but I had no idea a team had spotted me until I received a letter from Leeds United inviting me to trials. To me this was a big deal, as I really wanted a chance to become a footballer.

The trials seemed to go well but until an offer came in, it was a nervous time. Eventually, I got the news I'd been waiting for but there was a problem, as my start date was before my O levels, so I had to get permission from school to leave before sitting them.

When I went to see the headmaster with my mam, he made it clear that if I joined Leeds as an apprentice, my school place would be given to someone else. And if I didn't make the grade, I would not get a place back at the school. That put a lot of pressure on me but I really wanted to give it a go. Mam had always backed me when it came to football and without batting an eyelid she told him I'd make it at Leeds.

McConnell had never travelled further than Cleveleys, a coastal town four miles north of Blackpool, for annual summer holidays, but crossed the Pennines and moved into digs in Beeston. One of eight 'ground staff boys', life at Leeds United began in earnest.

We cleared the terraces after a match and cleaned the players' boots, but the worst job was rolling the pitch after games because the equipment was hard to use. The banter between the lads was terrific and we used to hide a football behind the stand for a kick about if the head groundsman, Ces Burrows, was not watching. Money was tight though because half of my £5 weekly wages went on digs.

Ivor Powell coached the apprentices and was a real character. There were so many times when he came out with the best comments without realising it. He was really annoyed at half time in one match against Barnsley when we were 2-0 down. Turning his anger to the strikers, he said, "Take a leaf out of Barnsley's forwards … every Tom, Dick and Angle is having a shot at goal,"

Of course, Ivor meant, Tom, Dick and Harry, but the lads were in fits of laugher.

Ivor soon cottoned on to his mistake and saw the funny side of it. But comments apart, Ivor was a great coach and I would team up with him later in my career at Carlisle United.

United's U18 side played in the Northern Intermediate League and was a competitive side but they had no answer to Manchester United's 'Busby Babes' in an FA Youth Cup clash at Old Trafford during the 1952/53 season.

The Youth Cup was the big competition every season so we gave it everything. Duncan Edwards was United's star player and really stood out. We lost 4-0 but it could have been more.

A lot has been written about the 'babes' and they really were something special. Edwards had played for United's first team; he was that good, and in my view, Bobby Moore would not have won so many England caps had Duncan not died in Munich. Bobby played in the perfect position for his skills but Duncan could play anywhere, even centre forward, because he had pace, strength and was unstoppable whether heading or striking a ball. Playing against Edwards was like trying to stop a train because he was such a powerful lad with a massive build.

I played alongside some great players including John Charles at his peak. Big John was a great mate of mine and equally good as a centre forward or centre half. John could score goals for fun but Edwards for me just had the edge on him.

When news broke about Munich it was a huge shock, especially for Jack Charlton because his brother Bobby was on the plane. There was only sketchy news at first about fatalities so it was a tough time. Jack rushed home to see his mother Cissie and we were all relieved when news came through that Bobby had survived. But the world of football mourned the loss of his teammates. I'd known Eddie Coleman in my army days and it was a tragedy.

United's youngsters enjoyed a memorable Youth Cup run during the 1953/54 season by knocking out Blackburn Rovers, Blackpool and Bury to set up a fifth round clash against Manchester City.

John Reynolds scored a hat-trick before a 10,000 crowd at Elland Road but had to retire after sustaining a bad knee injury in the next round against West Brom. He went on to become head groundsman at Elland Road.

We had a fantastic 3-1 win over City, which made local headlines but West Brom knocked us out, which was a massive disappointment although we'd had a great run to the quarterfinals.

John was a great footballer and his injury was terrible. It showed how fragile a football career could be and the lads were all upset for him but unfortunately it is a part of the game.

McConnell progressed to United's reserve team under the watchful eye of Bob Roxburgh and manager Major Frank Buckley but would soon have to impress new boss Raich Carter.

Roxburgh was a straight talking Geordie and not the type of guy you argued with about duties. But I was surprised when, apart from my dressing room duties, he asked me to make sure John Charles arrived at training on time. And I quickly discovered the role was no easy task. Big John lived near the ground but when you knocked on his door he'd not always answer. Eventually he would come down but was often late and it drove Roxburgh mad. John was his own man but when he ran out to play on a Saturday was capable of knocking in a hat-trick so he always got his way!

Carter's appointment was well received and I respected him enormously because of his playing career at Sunderland then Derby County. Some duties were a pain such as running the players' bath, and after his arrival I had the added honour of cleaning his car but it went with the territory.

Duties aside, Carter was great with me and could still play a bit. Every so often, I'd face him in practice matches but daren't tackle him as I wanted a full-time contract on my 17th birthday!

McConnell, on his day of destiny, duly received a full-time contract. In an era of the maximum wage, he was offered a £20 signing on fee, £12 a week during the season and £10 in the summer. But this teenager wanted a better deal.

There was a great sense of achievement getting a contract but I'd spoken with the senior lads and they egged me on to push Carter for a bit more. Raich was always up for a bit of banter so I asked for £12 in the summer like John Charles.

Smiling at me, Raich pointed out John was a far better player.

"Yes," I replied, "But not in the summer!"

Raich took a pause and smiled, then offered me £12 if I became as good a footballer!

Shortly afterwards, I moved into new digs in Beeston. Dilwyn Jones was my roommate and we got on really well.

There were perks playing for Leeds because if you wore your club blazer and showed a players' pass at the Majestic dance hall or La Scala cinema or Mecca ballroom, you got free entry, so our social life was sorted but it was only for a short time because my National Service was only a year away.

McConnell was based in Catterick for National Service and after basic training passed out as a B3 Wireless Operator, prior to taking up a gym instructor role. Posted to Germany, he played for the British Army 1st Armoured Division then resumed his football career with Leeds United in the First Division.

Following promotion in 1955/56, John Charles had plundered a hatful of goals in top-flight football but had now joined Juventus in a world record deal. Bill Lambton succeeded Carter as manager at the end of the 1957/58 campaign and soon new players arrived at the club, including Don Revie from Sunderland in November 1958.

Revie's arrival coincided with consecutive wins against Newcastle United, West Ham and Nottingham Forest. McConnell was 20 years of age when he made his first team debut in United's next match against Bolton Wanderers just before Christmas, 1958.

Crowe (penalty), Gibson and Shackleton scored for Leeds but Bolton won a thrilling game 4-3 with goals from Lofthouse (2), Gibson (og) and Edwards.

Leeds United v Bolton Wanderers, December 20th, 1958

Leeds United: Wood, Ashall, Dunn, McConnell, Charlton, Gibson, Humphries, Crowe, Shackleton, Revie, Overfield

Bolton Wanderers: Hopkinson, Banks, Edwards, Hartle, Hennin, Higgins, Hill, Holden, Lofthouse, Parry, Birch

Promotion was massive for the club, but without Big John the first team picked itself. Leeds made headline news when they signed Don because of his Manchester City days, but he was at the back end of his career. Even so, it was something of a coup. Facing Don in training, he wasn't the quickest of players but was still a great passer of a ball.

Our team bus was about to leave for a reserve match when Roxburgh got on and called out my name because Wilbur Cush had pulled out against Bolton. I was in the starting line-up but everything happened so quickly there was no time for nerves, which was probably a good thing.

It was by far the biggest crowd I'd played before and running out you could sense the excitement. It was a cracking game and although we lost, the team got a standing ovation at the end. Our right half, Archie Gibson, scored at both ends, but Bolton edged it. Nat Lofthouse was an unbelievable player and scored twice that day. Marking him was really tough because he so powerful in the air and strong on the ball. Lofthouse was known as the 'Lion of Vienna' following a famous win for England against Austria (May 1952) when he scored the second goal after being elbowed in the face, tackled from behind and brought down by the goalkeeper.

Nat was brave as they come and during a quick drink afterwards, I asked him who he preferred playing alongside in international football, Stanley Matthews or Tom Finney. Without hesitating, he quipped Matthews, because when Stan crossed the old style football, he'd make sure the lace was away from his forehead!

Following the Bolton match, I was confident of playing first team football, but knew I'd return to the reserves once Cush was fit and that was the next game.

McConnell came back into the first team towards the end of the season when Leeds enjoyed an unbeaten six-match run.

Archie Gibson was not in the best of form so Lambton picked me to play at Blackpool.

Matthews was such an influential player for Blackpool and didn't disappoint home fans because we lost 3-0. But I retained my place in the team which gave me hope I'd become a regular starter.

Jack Taylor had taken the managerial hot seat by the time United's first team squad assembled for pre-season training in 1959/60. But in a dreadful campaign, Leeds hit rock bottom with relegation to the Second Division.

Lambton's appointment baffled me because his training ideas were bizarre. One day he had us diving under and over hurdles on an obstacle course to improve our agility. Needless to say the lads were not too keen. I also remember target practices that often ended with the lads peppering footballs at him. However, some of his ideas stuck including the 'Keep Fighting' sign that stayed up in the changing room for years.

Taylor was a nice feller but had little idea when it came to training or tactics. However, I was in the first team, but pulled a hamstring against Leicester City early in the season. I was desperate not to lose my place so declared myself fit after treatment for a trip to West Ham. But it proved a harsh lesson because my hamstring went inside 10 minutes and I only played a handful of matches the rest of the campaign.

I was not in the team when relegation was confirmed. Confidence had been low throughout the season and going down was dreadful for everyone connected to the club.

When United's woeful form continued into the 1960/61 season, it was clear that a new direction was required at the club. McConnell was preparing for training when Revie was introduced to the first team squad as player-manager.

> The lads were about to go out when Harry Reynolds came into the changing room. Harry was a self-made millionaire and a real character when you got to know him.
>
> "Right lads, I've got some news for you," he said. "We've sacked Jack Taylor and appointed a new manager."
>
> Next thing, Don walks in.
>
> "You all know Don," said Harry. "He's now player-manager but will mainly be managing the team."
>
> Don said a few words, he wanted to be called boss and that was it, then we went out for training.
>
> Of course, we were all shocked and I was really surprised because the day before Don had asked me if I fancied going to Bournemouth as he'd been offered the player-manager's job. I'd only just discussed a possible move with my wife, Mary, who had mixed feelings, but now Don was manager she was pleased, and it didn't take me long to think, I've got a chance here because he likes me. Going to Bournemouth never came up in a conversation again.

Twenty-four hours on and Revie named his team to face Portsmouth at Fratton Park, and though Leeds lost the game 3-1, times were about to change at Elland Road. For the record, Priscott, Saunders and Campbell scored for Pompey with Charlton scoring a consolation goal for the visitors in front of 16,230 spectators.

Portsmouth v Leeds United, March 18th, 1961

Portsmouth: Beattie, Thomas, Wilson, Dickinson, Snowdon, Harris, Priscott, Gordon, Saunders, Brown, Campbell

Leeds United: Humphries, Jones, Kilford, Cameron, Goodwin, McConnell, Francis, Fitzgerald, Charlton, Bremner, Grainger

McConnell recalled:

> We played in the old fashioned W-M 2-3-5 formation. John McCole had replaced Shackleton at centre forward but we were finding goals hard to come by so Big Jack was playing as a makeshift striker because

he was good in the air. I played right half and we were really fired up to do well.

During the first half, I went up for a ball with their centre forward, Ron Saunders, who clattered me and split my eyebrow open. All these years later, my eyebrow still grows funny so I have a legacy from that game. Les Cocker ran on with his 'magic sponge' and Billy Bremner came running over.

I was a bit dazed and while Les was sponging my eye, Billy grinned at me and said, "That's a bad one isn't it," which made me feel a whole lot better!

There were no subs then so one of the lads helped carry me off but I came back on to finish the game. That's how it was in those days, if anyone got injured you were down to 10 men, so unless it was a leg break or something serious, you just got on with it.

I kept a sponge over my eye travelling home to keep the swelling down but I had a 'shiner' for days.

Revie kept faith with McConnell despite the 'shiner' during an inauspicious nine-game run to the end of the season that yielded one victory. However, it was a terrific win as McConnell scored his first goal for the club in a 7-0 romp against Lincoln City. United's scorers aside from McConnell against Lincoln were McCole (2, 1 pen), Bell, Peyton, Bremner, Drysdale (og).

Leeds United v Lincoln City, April 22nd, 1961

Leeds United: Caldwell, Hair, Kilford, Smith E, Charlton, Bell, Bremner, McConnell, McCole, Peyton, Johanneson

Lincoln City: Burden, Barnard, Smith J, Middleton, Jackson, Drysdale, McClelland, Holmes, Punter, Chapman, Bannister

McConnell recalled:

It was one of those days when everything went for us; we won easily and could have scored a few more.

Getting my first goal was a great moment for me but more important, at last I felt a part of the first team set up.

Revie, Les Cocker and Syd Owen went about establishing a professional approach in terms of preparation for matches.

Les and Syd were Don's right hand men and got us ready physically and mentally for matches. Syd was fit as a fiddle and a real disciplinarian. If you were not pulling your weight, he'd tell you straight, whereas Les was more approachable but still got his message across.

Les was really enthusiastic in training sessions and great when it came to banter with the lads. Big Jack liked winding up the lads and thought nothing of having a go at Les about his playing days for Accrington Stanley. Les might have been a foot shorter but would have a go back and chase Jack round the training ground with the lads killing themselves!

Revie had begun to change the philosophy at the club but was under no illusions about the task at hand.

Some of the first team lads played in reserve games to keep up their fitness but didn't always take it seriously. And after Huddersfield Town hammered us in a reseve match 'steam' was coming out of Syd's ears back in the changing room.

"You chuffing lot, you think you're all superstars," he yelled. "You, you and you would not be in a second XI if you were a superstar. I want you all down at Elland Road, tomorrow, Sunday morning, at 10.00am and don't be late."

Next day, Syd set us running off down the main road at a fast pace. I was just a young lad so did what I was told, but a few of the lads jogged along.

Syd then wanted us to sprint between two lamp posts, but again some of the lads just jogged. Syd was now seething. "You chuffing lot, that's it, back to the ground," he screamed.

Back in the changing room, Syd told four lads to see Don on Monday morning.

The following day, Don called me over to tell me the lads that gave Syd a hard time were on the transfer list but I'd impressed him with my attitude so was playing for the first team against Huddersfield Town in a West Riding Cup game on the Tuesday night.

I was chuffed but it was clear that Don was having a clear out of players. He would eventually bring promising apprentices into the first team but that would take time. Until then he had to firefight with players willing to work hard and I came into that category.

United wore an all-white strip for the first time when the 1961/62 campaign kicked off. Early results were encouraging and McConnell enjoyed a mini-scoring spree, but the first team soon struggled for consistency.

> We won our opening two fixtures against Charlton Athletic and Brighton, which was great, but I missed a penalty against Brighton in front of the Kop. And it was just my luck because during the close season, we'd had a competition to be penalty taker as we'd missed a few and Don decided to find a new first choice. Tommy Younger was in goal and a few of the lads stepped up to practice them on Fullerton Park.
>
> I didn't miss one so got the nod, but its one thing banging them in on the training ground then stepping up when the crowd is shouting and carrying on behind the goal. I don't know what came over me against Brighton. Whether it was nerves, who knows, but in training I'd been knocking them in for fun. I'd been side footing them inside the left hand post but on this occasion stubbed my foot and topped it over the stand, so Billy took over the role.
>
> I did hit a 25-yard winner in a League Cup win over Huddersfield Town and then scored in draws against Plymouth Argyle and Southampton. The Town match was one of my best games for Leeds but only playable because the lads helped clear snow off the pitch. And it was enjoyable getting some good press after my goal against Southampton when in fact I'd actually miscued my shot! Don was great though because he praised me, then gave me a knowing wink because he realised I'd not meant it.
>
> My favourite goal, however, was at Swansea Town in a really tough encounter. Don had come back into the side because of injuries and played me in with a great through ball, which I put away to give us the lead, but we went down to a 2-1 defeat.

Following a home loss against Plymouth Argyle on February 24th, 1962, relegation was a real possibility.

Desperate times called for desperate measures as Revie signed Ian Lawson, Cliff Mason and a player that would change the fortunes of Leeds United … Bobby Collins. But with new players coming in, the writing was on the wall for McConnell.

> Don asked me to pop into his office after the Plymouth match and asked if I'd be interested in speaking to Carlisle United because they'd made an inquiry. He could not guarantee first team football anymore so I could talk to them but it was up to me.

Of course, I was disappointed, and with Bobby's arrival I'd be back in the reserves so agreed to think about it, but the interest went quiet.

Bobby scored a smasher from 25 yards on his debut against Swansea, which endeared him to the fans straight away. It was a dream start and suddenly there was a feeling we'd survive.

McConnell's final game for Leeds was against Preston North End. It was also fitting that he was wearing his favoured number 4 shirt.

Preston North End v Leeds United, April 9th, 1962

Preston North End: Barton, Cunningham, Ross, Wylie, Singleton, Smith J, Alston, Biggs, Dawson, Spavin, Thompson

Leeds United: Younger, Hair, Mason, McConnell, Charlton, Smith E, Bremner, Collins, Lawson, Peyton, Hawksby

My job was to look after Peter Thompson who played on the left wing and was a dangerous player. Thompson, who would eventually star for Liverpool and England, used to drop his shoulder and come in on the inside. Don made it clear that it was my job to stop him and I had a good game. We drew 1-1, which was a satisfactory result. Then walking off, Bobby came over to tell me the boss couldn't leave me out again.

Don didn't say much to me afterwards, then after changing, I was about to get on the team bus when someone shouted my name. Looking round, it was Ivor Powell, who used to coach me at Leeds and was now manager of Carlisle. Don must have let him know I'd be playing so he came to watch me. Ivor told me that Carlisle would give me a club house rent free, double my salary and I'd also be captain and play every week. I had a lot to seriously think about on the return journey.

When Carlisle made a formal offer later that week, I had a good feeling so agreed to join them for the 1962/63 season.

When Leeds enjoyed an unbeaten run to survive on the final day of the season at Newcastle United, I was delighted for the lads but knew it was time to move on.

Appointed skipper of the team, McConnell made over 300 appearances for Carlisle during seven seasons in Cumbria. Following relegation in his first season to the Fourth Division, Carlisle immediately won promotion when they finished runners up to Gillingham on goal average.

Then in the following season, in a remarkable campaign, Carlisle recorded a 3-0 home win in their final game against Mansfield Town to clinch the Third Division title by one point ahead of Bristol City, resulting in huge celebrations in the town.

Bristol snatched second spot on goal average from Mansfield with Hull City a point back.

Ken Wagstaff was top league scorer and could have been a member of two promotion squads as he scored eight for Mansfield then 23 goals for Hull.

Carlisle was a long way from Leeds and Ivor was true to his word because he made me club captain, although it took me a bit of time to win over the fans because I'd taken over from a club legend called Ron 'Ginger' Thompson.

During those early days I often wondered if I had made the right decision. And back at Leeds, Freddie Goodwin and Eric Smith had both suffered a broken leg early on in the season, so I'd have come back in at one of the half back spots. It was at this point Billy first took over the number 4 half back position, and as they say, the rest is history.

I've always believed that as one door closes another opens, and I didn't have long to ponder on any possible misfortune because Carlisle trainer, Dick Young, told you things straight. Dick made it clear to me with a few choice words that I was not at Leeds anymore so it was time to knuckle down and it helped my performances.

After I scored a cracking goal to win a local clash against Workington Town, Dick came over at full time to pat me on the back. Looking at me, Dick said, "Nice one Skip," which was a simple comment, but the phrase meant a lot to me and things went from strength to strength afterwards.

When we won the League, it all came down to our match with Mansfield and we raced into a three-goal lead after 20 minutes in front of a packed house and then saw the game out. It was a marvelous occasion and after the game our fans invaded the pitch, so we went in the director's box and threw our shirts to them.

Being captain was important and I always found out where a referee travelled from for a game. Before kick off I'd ask how his journey was then tell him if any of the lads got stroppy I'd have a word. The tactic worked a treat because I got away with murder over the years!

Mary and I brought our three children, Debra, Catherine and James, up in the area and it was a good move for us. Whenever I visit Carlisle, I still get a great reception and it was a very proud moment a few years ago when the club asked me to open McConnell's Bar in the East Stand in recognition of my time at the club.

McConnell went close to promotion with Carlisle in 1966/67 before seeing out his career with Bradford City at the start of the 1970s. Then following a brief spell as Scarborough coach, the McConnell's became licensees at The Angel then Hare & Hounds in Leeds, which heralded a new association with Leeds United.

Lots of former players went into the trade and though I was not a household name in Leeds, playing charity games with my former teammates into my early 50s certainly helped.

When we opened The Angel a few of the lads supported us, which swelled the attendance. Harold Williams was an ex-Leeds player who also had a pub and was really helpful in passing on his experience.

When two Leeds United supporters' clubs departed from our pub for away games, it was great to be involved. We'd open at 8.00 am to put on breakfast and help get their day off to a good start. On the social side we ran a football team, dominoes and darts teams, karaoke nights and our Christmas and New Year's Eve celebrations were always popular. Lots of the lads came to events but the best night was after the FA Cup Final in 1972, because Billy brought the trophy to The Angel. The pub was absolutely packed and it was a brilliant night.

Getting together with the lads was always enjoyable, and through one of our regulars, Tommy Kneeshaw, I started to commentate on games at Elland Road for Leeds Hospital Radio. Tommy and Barney Coleman showed me the ropes and it was great fun, but more important the organisation offered a valuable service for patients in hospital.

Covering Leeds was great and when Billy got the manager's job it was terrific seeing him on a regular basis in his office for a chat about the game and old times.

Whenever I've been back to the club, I've been made to feel really welcome and its something that I've always appreciated because my time at Leeds was a special period of my life.

Looking back at his time at Leeds United, Peter, who has seven grandchildren, has fond memories.

When Carlisle got promotion Don was the first to send me a telegram, and that was typical of him because he had that personal touch and his management style was terrific. Don had aspirations for Leeds United and knew the youth team was the future. But at the start he had players like Freddie Goodwin and Granville Hair who were seasoned professionals.

Big Jack was also a key member of his team, though not the easiest of players to handle in the early days but Don was well aware of his strengths. Jack was a real character. At one time we shared digs and he drove me crazy borrowing my clothes, but you could not help but like him. On away trips, he would leave his shoes out so the night porter would clean them and he was also an expert at cadging cigarettes off the lads but rarely returned the favour, making out he only had one left when there was a full packet in his jacket! John Charles cottoned on to this routine when he was at the club and had equal success.

Don knew he had to get the best out of Jack and helped him develop into one of the Boys of '66.

There was also Noel Peyton who was not a bad little player but ought to have scored more goals because he got into a lot of good positions, but his finishing was lacking.

Albert Johanneson was from South Africa and had recently joined the club. He was an amazing athlete and during training exercises we'd be screaming at him to slow down! Albert on his day could destroy any team, but we had to toughen him up because unscrupulous opponents intimidated him and he was also subjected to racist remarks.

Players had different ways to prepare and some were more nervous than others. Don would leave out a bottle of whisky if anyone wanted a nip to calm nerves before a game. Albert was one who liked a nip but this had nothing to do with his later drink issues and I choose to remember him for the way he destroyed teams with his pace and skill.

Hindsight is easy, but Bobby Collins was Don's best signing, though he could not have predicted the success that would follow in the coming years. As a footballer, Bobby had a great range of passing and could shoot from distance, but did go over the top at times. He took no prisoners and was just the type of player Don needed at that time. He took the team by the scruff of the neck and dragged it to safety from relegation.

Off the field, Bobby was just as committed as if he were playing a first team game. Five-a-sides were really intense and the lads soon started wearing shin pads! But it was more than that because on the park, Bobby carried out Don's instructions. Full marks to Don for having the foresight to get a player like him because his impact was incredible, especially in those early days while the young players developed.

Of all the lads, Billy Bremner was a terrific player and Don's blue-eyed boy. Billy wanted the ball all the time and once they moved him from right wing to central midfield, he showed he had the ability to pass a ball then get in the box to finish off a move. Billy was also a skillful player and I often thought this element of his game was underrated. But when Don made Billy captain, he flourished with the extra responsibility.

In football, sometimes you need to be in the right place at the right time, and Don was, because there were lots of talented lads coming through. Whether Don realised just how promising kids like Norman Hunter, Paul Reaney, Gary Sprake, Rod Johnson and Terry Cooper were I don't know, but he quickly brought them through. Then the likes of Peter Lorimer, Paul Madeley, David Harvey, Mick Bates and Eddie Gray all made a mark.

When I signed for Bradford City, Don helped me out whilst we moved back to Leeds by letting me train at Elland Road. And playing for the reserves against the first team in practice matches, it was amazing to see how the team had developed.

Apart from the lads during my time, Don had signed Johnny Giles, Mick Jones and Allan Clarke. Playing against Don's first string was an experience because they had everything. The way they passed the ball then found space was incredible.

From a distance, I kept an eye on results and was delighted at their success.

I've always retained a soft spot for Leeds United and still have my club blazer because it was an honour playing for them.

2

John Hawksby

JOHN Hawksby enjoyed a sensational start to his Leeds United career when he scored in his first two games for the club at the start of the 1960/61 season. United had recently been relegated to the Second Division when manager Jack Taylor made the talented teenager one of the club's youngest debutants. Following Don Revie's appointment as player-manager towards the end of an inauspicious season, Hawksby enjoyed first team status for much of the following campaign when United avoided relegation on the final day of a fraught season. Hawksby's potential would ultimately not be realised at United but he did hit the headlines during one of the toughest periods in the club's history.

Born in the historical city of York in June 1942, James and Marjorie Hawksby's son was educated at Tang Hall Junior and Burnholme Secondary Modern Schools. John's father was a talented amateur footballer until injury curtailed his career, but realising his son had a natural ability for the game encouraged his ambition to succeed.

Hawksby recalled:

> Dad was an electrician with North Eastern Region Railways and was a huge football fan, so when he got free passes, we'd go by train to see Newcastle United play on a Saturday afternoon.
>
> Jackie Milburn was Newcastle's star forward and the atmosphere at St James' Park was fantastic at every game. There were loads of players to admire, including Jimmy Hagan of Sheffield United because he was a real entertainer. I remember in one match Hagan getting the ball on the touchline and then dribbling round opponents before sitting on the ball. You could not help but feel sorry for the defender, but it was brilliant to watch.

The Hawksby's also followed the fortunes of York City who played in the Third Division (North) and were among supporters when they reached an FA Cup semifinal in 1955. A remarkable campaign saw York defeat Scarborough then Dorchester Town, who were hosting league opposition for the first time and welcomed away supporters with a rendition of 'On Ilkla Moor Baht At', but went out to an Arthur Bottom hat-trick.

A plum third round clash with First Division giants Blackpool followed when City recorded a stunning 2-0 win against the 1953 winners with Stanley Matthews in the line-up.

York then overcame giant killers Bishop Auckland before taking on mighty Tottenham Hotspur at a snowbound Kingsway Stadium and caused another shock with a 3-1 triumph. *The Daily Express* headline after the game read: "NO FLUKE, IT MIGHT HAVE BEEN 6".

Correspondent, Henry Rose wrote:

The humiliation, the unmistakable Cup blitz of London's aristocrats was achieved by a team who played Spurs' own immaculate stylish soccer, but played it more quickly, more accurately, with more sense of urgency and more spirit.

Bottom was the hero again as underdogs York defeated Notts County in the quarterfinals before a record 47,000 crowd at Meadow Lane. Hundreds of fans welcomed back the victorious team who now faced Newcastle United in the semifinals.

Newcastle took an early lead at Hillsborough before Bottom sent York fans wild with an equaliser, and roared on by 21,000 fans, only a controversial decision ruled out a late Bottom winner.

Alas, cup glory was dashed when Newcastle won the replay 2-0 at Roker Park. In York, live updates were relayed of the semifinal at cinemas and a loudspeaker in the market place broadcast commentary of the replay. Pathe News footage showed highlights in cinemas.

Hawksby remembers York's cup run:

York didn't have any famous players but had a spirit that made them a good cup side. Beating Blackpool was an incredible achievement but then to defeat Tottenham was amazing. The atmosphere inside the ground against Tottenham was fantastic and the further York went in the competition, the more the excitement grew. It was an amazing time to follow York because, when you consider they'd started the tournament in the first round, it had been unthinkable that they would eventually face Newcastle in the semifinal.

The FA Cup Final was the biggest match of the season. Domestically it was the only game televised live and top teams never played weakened line-ups in early rounds as they do now. The competition has lost some of its sparkle because of the Champions League and Premier League but in the 1950s it was the biggest competition for players and supporters. It would have been miraculous for York to make the Final, but I followed Newcastle with dad, so enjoyed seeing them win the FA Cup against Manchester City at Wembley.

Hawksby was showing potential as a footballer by the mid-1950s. Having represented York City Schoolboys and Yorkshire Schoolboys, a host of clubs approached his parents, hoping to sign their son as an apprentice professional. It was only a question of time before he signed for a Football League club, especially when scouts saw him play in an England 'north v south' game.

Weighing up his options, Hawksby joined Leeds United, initially as an amateur in July 1957. Raich Carter was manager at Elland Road and star striker John Charles had led the club to an eighth place finish in the First Division. United's colossus though had just joined Juventus in a world record £65,000 transfer.

> First Division clubs were interested in signing me and Newcastle United was really keen but I was not ready to leave home and move into digs. I was only 15 years of age so chose Leeds, as they were the biggest club on my doorstep. Looking back, who knows what would have happened if I'd felt ready to join Newcastle. Maybe it would have toughened me up as a player but you can't change the past.
>
> On the day I went over to Elland Road to sign my apprentice forms John Charles dropped in to pick up fan mail and it was the biggest pile of letters you've ever seen on a desk. You could not help but be impressed.

Hawksby travelled to Leeds by train when pre-season training began. Throughout the season, details of where and when to report for matches were sent by telegram.

On the first team front, United struggled during the 1957/58 campaign without Welsh talisman Charles, and with goals at a premium, finished in 17th place in the First Division table.

Bill Lambton took on a caretaker manager role when Carter failed to agree a new contract, then accepted the managerial post in December 1958. Lambton signed Don Revie from Sunderland in November 1958 to add experience to his squad, then appointed him captain when Wilbur Cush relinquished the role. However, Lambton's training methods were unpopular with players and directors alike. His tenure lasted just three months.

> Don had been a big footballing name, but was finished as a top player when he came to Leeds. At Manchester City, he played a deep lying centre forward role, which was seen as visionary, because strikers in that era such as Nat Lofthouse and Stan Mortenson would run through a brick wall. Don was what I'd call an educated forward because he had good ball control and vision, so in possession would look up then spread play as he could pick a pass.
>
> Lambton was a fitness fanatic so we knew training would be tough. We did a lot of strength training and at every opportunity he had us running with sandbags on our backs to build stamina. There weren't too many players disappointed at his departure, but it was not the best timing for me as my 17th birthday was coming up.

Hawksby was a young player with great promise, and after the managerial shake-up, played for England Youth in a 3-0 victory against Wales and 1-1 draw with Scotland. John then took part in the 12th UEFA Youth Tournament in Bulgaria, in March 1959. During the tournament, England failed to get out of the group phase following games against East Germany, Italy, Turkey, Romania and Greece.

> Playing for England was a great experience and I'm proud of my youth cap. Against Scotland, I scored with a header, which is what I was not noted for, so was delighted. It didn't matter how many games you represented the youth team for at that time, you just received one cap, unlike nowadays when you get a cap per match. We had talented players in our side, including Nobby Stiles and Geoff Hurst, but no one realised their careers would take off in the way they did, as they both became 1966 World Cup heroes.

Jack Taylor took up the managerial mantle in May 1959 and a month into his appointment was on hand when Hawksby signed professional forms.

I'd been playing well for the juniors and Taylor knew clubs were interested in me. He told me I'd get opportunities if I continued to impress, and with the first team struggling, I felt that my chance would come, so it did not take me long to sign a professional contract.

Billy Bremner arrived at Elland Road shortly after Hawksby signed pro forms for Leeds. A Scottish schoolboy international, Bremner made his debut against Chelsea during a tortuous 1959/60 season that would end in relegation to the Second Division.

Billy had a host of clubs after him when he signed for Leeds. He clearly had talent but no one could foresee the impact he'd have on the side in years to come.

Taylor handed Hawksby his senior debut, with Revie sidelined through injury, in the third league game of United's 1960/61 season. And the teenager grabbed the headlines when opening the scoring against Rotherham United.

John McCole scored Leeds' second goal in a 2-0 win against the team from South Yorkshire.

Leeds United v Rotherham United, August 27th, 1960

Leeds United: Burgin, Jones, Hair, Cameron, Charlton, Goodwin, Francis, Hawksby, McCole, Peyton, Grainger

Rotherham United: Ironside, Perry, Morgan, Lambert, Madden, Waterhouse, Webster, Kettleborough, Smith, Kirkman, Sawyer

Before the match no one came over to me at training to give the nod, I just received a telegram to turn up at the ground for the match.

On the day, I did okay but faded in the second half, which was understandable given my age. Grabbing a goal was thrilling and I got headlines in the local papers, which my dad kept. In fact, he saved newspaper cuttings throughout my career, which has been a great keepsake.

Taylor selected the same team to face Bristol Rovers two days later and Hawksby repeated his goal-scoring feat with the opening goal, but United let a 4-0 lead slip to eventually draw an extraordinary game when McCole, Colin Grainger and Noel Peyton also scored.

A replacement for Revie in another 4-4 thriller at home to

Middlesbrough a few weeks later, Hawksby then played in defeats at Swansea Town and Ipswich Town.

Shortly after the 4-0 loss at Ipswich, Revie took up the managerial 'hot seat' at Elland Road.

> The match against Bristol was crazy because, after I scored a tap-in, we had a four-goal lead at half time so expected to go on and win comfortably, but somehow drew 4-4. Taylor was not pleased to say the least at full time.
>
> In the dressing room you sit there and think, how did that happen? What went wrong? At the end of the day though as a player you are concentrating on your own performance. You can't really see from where you are on a pitch what happened. All you assume is someone must have had a blinder, but being so young, I didn't really analyse things like that, I was just a kid making my way in the game. Maybe psychologically we switched off but incredibly, in my next game, we drew 4-4 again, this time against Middlesborough. Looking back, what were the odds on that happening?
>
> When Don got the job, it did not surprise me because he was popular with the lads. Harry Reynolds had recommended him to the board and was really supportive of young lads coming through but that would take time. Like Don, he wanted young players to shape the future of the club. Don was a players' manager, treated us well and wanted us to believe in ourselves more.

Following Revie's appointment, Hawksby played against Luton Town and Scunthorpe United as Leeds avoided relegation for a second successive season. Hawksby had shown a lot of promise during a challenging time and now looked to cement a first team spot in Revie's first season at the helm.

> There were established pros and plenty of characters in our dressing room. After a kick-a-bout, the lads would be 'effing and blinding about everything. Mentally I was a schoolboy thinking, is this for real? But I soon learned it was just banter and joined in. Grenville Hair in particular was like a father figure to me. He kept an eye out for me and gave advice, which I appreciated as it helped me settle in.

Albert Johanneson joined Leeds United, initially on loan then signed professional forms, just after Revie took up his managerial duties. The South African winger was in Revie's starting line-up when the 1961/62 campaign kicked off, but after a woeful start Hawksby came into the side and went on to make 25 appearances.

United had struggled for goals throughout the season with John McCole and December signing Billy McAdams both failing to hit the target on a regular basis. In a desperate move to pep up his attack, Revie switched Jack Charlton to a central striker role with limited success.

United were in danger of relegation for the second time in three seasons with 12 matches remaining. Revie responded by signing Burnley striker Ian Lawson, Sheffield United defender Cliff Mason and former Celtic legend Bobby Collins from Everton.

Scottish international Collins strengthened the midfield and had an immediate impact on and off the pitch. United survived the drop following a run of form where they lost only two games from the final dozen matches. Hawksby played in seven of these crucial games including wins against Swansea Town and Middlesborough before an injury at Preston North End ended his season.

United's 'must-win' game on the final day of the league campaign was at Newcastle United when Johanneson, McAdams and a Keith own goal ensure safety.

> Our lack of goals was a serious situation, so Big Jack led the attack after McCole was dropped but it was not the answer. Don then decided to bring in McAdams who was an old-school striker ... butch, strong and battled away for the team, but we were in a terrible run of form. Inwardly, Don must have been concerned but he didn't show it to the lads. He just wanted us to get out and do our stuff.
>
> There are times when I think a manager's job is impossible. They have ideas but on a matchday it's down to the players when they run out to play. Nowadays there are substitutes to freshen things up, but then that was not an option. It was down to the team selected and they determined the success of a manager. Revie was under massive pressure and had to do something with games running out. Jack had moved back up front when McAdams picked up an injury but we needed a boost, which Lawson provided, then he signed Mason because Willie Bell was injured. Collins though proved to be the key signing and gave us the fillip we needed. But I didn't realise Everton wanted me in an exchange deal.
>
> Don never informed me about a potential move; Bobby told me some time later. Everton had a heck of a side with Roy Vernon,

Brian Labone and Alex Young playing for them so it would have been interesting speaking to them, but it was not to be. In any case, I had a future at Leeds at that particular time so it did not really cross my mind.

Bobby was the main man and a really big influence because he got us organised on the pitch and added steel to the team. He brought class, vision, control and experience, which is what we needed but also had a nasty side and would not flinch at taking out an opponent. I really enjoyed being a part of the team with Bobby leading us. He scored a screamer against Swansea on his debut but I did my ligaments at Preston, which was a huge disappointment, as I wanted to help see us to safety.

I wasn't at the Newcastle match but was delighted when news of the result came through. There was huge pressure on the lads and it was a surprise when I heard we were 3-0 up at half time but what a great result.

Come the close season, there was relief United had survived relegation but also a determination that they would not come close to the drop again. Football though has a habit of providing a reality check and during the previous season a dreadful incident involving Terry Casey would resonate with Hawksby. The pair had played together in the juniors and then a League Cup game against Rotherham United before a car crash ended Casey's career at the age of 19.

We were on our way from the ground into town when the accident occurred. Terry was badly injured and by the time police arrived there were loads of people around. A number of lads were in the car and in a state of shock.

A copper offered a cigarette, which helped to calm me down but that was the start of my smoking. The whole incident was a tragedy, especially for Terry, who never got back to full fitness.

Don Revie, Les Cocker and Syd Owen were thorough when it came to pre-season planning. Following United's great escape, Revie was determined his squad would be ready for the big kick off in August 1962.

Training started in the middle of July and was really strenuous, especially the long runs. I was okay with the short stuff but the 'Roundhay Park runs' were pretty stiff.

> During training, Les used to give me stick all the time because he thought I could do more. I was only a kid, but he was always on my back and it did knock my confidence. It was tough going, but looking back I had a lot of talent and Les just wanted more and more, but his way of trying to get it from me was demotivating.

The surprise news during the close season surrounded the return of John Charles in a blaze of publicity following his £53,000 signing from Juventus, a club record at the time.

Hawksby was out of the first team picture when the campaign kicked off against Stoke City at Elland Road but did come in for Johanneson during a 2-1 defeat against Rotherham United.

Charles' brief spell ended after 11 appearances when he returned to Italy in a £70,000 transfer to Roma.

> Big John was a megastar at Juventus but his best days were behind him. I remember watching him in his heyday for Leeds at centre half and centre forward. In one game, he headed a George Meek corner with such power it hit the crossbar and bounced back out of the penalty area. John in his pomp was a world class footballer but also so modest. What would he be worth today? He'd be up there with Ronaldo and Messi.

With Johanneson enjoying an extended run on the wing, Hawksby had to wait for an opportunity, which came in a League Cup tie against Crystal Palace at Elland Road.

United also had a new look as teenagers Gary Sprake, Paul Reaney and Norman Hunter were now in the first team after changes in the side following an indifferent start.

Results picked up and continued when Leeds defeated Newcastle United and Norwich City. Sadly for Hawksby, his appearance against Norwich, when Leeds enjoyed a 3-0 win in early November, would be his final one of the season due to a bad injury.

Norwich City v Leeds United, November 3rd, 1962

Norwich City: Kennon, Burton, Bell, Allcock, Hill, Oliver, Miller, Mullett, Kelly, Bryceland, Worrell

Leeds United: Sprake, Reaney, Mason, Bell, Goodwin, Hunter, Hawksby, Bremner, Storrie, Collins, Johanneson

Hawksby recalled:

> When Don put Sprake, Reaney and Hunter in against Swansea Town
> on September 8th, you could sense things were changing at the club,
> so I was hoping my luck may change.
>
> I played on the right wing against Norwich when my opponent
> came over the top. I left the ground on crutches knowing I'd be out
> for some time. It was a massive disappointment and I never really got
> fully fit again.
>
> Of all the lads, Johanneson was the most naturally fit player I'd
> come across and made the wing position his own. He was a smooth
> runner and could destroy full backs with his pace. If you asked Albert
> to run 100 yards, he'd finish two or three yards in front of everyone
> and if he had to run 25 miles he'd have finished a mile in front.

The arrival of Johnny Giles from Manchester United in August 1963
effectively ended Hawksby's chances of breaking back into the first
team. Linking up with Bremner and Collins in midfield, Revie's promotion
side was taking shape with Johanneson supplying crosses for Lawson,
Storrie, Don Weston and Alan Peacock to strike.

On the sidelines throughout United's Second Division campaign,
Hawksby played in United's League Cup defeat against Manchester
City and his final appearance was in an FA Cup fourth round replay
when United went out at Everton before a capacity 66,000 crowd.

Everton v Leeds United, January 28th, 1964

Everton: West, Brown, Meagan, Harris, Labone, Kay, Scott, Stevens, Gabriel, Vernon, Temple

Leeds United: Sprake, Reaney, Bell, Bremner, Madeley, Hunter, Henderson, Giles, Lawson, Collins, Hawksby

> Playing at Everton the atmosphere was fantastic but, after the civic
> celebrations, I realised my days were numbered at the club. Lads
> from the next group of ground staff such as Jimmy Greenhoff, Terry
> Cooper, Paul Madeley and Peter Lorimer had begun to come through.
> And then there was Eddie Gray, who had a heck of a reputation as
> a schoolboy international when he came to the club, about to make
> his mark. All of them became top players and that's the fortunes of
> football.

Lamentably for Hawksby, the Goodison clash was a taster of things to come for the club, and at 22 years of age he joined Lincoln City in August 1964. He went on to play for York City then a number of non-league clubs in a career lasting over 25 years.

> Lincoln City manager Bill Anderson had been chasing me, so when Don told me I might like to have a go at another club it came as no surprise. And I had some good times at Lincoln but when a chance came to move back to my hometown club, who were fighting relegation from the Football League, I decided to join them.
>
> There was a lot of pressure at York so it was a relief for everyone connected with the club when we avoided the drop. But when Joe Shaw came in and cleared out the squad, it was time to find another club.
>
> Chelmsford United was the 'money team' outside the Football League and we agreed terms, but the night before signing, Kings Lynn manager Reg Davies rang and I agreed to drop by on my way. Arriving at the club I loved the set up and surroundings, so decided to join, but left Reg to speak with Chelmsford.
>
> Playing at this level you soon know which teams are run well, so after a spell at Bedford Town, I was delighted when Ron Atkinson made me his first signing at Kettering Town and he led the team to promotion.

John and his wife, Sue, moved to the area and have lived there since. The couple have two children, Martin and Nichola, and four grandchildren.

Hawksby was sent off only once in a 20-plus year career. At the time he was playing for Bedfordshire side Dunstable Town.

> I had a real go at a referee when he did nothing after I just managed to evade a leg-breaking tackle. Walking off the pitch after the referee gave me my marching orders, that was it for me. I could not believe the standard of refereeing, so called it a day.

Retiring from the game, after brief spells with Stevenage Borough, Rushden Town and Desborough Town, Hawsby worked in various industries including share registration for 25 years. Looking back on his football career, he has mixed feelings.

> I was just a kid with a talent, but in football you get knockbacks which dent your confidence. If I'd worked on civvy street then got spotted by a club, maybe things would have been different because I might

have been given a longer run in the side.

Injuries play a part, and without making excuses I had a bad ligament injury in my left ankle and knee. Treatment was different all those years ago and I never fully recovered. Don and Les did their best for me but maybe everything happened too quickly. Technically I was on a par with Billy, but did not have his desire to make the most of my ability. Billy's a legend and deservedly so because of what he achieved.

I was blessed with natural ability on the ball but my attitude towards training was not always right. I didn't work hard enough, which I regret. Don told me once that I was the best youth player he'd seen, which means a lot now. If I'd stayed at Leeds and matured, who knows?

Coaches always feel that you can do better, but I was probably a bit soft when it came to criticism, so took comments the wrong way.

Meeting up with former teammates at a Revie reunion dinner a few years ago brought back many memories, and once we got chatting it was as if we were at the club again. Although I was not part of the glory years that followed my time at Leeds, it was unbelievable how many supporters asked me to sign books and pictures. I really thought that I was a forgotten name so it was a massive surprise.

The lads associated with Don were part of something special, which is humbling. Leeds United were fighting relegation when I played for the club, but I tasted a little bit of stardom and I remember those moments because it was something very special.

3

Ian Lawson

THERE are times in a football club's history when key decisions have to be taken. Leeds United boss Don Revie illustrated this point with his team spiraling towards relegation from the Second Division in March 1962 when he signed three players in a bid to avoid the trapdoor into the Third Division.

Burnley centre forward Ian Lawson was first to arrive for £20,000 and immediately made his debut against Huddersfield Town in a game that signaled the end of Revie's playing days. Lawson, Cliff Mason and veteran Scottish international Bobby Collins lined up against Swansea Town at Elland Road in the next match. When Collins opened the scoring in a 2-0 win, the road to recovery had begun. Lawson went on to play his part in United's Second Division Championship success in 1964.

Born in Ouston, County Durham to parents Joe and Lily Lawson in March 1939, Ian was educated at Pelton Secondary Modern School where he excelled at athletics and tennis, but football was his first choice sport. Amongst his earliest memories was playing 20-a-side games near his home, and watching his father, an electrician by trade, play right half for Blyth Spartans in the North Eastern League.

Lawson recalled:

> Football meant everything to me, so at every opportunity I'd be in the back yard hitting a ball against the wall into a false net, or playing on cobbled streets with coats for goals, long into the night.
>
> I started out as a centre half then moved into attack and couldn't stop scoring goals, so stayed as a striker. My school was small but our enthusiasm for football was massive and we became the best team

in the region. From school, I progressed to our district team, Chester-le-Street, who won the Sunderland Hospitals Cup which was a big achievement.

As for following a club, there was only one choice for this football-mad youngster.

Newcastle United was my team and I'd watch them from the Gallowgate End at St James' Park. Singing 'Blaydon Races' was always a highlight and you could not believe the noise in the ground at each game. There was so much passion; it was just fantastic.

Another reason for going was of course to watch Jackie Milburn lead the attack. Wor Jackie, as fans called him, was an incredible footballer because he was strong, direct and fearless. Newcastle were known for their attacking football and they had a fantastic forward line in Milburn, Tommy Walker, Ernie Taylor, George Robledo and Bobby Mitchell. Sunderland was the big game each season and as a derby clash it was a special occasion.

When Newcastle United won the FA Cup three times in five years during the 1950s, the Toon Army were in dreamland.

The FA Cup was the glamour competition every season, so we'd get up in the early hours to queue for tickets, and once you had one, it was brilliant. I didn't miss a home match during the '51 Cup run and was at the Hillsborough semifinal when we defeated Wolves to reach Wembley. I tried everything to get a ticket for the Final but it was impossible.

On Cup Final day, we did not have a television so all the family crammed around a wireless listening to the commentary. At the final whistle after we'd won 2-0 against Blackpool we all ran out into the street celebrating. And when Newcastle paraded the Cup through the streets, I was amongst thousands of fans cheering them home dressed in black and white club colours.

Newcastle retained the trophy against Arsenal in 1952, and then won it again in 1955 when Milburn scored a bullet header against Manchester City in a famous 3-1 win. In the midst of these cup heroics, 15-year-old Lawson was attracting the attention of scouts across the country and within a fortnight of leaving school, Ian had joined the ground staff at Burnley FC.

I'd seen the set up at Newcastle and Sunderland but decided to get away from my home environment. Of course, playing for Newcastle would have been great but I knew that I'd be distracted. If apprentices went into town, I'd have gone, and not concentrated on making it as a footballer, which was my goal. Burnley chief scout Charlie Ferguson had seen me play for the school team, met my headteacher and parents, then everything went from there.

After signing apprentice forms with The Clarets, Lawson lived in digs with Jimmy Robson and John Angus. Budgeting on £5 a week over this period was challenging, but Lawson embraced the apprentice lifestyle.

Of my weekly wage, £2 went on digs and the club put £1 in a post office account, so I was left with 18 shillings pocket money. Going out on the town was never going to be an issue!

Ground staff duties included cleaning the first team players' boots and painting the goal stanchions. If we had a Saturday game, we'd sweep the terracing on a Monday morning then have a training session in the afternoon. We also helped look after the pitch at Turf Moor, which was not one of the best surfaces. Tommy Danns was groundsman and knew every swearword in the book. Tommy was a real character and had us in stitches if he had a strop. We rolled the pitch after every game, but in the winter, if it was impossible to put a heavy roller on, we had to hand roll it, which was not much fun.

Alan Brown was manager but Billy Dougall coached the first team and was years ahead of his time with training methods. Billy Morris looked after the apprentices and was brilliant with us. In the early days, some of the lads seemed like world beaters to me, but when they went out in front of a few thousand supporters froze, whereas I felt fine.

Lawson had held his own in Burnley's reserve team and signed as a professional in March 1956. By now sharing digs with John Connelly, who would play for Manchester United and then England in the 1966 World Cup, Lawson made an astonishing first team debut against Chesterfield in an FA Cup third round tie in January 1957.

Scoring Burnley's first goal after four minutes, he completed his hat-trick nine minutes from full time and there was still time to hit a fourth as Burnley finished 7-0 victors. The teenage sensation was headline news in Saturday's evening sports paper.

Burnley's 14-man squad was pinned up next to the changing room door for the Chesterfield tie. When I saw my name, I thought it was just for the experience of being around our first team, but the manager had phoned my dad and invited him to watch the game. I had my boots with me when the squad met up and it was only at that point that I realised I'd be playing. I thought, that'll do me.

Looking back, Brown handled the situation well because I was not too nervous, just excited to finally be involved and determined to make an impression. When the game kicked off, I just played my game and managed to put four goals away.

There was a great feeling of elation afterwards and I knew I'd make the headlines, but there was no great celebration with a night out on the town. I went out with my girlfriend, Maureen, who I'd been courting for a while to see the World War 2 film *Attack!* starring American actors Jack Palance, Eddie Albert and Lee Marvin at the Odean!

Following his FA Cup exploits, Brown kept Lawson in the side and he continued his stunning form with a hat-trick when Burnley thumped New Brighton 9-0 in the fourth round. But the Cup run ended when Aston Villa won a quarterfinal replay 2-0 at Villa Park.

Villa knocked us out, which was ridiculous because we should have hammered them. I missed a couple of sitters that day and they went on to win the Cup against Manchester United.

Lawson made seven League appearances, aside of his Cup exertions, including a memorable match against his boyhood hero when Newcastle United came to town.

Jackie Milburn was the most exciting player I'd ever seen play football. I'd idolised him as a kid, and still did, but now I was playing against him for Burnley in a First Division fixture so there was no time for sentiment. If our paths crossed and I had to kick him, then I would, but on the day I couldn't get near him! Over the years, I was fortunate to meet Jackie numerous times and he was always a top man.

Lawson had shot to prominence, which brought him an England Youth appearance against Spain in a thrilling 4-4 draw at Birmingham City's St Andrew's ground in September 1957 but bizarrely, after his debut season for Burnley, he did not feature in the side for two seasons.

Playing for England was a proud occasion but the Football Association would not let players keep their shirt as a memento. We were allowed to take the badge with the three lions off the shirt, which seemed strange at the time, but I still have it along with my cap for playing. Both mean a lot to me.

Manchester United as League Champions had entered the European Cup in 1957/58, which was groundbreaking for English football. But tragically the world of football would soon mourn the loss of many talented players after the Munich air disaster in February 1958.

Everyone was stunned when we heard about the crash on the radio. When I started out at Burnley we played some tough teams and the 'Busby Babes' were by far the best side I'd faced with the likes of Pegg, Coleman, Taylor, Violett and Charlton in their side. When the 'Babes' ran out to play we knew that we had a game on. There was something special about them and from the kick off they attacked at will.

Duncan Edwards was such a nice guy, so modest and a magical player. They were an incredible group so it was a tragedy for the club and British football because they could have competed with the great Real Madrid team from that era.

Lawson's National Service at Chatham, which began in November 1958, was eventful. Apart from his marriage to Maureen the following April, he played his part in a remarkable First Division campaign when Burnley competed with defending champions Wolves and Tottenham Hotspur for the Championship in 1959/60.

Lawson played eight games at inside right as understudy to Jimmy McIlroy, scoring three goals, including the winner against Manchester United at Old Trafford. Burnley went on to stun English football when they clinched the title in the last game of an astonishing season (Tottenham would be the first 20th century team to win the League and Cup 'double' in 1960/61).

I trained with army sides during the week then had permission to play on a Saturday afternoon. Burnley had great senior pros and young players in a balanced side. We had a strong defence in front of goalkeeper Adam Blackwell, who was my best mate. Jimmy Adamson was an influential captain but McIlroy was the key player and you really respected him as a footballer.

Going into the last game against Manchester City, only a victory would allow us to overhaul Wolves who had a one-point advantage with a superior goal average. We were dark horses for the title but had thousands of fans amongst a capacity crowd. Brian Pilkington scored then City equalised before Terry Meredith, who was in for Connelly, clinched the title.

I watched from the stands but back in the dressing room the champagne was flowing. Afterwards we went to Burnley Town Hall and Nelson Golf Club for a few sherbets! For little Burnley to win the Championship was incredible for the town and major news. Everything came together and it was an amazing achievement. I only played eight games that season, scoring three goals, but was always involved on matchdays so received a Championship medal, which I've been proud to own.

Lawson was out of the first team frame when Burnley made a spirited defence of their title, then progressed in the FA Cup during the 1961/62 season. Then out of the blue, Leeds United offered Burnley £20,000 in a bid for Lawson's services in February 1962. After 30 appearances and 15 goals for Burnley, Lawson but had a big decision to make over whether to stay in the First Division and fight for a place in the team or drop down to a side struggling in the Second Division but with more certainty of playing regular football.

At this time, Leeds manager Don Revie had moved Jack Charlton into an emergency centre forward role with some success and Billy Bremner had hit nine league goals (and would finish top scorer on 11) but United's manager needed a centre forward to bring firepower to his ailing team.

Lawson explained:

Harry Potts was now the Burnley manager and made it clear I'd be in the reserves every Saturday. When he came round to my house it was a surprise, as it was our day off, but I was even more surprised when he told me Don and Les Cocker would be down at the ground by 2pm. Don had seen me play for Burnley's reserves against Leeds and was impressed with my attitude. It might have also helped that I scored a hat-trick that day!

I knew nothing about Leeds, apart from Charlton being a Geordie, and they looked to be on their way to the Third Division. But Don had a clear vision for the club. He'd changed the strip to all white like

Real Madrid and was determined they would make it back to the First Division and wanted me to be a part of it.

Looking at the League table, Don's views seemed crazy, but he was so convincing that I went over on the Wednesday to have a look around, met the coaching staff and signed. I'd enjoyed my time at Burnley, our children, Sharon and Michael, were born there, but it was time for a new challenge and that meant helping Leeds survive relegation.

When Lawson met his new teammates at Elland Road there was no time to settle in to his new surroundings. He had to hit the ground running and was thrown into the first team three days after his arrival, for a fixture at Huddersfield Town.

Huddersfield Town v Leeds United, March 3rd, 1962

Huddersfield Town: Wilson, Saward, Coddington, Dinsdale, McHale, Stokes, Massie, O'Grady, Atkins, Wood, White

Leeds United: Younger, Jones, Hair, Cameron, Goodwin, Smith, Bremner, Revie, Charlton, Lawson, Peyton

Big Jack had been playing up front, which showed how desperate things were, and the game turned out to be Don's last game for the club. I had played against him in his Sunderland days, but he was now past his best, so it was not a surprise when he decided to call it a day.

We lost to Huddersfield 2-1 and it was clear that we were in a real scrap for survival. I partnered Jack in attack against Town but it would be his last appearance as a striker.

A few days after the Town defeat, Revie pulled a masterstroke by adding Bobby Collins to the playing ranks at Elland Road. Cliff Mason also joined the fight for survival. Ten games remained for Leeds to avoid slipping into the Third Division. Relegation would be a shattering blow and could end Revie's tenure at the club before it had started. The trio of signings played against Swansea Town and recorded a first win in eight games.

Leeds United v Swansea Town, March 10th, 1962

Leeds United: Younger, Hair, Mason, Cameron, Goodwin, Smith, Bremner, Collins, McAdams, Lawson, Hawksby

Swansea Town: King, Purcell, Sanders, Johnson, Nurse, Williams, Jones, Davies, Webster, Donnelly, Griffiths

Bobby was an incredible signing and his effect was immediate. The dressing room atmosphere changed when he arrived and I'd only been there a few days. It was no surprise that Bobby scored on his debut against Swansea. He led by example; it was a crucial win and built our confidence.

Lawson scored his first goal for the club in the next match against Southampton but the game is remembered for a goalkeeping crisis.

Southampton v Leeds United, March 17th, 1962

Southampton: Chadwick, Clifton, Godfrey, Huxford, Knapp, Mulgrew, Payne, Patrick, Penk, Reeves, Traynor

Leeds United: Sprake, Hair, Mason, Cameron, Goodwin, Smith, Bremner, Collins, McAdams, Lawson, Hawksby

We went down 4-1 to Southampton when I got my first goal for Leeds, but we had been unlucky, because after traveling down by train our goalkeeper, Tommy Younger, fell ill so they had to fly down Gary Sprake, who was only 16, as a late replacement. Gary showed though that he could command his area, had class and the temperament to make it.

The coming weeks would see Leeds grind out an unbeaten run to give themselves a chance of survival.

Billy scored both goals in a win against Luton Town then we defeated Middlesborough, which gave us momentum. From there the run-in brought a spate of draws as we scrambled for points, including a 0-0 draw with Bury, which was my last game of the season because I'd picked up an ankle injury.

It was all a bit desperate but we were at a stage of the season when points meant everything. Things were moving forward although there was a lot of work to do on the training ground because in games the lads had been so disorganised, but Bobby got into them. Big Jack was also his own man and did his own thing. He'd defend then suddenly join the attack but Bobby sorted that out too.

Don knew what he was getting with Bobby and he made a difference in our approach to succeed. We feared Bobby more than

Don at times. He'd yell at us, "Do you want to be chuffing playing in the Third Division or do you want to get organised and avoid relegation?"

Bobby was so determined and suddenly we were moving in the right direction.

With one match left, Leeds travelled to Newcastle United where a win at St James' Park would guarantee staying up.

Missing the game was really disappointing on a personal level but Billy McAdams came in and played his last game for the club. I travelled up with the lads by coach and we all knew how big the match was for the club. There was tension but we'd been on a good run and just needed to finish the job.

On the day, we knew what we had to do and there was an overriding feeling that we were going do it. Bobby was really fired up and made sure everyone was ready from the first kick. I was in the dugout watching the game with Don and Les. Don was quite calm but Les was kicking every ball and yelling at everyone. We had more to play for than Newcastle and by half time led 3-0 then saw out the game.

There was huge relief that we'd done it and a feeling that we'd never be in that position again. It was a happy coach journey back to Leeds after the game.

Lawson was still struggling with ankle problems throughout the close season. To pep up his attack, Revie signed Airdrie striker Jim Storrie, for £15,650, and sprang a surprise by bringing back former legend John Charles from Juventus to the club in a £53,000 transfer.

Big John was a superstar and arrived at our team hotel dressed in a well-cut Italian suit, looking like a Greek God. You could not get near him because every lady in the hotel was swooning around him! John was such a modest guy though and took it all in his stride.

The first day he arrived for training, John asked where we wanted him to change, so we decided to wind up little Billy who was always late. Billy, all white and freckles, came rushing in and went straight to where he normally changed. Standing beside his peg, John was stripped and bronzed. Billy looked around at us, "Jesus Christ, thanks guys".

It was brilliant; the banter was great. We were all mates on and off the field, and Don must take a lot of credit for the atmosphere in the dressing room. There was a tremendous feelgood factor and a determination not to endure another nightmare season.

Storrie began firing in goals when the 1962/63 season kicked off but, with the first team struggling for results, Revie blooded four teenagers in a league clash at Swansea Town on September 8th, 1962. Gary Sprake, Norman Hunter, Paul Reaney and Rod Johnson came into the side for the match, which Leeds won 2-0, and results soon picked up.

> My ankle was still causing issues, so it was no surprise Storrie and Big John got the nod. I played alongside both in a defeat against Rotherham United but was then out for a month. By the time I returned for a League Cup tie at Blackburn Rovers, John had played his last game for Leeds and he was past his best. Things did not work out for him, but John in his prime was up there with the very best players. In today's game he'd be alongside Messi and Ronaldo because John was that good a footballer.
>
> Don was right to bring in the kids, as he did at Swansea with the first team struggling. I'd got my break at 17 for Burnley, so had no complaints. I've always felt that if you're good enough it does not matter how old you are for the first team. Hunter was a skinny kid but had that timing in his tackling he became famous for as a defender. Yet off the pitch, he would not say boo to a goose, but clearly had bags of talent. Norman was professional from an early age, straight up, and you knew what you'd get with him.
>
> Reaney always worked hard and was so determined to make it. He wasn't naturally gifted like some of the other young lads but got the best out of his abilities.
>
> Sprake was a smashing lad and had already been in the first team, but this was his break, and he showed he was a terrific goalkeeper.

Following United's 4-0 defeat to Blackburn Rovers, Lawson would not enjoy first team action until late in the season when he teamed up alongside Storrie and recent signing Don Weston. But it was some return as he scored both goals in a 2-0 victory at Scunthorpe United.

Another brace followed at Chelsea in a 2-2 draw but with his ankle playing up, Revie played Lawson sporadically in United's remaining five games of the season.

The season ended on a high with Leeds thumping Swansea Town 5-0. Storrie (2), Lawson, Collins and Johanneson scored the goals in a fine victory.

It was frustrating playing for the reserves but I was pleased with my comeback, however, that didn't stop Don resting me after scoring two goals against Chelsea, and after my goal against Swansea when I ended the game playing centre half because Big Jack got injured. We finished in fifth place, which was a remarkable turnaround from the previous season.

As the 1963/64 season approached, a promotion push appeared on the cards. Revie, Les Cocker and Syd Owen had created a professional environment for players. There was a meticulous training and matchday routine but also a special atmosphere around the club. United were going places.

Pre-season was tough with the initial workouts then running round Roundhay Park. First though I had to get down to my target weight. The heavier lads, including myself, used to go in two weeks early to make sure we'd hit our weight, and once I hit mine I was fine throughout the season. There was also plenty of fun in between the sessions, especially cricket matches to lighten the mood. Confidence had returned to the squad and we had coaches who got the best from us in training. Cocker was so enthusiastic whereas Owen was a great organiser though a hard character. There was a sense among the lads that we'd be up there and were from the start. Promotion was the target and our bonuses were set for a win, if we were top of the table and for attracting bigger gates.

When it came to man-management, the boss was terrific and ran a tight ship. With Don, everything he did was for the players. Away from training, we had regular golf days and at Christmas the young lads and staff behind the scenes would join us. The atmosphere was fantastic and you felt a part of something special. Before a game, we'd meet up at the team hotel, have our pre-match meal then Don would go through his dossier on our opponents. We travelled to games by coach or train depending on where it was taking place. If we stopped overnight before a game, we played carpet bowls and bingo to relax.

Don was meticulous but also very superstitious. Some of the lads ran out in a particular position, like Jack, who was last out, however Don was on another level. When a game came around we were prepared but Don would still have a quiet word with each player in the dressing room. There was no team warming up session as you see now, I did my stretches an hour before kick off then ran out when it was time. Looking back, it's amazing there were not more muscle pulls.

All the lads had a routine and whereas I'd take ages, Weston would walk in 15 minutes before the game and be ready in no time at all. Billy also seemed ill prepared but he'd go out and have a blinder! Before running out some lads would be shouting and balling while others would sit quietly but we went out as a team.

The atmosphere was great behind the scenes where a lot of people were behind us and none more than chairman Harry Reynolds. Harry was a larger-than-life character and loved being with the lads. On journeys to games he'd sit with us, not the directors. "My boys," he'd say, "there is nothing better than having a beer with my boys, you do us proud."

Big Jack and Billy were also real characters. Jack was a fantastic personality, his own man and never deviated from what he believed in. On a club tour, he'd say I'm going for a drink, so we'd say, "Right you are, Jack, you do that." We'd have a bet that after his second pint, he'd be back. And true to form, he'd come strolling in!

I roomed with Billy who was not the tidiest of roommates and roped me into all sorts. We were always doing something crazy and, more often than not, Willie Bell would be on the receiving end. Willie, on occasions, would not go out on a night out so we'd ring him up and make out we were from the Water Board then get him to fill his bath, which for some reason he did. Then if we got back late from a nightclub we'd run into Willie's room all dressed up. "Willie, what are you doing man, it's time to go," we'd scream.

Poor Willie would get up dazed, dress and then we'd put him out of his misery. Willie got the brunt of our daft capers! On the field though, Willie was a crucial member of the team because he added balance.

Revie's line-up was taking shape, building from a settled defensive unit of Reaney, Charlton, Hunter and Bell in front of Sprake in goal. Midfielders Bremner, Collins and Johanneson were bolstered by the signing of Johnny Giles from Manchester United for £33,000 promising guile, strength and pace. Two of Storrie, Weston or Lawson would lead the attack.

Bobby Collins was number one in my book. For me, he is the most important signing in the club's history when you look at his impact on and off the field. Bobby brought in a winning mentality, even in five-a-sides, he was so competitive and had to win. Giles had a winning mentality from his years with Manchester United but he could also play. Blessed with great vision, Johnny prepared well and could ping a ball anywhere around the park. When Johnny teamed up with Billy, they were magic together, and on another level to other midfield partnerships.

As for Albert Johanneson, he was a dandy fellow and loved to be smartly dressed. Back in Johannesburg where he grew up, Albert experienced segregation, so despite his talent it took him time to settle at Leeds. Albert wouldn't shower with the lads at one time but we soon put him right. I also remember sitting with him at a plush hotel in Birmingham before a game when waiters served us. Albert laughed nervously, and when I asked him why, he said he was wondering what it would have been like if white people had served him back in South Africa. Albert had to overcome racist chants from fans at some grounds, which was a disgrace, but he channelled his efforts into football, was exceptionally quick and could be a match winner.

Lawson was in the starting line-up when United got their league campaign off to a winning start against Rotherham, but would not feature again until opening the scoring in a 3-0 win over Northampton Town on October 1st, 1963.

Swindon Town were surprising early league leaders ahead of Leeds, Sunderland and Preston North End, but United were in the midst of a winning streak and headed the table for the first time on goal average following a 4-1 win at Southampton near the end of the month. Scoring four goals in the opening 33 minutes, Lawson bagged a brace in a memorable win.

Southampton v Leeds United, October 26th, 1963

Southampton: Burnside, Godfrey, Huxford, Kirby, Knapp, O'Brien, Payne, Penk, Traynor, White, Williams

Leeds United: Sprake, Reaney, Bell, Bremner, Charlton, Hunter, Giles, Lawson, Weston, Collins, Johanneson

Correspondent, James Hastings:

Seven coaches of a special train and a chartered aircraft took Leeds

United fans to The Dell, and what a worthwhile journey it proved to be for the Yorkshire club who gained their fourth successive away win to emphasise their strong challenge for promotion. Southampton are a difficult side to beat at home but they were completely outplayed by the slick moving and direct Leeds attack.

Lawson was back in favour ahead of Storrie and continued his impressive form in wins over Grimsby Town and Bury.

Lawson recalled:

Don was always fair with the strikers if goals were hard to come by, as he'd give you extra games to find your form, but it would come to a point when you would be out of the line-up. As things turned out, Storrie's goals dried up so I was back in the side and knew if I played well the attacking spot was mine.

United and Sunderland came up against each other in a double-header over the festive period. Anticiptation in both cities was huge for the Boxing Day clash at Elland Road and return fixture at Roker Park two days later. The victors would gain a huge boost of confidence for the remainder of the campaign.

Leeds United v Sunderland, December 26th, 1963

Leeds United: Sprake, Reaney, Bell, Bremner, Goodwin, Hunter, Giles, Weston, Lawson, Collins, Johanneson

Sunderland: Montgomery, Irwin, Ashurst, Harvey, Hurley, McNab, Usher, Herd, Sharkey, Crossan, Mulhall

After Mulhall scored against the run of play, Leeds searched for an equaliser and eventually got it through Lawson's poaching ability.

By a special correspondent:

Leeds' efforts became almost frenzied but their directness seemed to desert them when it came to shooting at goal. Finally, however, they managed to equalise. It was a pity that such a long awaited goal should be so scrambled. Weston and Lawson challenged Montgomery, the ball dropped from his hands and Lawson scored. In spite of Sunderland's protests the goal was allowed.

Following the match, *Soccer Star* correspondent John Helm summed up Lawson's upturn in form in his Yorkshire Round-Up column titled

'Ian Is The Comeback Man'.

Nothing delights the football fan more than a good comeback story, and a man who can undoubtedly claim to have done just that is Leeds United's bustling centre forward Ian Lawson.

Remember Lawson, the 17-year-old youngster who first hit the headlines of the sports pages way back in 1957, when in two cup ties against Chesterfield and New Brighton, he slammed seven goals for Burnley in wins of 7-0 and 9-0?

He was hailed as the greatest centre forward discovery since Tommy Lawton, but the reputation proved harmful to Lawson, who was never able to reproduce similar form in subsequent seasons. Finally, in February 1962, Leeds United decided to take a gamble, and Don Revie signed Lawson from Burnley, for a fairly substantial fee.

But the fairytale did not materialise even then for Lawson. He had to fight his way back to the top, and it was not easy. He still found goals hard to come by, and the Leeds crowd did not take kindly to a costly flop.

However, manager Don Revie was convinced he would come through with flying colours. For practically the whole of last season, Lawson had to be content with Central League football, as United's new signing from Scotland Jim Storrie was getting the goals regularly.

But this time it is Lawson's turn to get the glory, and Storrie's turn to fight to recapture his form. Nothing has stood out more prominently in United's rise to the top of the Second Division than Lawson's ability to take the half-chance. So perseverance has paid off at last. Lawson is once again in favour with the crowds, and the goals are flowing fast from his boots.

It was Lawson who got the point-saving goal in the Boxing Day clash with challengers Sunderland, just when it seemed the Roker boys were going to score a valuable success at Elland Road. Incidentally, the attendance that day of well over 40,000 was the best at Leeds since the golden era of John Charles. There was a fair sprinkling of red 'n white clad supporters there too, in one of the keenest fought matches I have seen this season.

Forty-eight hours on and the Wiersiders inflicted a 2-0 defeat on United, only their second in 25 matches to throw the promotion race wide open. Going into the New Year, Leeds headed the way on 37 points with Preston and Sunderland a point back.

Lawson recalled:

The atmosphere in both games was fantastic but we did not perform because we drew 1-1 at home then lost 2-0 at Roker Park. The lads were so disappointed because you want to defeat your biggest rivals but there were plenty of games to go and we felt we could still achieve our goals. Don didn't go overboard about the Sunderland results, it's a cliché but you quickly move on to the next games. We vowed to send them a telegram after we won the title and did!

Away from the promotion race, Leeds turned their attentions to the FA Cup. And continuing his run of form, Lawson hit his first FA Cup goal since his Burnley days when Leeds pushed First Division Champions Everton all the way during a fourth round clash when they drew 1-1 in front of 48,826 fans at Elland Road.

Leeds United v Everton, January 25th, 1964

Leeds United: Sprake, Reaney, Bell, Bremner, Madeley, Hunter, Henderson, Giles, Lawson, Collins, Johanneson

Everton: West, Brown, Harris, Gabriel, Labone, Kay, Scott, Stevens, Young, Vernon, Temple

The ground was packed to the rafters against Everton and when crowds are massive you are more energised and want to perform. Big matches are why you play the game; you want to impress in front of full houses. Everton were a star team and Cup fever had really gripped the city of Leeds. Don really felt we had a chance because we were winning games and playing with confidence. And we should have won after I gave us a first half lead at Elland Road. I should have scored a second and then the referee made a terrible decision when Sprakie saved a penalty and he said that he'd moved. You think to yourself, come on ref give us a break.

Everton defeated United 2-0 in front of 66,000 spectators at Goodison Park three days later.

Everton v Leeds United, January 28th, 1964

Everton: West, Brown, Meagan, Harris, Labone, Kay, Scott, Stevens, Gabriel, Vernon, Temple

Leeds United: Sprake, Reaney, Bell, Bremner, Madeley, Hunter, Henderson, Giles, Lawson, Collins, Hawksby

Everton edged the replay before another bumper crowd but it had
been a great experience. Both games made us realise we'd be able
to compete at a higher level, but first we had to make it out of the
Second Division. Consistency was now the key and I knew that we
could do it.

Sunderland held a two-point advantage over Leeds and Preston with
10 matches left. United's league form had dipped since the Boxing Day
showdown with the Roker men, arguably due to their cup encounters,
but Revie had strengthened his attack by signing Middlesborough and
former England centre forward, Alan Peacock, for £53,000 in February
1964.

Revie's hunch to link up Peacock and Lawson would bring dividends
in the midst of consecutive 3-1 victories against Southampton,
Middlesborough and Grimsby Town. Leeds opened the scoring against
Southampton with a fortuitous Lawson goal before skipper Collins
ignited United's promotion push in early March.

Leeds United v Southampton, March 7th, 1964

**Leeds United: Sprake, Reaney, Bell, Greenhoff, Charlton, Hunter, Weston,
Lawson, Peacock, Collins, Johanneson**

**Southampton: Godfrey, Willams, Hollywood, Wimshurst, Knapp, Huxford,
Payne, Chivers, Kirby, McGuigan, Sydenham**

Correspondent, Ronald Kennedy:

*The City of Leeds, hungry for success, breathed a sigh of relief in the
72nd minute of this rugged battle tinged with promotion glamour.*

*Bobby Collins, a little chunkier and a little slower than in his hey-
day, swept away with the ball towards the left edge of the penalty
area.*

*Elland Road groaned because it looked a thousand to one that
wee Bobby had thrown away a golden chance to settle The Saints'
clash once and for all. But suddenly the little general's foot struck like
the tongue of an angry viper, and the ball tore savagely into the net.*

*Till then, United, once a goal ahead (through Lawson) and then
level, had dangled the nervous fans on the end of a thread of suspense.*

*Collins' goal restored the balance and was a tranquiliser for the
fury that blasted from the terraces as United threatened to give the
game away in a fit of casual inefficiency.*

The Peacock-Lawson partnership then came up trumps against Boro' and Grimsby.

Seven games remained with Leeds on 51 points, Sunderland 50 and Preston 47.

> In all three games we were level at half time but Don was not the type to lose his temper. He made his points clear in encouraging us to win the game. However, Bobby was always fiery and made his viewpoint in no uncertain terms. He ripped into us all to get out there and do the business, which we did.
>
> Each game was so important because we edged in front of Sunderland and Preston. Peacock had really added impetus to the attack and I enjoyed playing alongside him. Alan was the best header of a ball I'd seen, so if he went up to head a ball, I knew he'd nod it down to me.

United now faced Easter trips to Newcastle United and Derby County before a return date with the Tyneside club on March 30th. Lawson helped Leeds win a tough encounter at St James' Park before sharing the spoils at the Baseball Ground. But United's 1-1 draw at Derby came at a cost with Lawson picking up a hamstring injury that would sideline him in the remaining games.

Leeds went on to clinch promotion at Swansea Town then the title at Charlton Athletic, courtesy of a Peacock brace, in a 2-0 triumph. Leeds topped the Second Division table with 63 points ahead of Sunderland with 61 and Preston on 56.

Correspondent, Phil Brown, *Green Post*:

> *Hail The Champions! Leeds United wound up a great season by claiming the crowning glory of Division Two at Charlton today.*
>
> *By rail, road and air, United supporters descended on this south-east London ground for the sight of United's final fling for the Second Division title.*
>
> *The win was completely deserved and it crowned the season ideally with the title again after 40 years.*

With the title wrapped up, chairman Harry Reynolds made a special trip to the Potteries to collect the Second Division trophy from last season's winners, Stoke City, in order for Leeds to have it available for their victory parade at Leeds Town Hall and civic reception. Leeds United were back in the big time and Lawson had played his part in a historic season.

> I travelled with the lads to Swansea and had a fitness test on the morning of the game, but was not right so knew I'd miss out. It was a huge disappointment but there were no substitutes so the boss could not take a chance. If I'd pulled up after a few minutes then the lads would be down to 10 men. Of course, players get injured in games but going out knowing I'd not get through was too risky.
>
> We got the right result, which was the main thing, and it was so exciting to get promotion. There was a great sense of achievement, elation and relief that we had reached our objective because that was the main target. We'd got what we deserved after the effort we'd put in over the season and the overriding feeling was that we'd cracked it; we were on our way. At the civic reception, we knew this was just a start for the club.

Top-flight football was back in the city of Leeds and a competitive football team was developing. United's success had brought positive media coverage, including snippets on the club's youth academy. Peter Lorimer, Jimmy Greenhoff, Paul Madeley and Terry Cooper had made debuts. Eddie Gray, Rod Belfitt, Terry Hibbitt and David Harvey would soon make an impression.

> When I first saw Gray and Lorimer play at 15 years of age, I knew they were going to make it. Don asked a few of the lads to put them through their paces in a five-a-side game, so we put in some hard tackles to see what they were made of but they shrugged them off and played well. When Don asked what I thought about them afterwards, I looked at him with a wry smile. There was no doubt about it, both would be stars.
>
> Madeley was only a kid but his character was spot on. Don knew he had the talent but he could not have predicted just how good he'd be all over the park. Paul's build allowed him to move with ease around the pitch and there was something about him that stood out. Some players were good at getting forward, which he could do, but Paul could also turn with the ball and defend when needed. He was a fabulous footballer and would be worth an astonishing amount in the modern game.
>
> Cooper was another kid with enormous potential, yet so modest. Terry started out on the left wing then switched to left back and you

knew he was going to make it to the top.

Harvey was a good kid and as a rookie keeper clearly had potential, though had to bide his time for years before getting an opportunity.

Of all the young lads, Hibbitt was cheekiest and the one you'd give a clip round the ear. As a prospect, he had a sweet left foot and could play but he never quite made it at Leeds. However, he was up against so many great midfield players it was always going to be tough. But Terry knew he'd be able to cut it somewhere, and did at Newcastle United when he teamed up with Malcolm Macdonald, sliding the ball through for 'SuperMac' to finish. Greenhoff and Belfitt also both had talent but like Hibbitt would enjoy better times at other clubs.

Football is a harsh business where apprentices are concerned. Barrie Wright captained England Schoolboys at Wembley but sometimes things don't work out. And then there were lads like Dennis Hawkins, whom you felt sad for because he worked really hard and had a great attitude but did not make the grade. Unlike Dennis though, there were ground staff lads who thought they were far better than they actually were, so you didn't feel sorry for them when they came and went. Don had a huge array of talent to serve the club but that was for the future.

United were not predicted to make a big impression when the 1964/65 season got underway, but the mass media sat up when Leeds won their opening three games against Aston Villa, Liverpool and Wolves. Lawson came in for Collins in a 3-2 win against Wolves at the end of August, before leading the attack alongside Storrie in a 3-3 thriller at Sunderland a week later.

Leeds United v Wolverhampton Wanderers, August 29th, 1964

Leeds United: Sprake, Reaney, Bell, Bremner, Charlton, Hunter, Giles, Weston, Storrie, Lawson, Johanneson

Wolverhampton Wanderers: Davies, Thomson, Harris, Goodwin, Flowers, Woodruff, Broadbent, Knowles, Crawford, Melia, Wharton

Correspondent, Edgar Turner:

I'll be the first to stick my neck out and say it, Leeds United for the Championship! I know that this was only the third game of the season, and I know there's a long way to go. But you can take it from me, Don

Revie's boys will be no pushover's for any team in the First Division. Far from it. They're soccer's new glamour boy's challenging the best in the land for a crack at that European jackpot.

Sunderland v Leeds United, September 5th, 1964

Sunderland: McLaughlan, Irwin, Ashurst, Harvey, Hurley, McNab, Usher, Mitchinson, Clough, Crossan, Mulhall

Leeds United: Sprake, Reaney, Bell, Bremner, Charlton, Hunter, Giles, Lawson, Storrie, Collins, Johanneson

Correspondent, John Dunn:

The symphonic sweetness of Leeds United's rhythmic soccer movement sent the far-travelled Yorkshire fans home in rhapsodies from Roker Park yesterday. And well it might have done for this United outfit have bridged the gap between Second Division clog and First Division finesse with admirable ease.

Sadly for Lawson, a 4-0 loss against Blackpool at Bloomfield Road would be his final game of the season due to a knee injury, and while United went close to winning the 'double', Lawson underwent an operation and wondered about his future.

Something had been wrong for a while with my knee but you just solider on in games. Against Blackpool it gave way and I ended up hobbling through the match because there were no subs. By the Friday, it was diagnosed as a cartilage problem and I had the operation a few days later.

The injury was a real blow and there were complications after the procedure so it took ages to get close to match fitness. I was fine running forward but turning was a real issue, so I realised my knee would not be right again. It was soul-destroying but all you can do is battle away and hope for a chance to get back into the first team. Don was great though because even though I was not involved on the pitch, he wanted me to be with the first team squad for away games and on short breaks after cup games.

Watching from the sidelines was not easy, especially seeing the lads lose the First Division title on goal average. But I was in the crowd at Nottingham Forest when Billy headed us into the FA Cup Final with a late winner against Manchester United. The atmosphere in the dressing room after was amazing and historic because it would be

United's first Wembley final.

For every footballer, to play in an FA Cup Final was a major ambition, and I missed out twice, which was the biggest disappointment of my career. Burnley let me go leading up to the 1962 Final against Tottenham Hotspur and now I was injured at Leeds. At least this time I was a part of the build up to Wembley when we recorded 'The Leeds United Calypso' with Ronnie Hilton. There were plenty of bad voices but it was all part of the experience, and it was top of the chart sales locally at Schofields and Lewis's department stores.

I was at Wembley for the big day and hoped they could do the business. Unfortunately we did not play well against Liverpool, which made the banquet afterwards at the Savoy Hotel tough on all the lads. We'd gone really close to the 'double' so to lose out on both was heartbreaking but it had been an incredible season.

Lawson, who scored 21 goals in 51 appearances for Leeds United, joined Crystal Palace in a £9,000 transfer during the close season.

After one season at Selhurst Park, where he made 17 league appearances, Lawson played briefly for Port Vale before moving to Barnsley in 1967. However, he never made an appearance for the Oakwell side as persistent knee problems forced his retirement from the game at 29 years of age.

During a career in the steel industry, the Lawson's, who have four grandchildren, moved around the country from Congleton to Stanley in County Durham, and later Tamworth, where they continue to enjoy retirement.

Before the FA Cup Final in '65, I realised it would be tough getting back into the first team, and not long after it was obvious I'd have to drop down a division to continue my career. When Palace came in for me, I was determined to give it a go, but my knee was still an issue.

One of the highlights during my spell at Palace was England captain, Bobby Moore, dropping in to our local pub on a Saturday night after a game for a drink. With the World Cup coming up, it was great chatting with Bobby, who was such a modest guy. Charlie Woods, Tony Millington and Keith Smith, like myself, also lived in Brighton, so we drove in together each day to training. We also watched the World Cup Final, and after England won, I did think about contacting Big Jack to join the celebrations, but there was no way after toasting the success we could have driven to London!

After Palace, my knee kept swelling up, so after a season not kicking a ball I hung up my boots. Retiring was tough though. You can only play football professionally for a short period and it was deflating to call it a day but I had plenty of memories and I would not change anything.

The highlight at Leeds was winning the Second Division title. There were not that many players under Don who won a title, so to achieve it with that group was really special. I played with three of the greatest footballers of any generation in Billy Bremner, John Charles and Bobby Collins. Playing with those guys, you can't help but think how great was that.

4

Rod Johnson

ROD Johnson was a central figure in a week that changed the course of Leeds United's history in September 1962. Manager Don Revie, backed by a board that believed in nurturing a youth policy, had come through a traumatic first season in charge when United avoided relegation to the Third Division with victory at Newcastle United in the final game. The spine of a new team needed developing after the club's great escape, but with a depleted squad at his disposal and senior players out of form, Revie gambled on youth for a Second Division away trip at Swansea Town on September 8th.

Seventeen-year-old striker Johnson was one of four players from United's reserve team that had just beaten Liverpool reserves to play at The Vetch Field and opened the scoring in a 2-0 victory. Thereafter, Johnson was unfortunate not to get an extended first team run, though did hit the winner on his First Division debut against West Brom, but when the story of the Revie period is recalled, his Swansea strike undoubtedly sparked the club into a new era.

The eldest of Ron and Vi Johnson's three children, Rod was born in Leeds in January 1945. Educated at Upper Wortley Junior School and Cow Close Secondary School, Rod was eight years of age when he attended his first Leeds United game on November 9th, 1953. Standing on the Kop when Hibernian came to town with his dad and granddad, Jack Johnson, it was a night the three generations of Johnson's witnessed 'floodlit' football arrive at Elland Road.

Johnson recalled:

My granddad lived in Tilbury Terrace off Elland Road so dad would

> park outside his house then we'd all walk to the ground. The Hibs game was a real occasion; granddad even took a buffet to the match.
>
> Nobody had seen a floodlit game before so there was great anticipation in the ground. The stand lights were on but you could not see the whole pitch. Then a few minutes before the match, the floodlights came on and it was an incredible sight seeing the pitch lit up. Both teams then ran out and got on with the game.
>
> Leeds played a number of Scottish teams that season and some joker cracked that we'd topped the Scottish First Division after beating them all under lights!

The 'floodlit' initiative also included St Mirren, Queen of the South and Aberdeen. And it didn't stop there because United took on Bradford Park Avenue in the West Riding Senior Cup then Admira (Vienna) and Rampla (Uruguay) under lights. And there was finally a testimonial style match against 'The Starlights' featuring giants of the game including Frank Swift, Bill Shankly, Peter Doherty and Wilf Mannion.

United manager Raich Carter, who led Sunderland and Derby County to major honours in his playing days, also lined up for the Starlights. But the big attraction for fans was Blackpool star Stanley Matthews although his appearance was not assured as the programme named 'A.N. Other' in the line-up should 'The Wizard of the Dribble' be unavailable.

A couple of years on and United's young supporter witnessed his team enjoy a successful Second Division promotion campaign in 1955/56.

> George Meek was one of my heroes along with John Charles before he went to Juventus. Jackie Overfield, Harold Williams, Wilbur Cush and Tommy Burden were also crowd favourites.
>
> It was exciting that Leeds would play top-flight football because great teams would come to Elland Road. After hanging up my boots I played with a number of lads from the promotion squad for the ex-players team and it was terrific fun.

As a sporting city, Leeds and Hunslet rugby league teams had enjoyed tangible success compared to Leeds United prior to the 1960s. And Johnson came from a rugby family. His maternal grandfather, Charlie Hirst, represented Hunslet RL whilst his father had played for the Leeds RL 'A' team.

A talented sportsman himself, Johnson represented Leeds City Boys at rugby league and football. Evaluating where to begin his sporting career, Rod signed for his hometown football club.

> I enjoyed all sports but my preference was always football and Leeds City had a strong team. Paul Madeley, Paul Reaney and Kevin Hector were among my teammates; all of them went on win England honours.
>
> As a perk for playing with Leeds City, players received passes to watch Leeds United games. We'd stand on the banking that became the Kop and was so close to the pitch you could head a ball back if it came your way.
>
> I trained with United's amateur players on a Tuesday and Thursday night at Elland Road but never had a formal trial, so it was a surprise when the club approached my parents about me joining the ground staff.

Jack Taylor was Leeds United manager when Johnson joined the club in January 1960. It was a time when three quarters of the population owned a television and a full Saturday afternoon results service was now broadcast live on BBC's *Grandstand* sports programme. Football fans tuned in to see how their football team had got on that afternoon, but becoming a professional footballer was no easy task, as archaic duties tested the determination of an apprentice to endure what was a tough programme.

> Leeds United were a Second Division team with no star players but there were lots of young lads with potential at the club. As apprentices we cleaned boots, swept the terraces, helped the groundsman or put kits out for the first team squad in the dressing room. Then, when the squad returned from training, we made sure cups of tea were ready for the players before tidying up. On top of everything, we also helped prepare the main pitch by sifting through soil at the bottom end of the club car park. After taking soil by wheelbarrow over to the pitch, head groundsman, John Reynolds, would seed the surface while we walked along planks spreading soil on top. We'd then go back to the car park and sift more soil. Once that task was finished we helped cut the grass down behind the stands.
>
> There was no under-soil heating for the pitch, which eventually became the norm at top clubs, so in the winter, to stop the pitch freezing, hay was laid on top of the playing surface. On a match day

we'd help clear the hay before a game. But there were also occasions when the weather was so bad coal burners had to be placed on the pitch to melt the snow. Can you imagine modern day apprentices rolling a pitch? I doubt it, but that's how it was in those days.

In March 1961, United appointed a new manager to succeed Taylor.

Before training a meeting was called in the dressing room, so we knew something was happening. Harry Reynolds walked in to announce Don Revie would be taking over as manager. Don stepped up and said, "You've all known me as Don, but when I walk out this door, you call me boss," that was it. Of course it was a surprise, but as a young kid you just get on with it.

Starting out in the junior team, which played in the Northern Intermediate League, Johnson moved into the reserves managed by Syd Owen and started banging in the goals against Central League opposition.

I'd scored regularly at every level so it was no different in the reserves, although one of my sweetest strikes was an own goal when I mistakenly volleyed a corner past our keeper into the top corner of our net. Syd was blazing in the dressing room afterwards but eventually got over it!

We mainly played every Saturday afternoon, so if the first team were at Old Trafford then Manchester United's reserves came to Elland Road. We had solid attendances for home games and I remember playing against Aston Villa at Villa Park when over 10,000 fans watched the game, which was a bigger gate than many clubs outside the First Division could attract for a first team fixture. It sounds crazy but that's how it was in the early 1960s.

United's reserve side had plenty of talent and included a South African player who would become the first black player to appear in an FA Cup Final.

Albert Johanneson had just come to Leeds and had no boots with him before a match against Blackpool at Bloomfield Road. Syd was not impressed but Albert borrowed a pair and was outstanding.

There were very few black footballers in the English game, so Albert was a target for racist taunts, especially at away games, and it did take him time to settle. On his day though he could open up a defence with his pace but struggled with the physical side, where defenders thought nothing of getting a tackle in early to put you off your game and you had to evade scything challenges from behind. You could not get away with those tactics now but it was part of the game and you had to cope.

Getting a professional contract on your 17th birthday was the main objective for all apprentices. But it was a nervous time for Johnson approaching the big day.

> When Don wanted to see me after the first team had finished training one day, my first thought was that he was going to release me. But after sitting down in his office, Don told me I was looking a bit peaky, which surprised me.
>
> Don arranged for me to take home a tender sirloin steak and bottle of Harvey's Bristol Cream to supplement my diet for a fortnight. A couple of weeks later, Don was pleased I looked healthier but I didn't mention my dad had feasted on the steak, as I didn't like them!
>
> I'd looked peaky because I was worried about being released!

Johnson duly signed for Leeds on a full-time basis in March 1962, and it was an exciting time for the teenager because he had also gained international recognition when he won an England Youth cap.

> Leeds had just signed Ian Lawson from Burnley who had been in their reserve side and I'd been at England youth trials in Reading. I played against Scotland at Peterborough and scored a goal in a 4-2 win, which was a memorable occasion for me. The headline in the *Evening Post* next day made me laugh: 'Leeds pay £20,000 for Burnley reserve and £20 for an International!'

On the domestic scene, it was an uncertain time at Elland Road, as Revie's team seemed destined for relegation. In a bid to avoid the drop, aside from Lawson, Revie had signed Cliff Mason from Sheffield United and Bobby Collins from Everton. However, during United's run-in, bureaucracy denied Johnson a first team debut against Middlesborough.

> Don was going to play me on the left wing in place of John Hawksby but the West Riding Football Association would not release me as they had first choice over my registration. I felt it was an injustice, but there was nothing the club could do so I played at East End Park, which was really disappointing. All you want is a chance to prove

yourself at first team level but I'd have to wait. Leeds beat 'Boro and eventually stayed up, which was a massive relief to everyone.

After surviving relegation, Revie signed Airdrie striker Jim Storrie for £15,650. And then, in a blaze of publicity, paid £53,000 for former United legend John Charles, following his Italian adventure with Juventus, to pep up his attack for the 1962/63 campaign.

Revie had already changed the club's strip from blue and gold to emulate the all-white of Real Madrid. Aiming high was laudable but United did not have the stature, players or talent to rival the Spanish giants, and made an uninspired start to their league campaign.

The day after a 2-1 midweek home defeat against Bury, United's third in six games, with Charles, Storrie, Freddie Goodwin and Willie Bell out through injury and other senior players struggling for form, Revie weighed up his options. United's reserves had won 2-0 at Liverpool 48 hours before the Bury debacle. Lining up at Anfield against Bill Shankly's second string outfit was a side blessed with nine talented teenagers who had impressed reserve boss Owen over an 18-month period.

Liverpool v Leeds United, September 3rd, 1962

Liverpool: Lawrence, Jones, Molyneux, Wheeler, Lawler, Corkhill, Graham, Scott, Arrowsmith, Smith, Wallace

Leeds United: Sprake, Reaney, Wright, Addy, Madeley, Hunter, Blackburn, Johnson, Lorimer, Hawksby, Cooper

Revie pondered whether some of his youngsters were ready for first team action. Deciding to take a calculated gamble, Revie dropped experienced pros Tommy Younger and Grenville Hair from his first team. Gary Sprake, Paul Reaney, Norman Hunter and Johnson were informed they would play against Swansea Town at The Vetch Field in the next fixture. For Sprake it was a second first team game, Reaney, Hunter and Johnson would make debuts. With the Welsh club winning their previous three league home encounters it would be a stern test for Revie's reshaped team.

Yorkshire Evening Post correspondent, Phil Brown, broke the news in the media:

After last night's setback by Bury, I expected changes, as I think did most supporters.

Mr Revie I know badly wanted a few more weeks at least for this crop of 'good uns' to mature in men's football in the Central League, but events have overtaken him.

Revie told the YEP: "I didn't really want to play the lads yet, I wanted them to get a bit more experience but I have to give them a chance now.

"We have to get cracking in the league."

Johnson recalled:

During pre-season I'd played on the left wing at Morecombe and Leicester City in friendly games. It was not my natural position but Don wanted me to play there and see how things developed. When the first team lost against Bury, we'd done well at Anfield. Don had a report on the game from Syd and decided the time was right to play us at Swansea.

When Don told me the news it was fantastic, but I was not totally surprised because I'd been knocking on the first team door for some months. Playing Swansea though was funny because my Nan's family was Welsh and lived in Cardiff, so they came to the game. My parents also travelled down from Leeds and were in the main stand for the match.

Certain games in the Revie era are acknowledged as pivotal and 90 minutes after Leeds United ran out at Swansea Town, on a muddy pitch in their away all-blue kit, the clash had entered club folklore.

Swansea Town v Leeds United, September 8ᵗʰ, 1962

Swansea Town: Dwyer, Hughes, Griffiths, Davies, Purcell, Saunders, Jones, Thomas, Webster, Williams, Morgan

Leeds United: Sprake, Reaney, Mason, Smith, Charlton, Hunter, Peyton, Bremner, Johnson, Collins, Johanneson

Revie's new-look XI made a bright start with Johnson opening the scoring for Leeds on 11 minutes. Johanneson darted down the left wing, linked with Billy Bremner who put Johnson in on goal. Journalists noted United's young striker showed composure beyond his years in evading two defenders before clinically firing home from a tight angle.

Bremner settled the match with a neat finish in the second half.

Johnson had impressed until a clash of heads with Swansea stopper Noel Dwyer saw him carried off on a stretcher before returning to the fray after lengthy treatment.

Saturday night's local sports paper front-page headline 'DEBUT DAY DRAMA – United boy scorer is a casualty' summed up the match.

A correspondent noted:

Leeds United manager, Mr Don Revie, took a real selection gamble at Swansea, and won. United were unrecognisable from their defeat at home to Bury.

United scored early in each half, Johnson, a mobile centre forward, steering in a difficult angled shot and Bremner crowning the best passing move in the match early in the second.

United moved faster and played more accurately than at any time this season or last, the youngsters bringing a zip the side badly needed.

Johnson's memory of the occasion has not diminished:

Tactically, we kept it tight at the back, played a pressing game and Bobby launched the ball forward at every opportunity. When I opened the scoring early in the game it was a great feeling, and things were going well until I jumped for a ball in the second half with their big keeper who flattened me.

I was out cold so had no idea I'd been stretchered off until I came round in the treatment room and the first person I saw was my mother in the bed next to me. I thought what are you doing here? Mum thought I'd been badly injured so had fainted.

Looking back, it was a bizarre incident and must be a one-off because I've never heard of a player getting injured and ending up in a treatment room with his mother! There was no time to chat though because in those days there were no subs so I wanted to get back out, and I felt okay so after I'd been checked over I finished the game.

Following his first team debut, Johnson went on to make four more league appearances during the season, including a win against Newcastle United. He also appeared in League Cup clashes against Crystal Palace and Blackburn Rovers.

By the close season, Charles had departed to Roma for £70,000, netting the club a quick profit, while other senior players had moved on. Revie was revamping his team and Johnson was aware changes were afoot.

> Don kept faith with Sprake, Reaney and Hunter, which was great for them and they went on to have long careers at the club. All three were in the right place at the right time, which is often the way with football. You need that break, and I did get an occasional game but had to wait for a real opportunity. With Storrie knocking in the goals I'd have to bide my time which felt okay as I was only a kid.

Johnson frustratingly missed out on United's successful Second Division campaign due to injury. Revie had strengthened his team with Johnny Giles coming into the midfield and seasoned campaigner, Alan Peacock, leading the attack alongside Jim Storrie or Don Weston. And from United's talented pool of players Peter Lorimer and Terry Cooper made first team starts during the season. Though delighted the team was back in top-flight football, it was discouraging sitting on the sidelines.

> Missing out on the season was a real blow because, when fit, I offered something different to the side. Our physio, Bob English, did his best but rehabilitation methods then were so basic. However, following promotion you really sensed the club was going places.
>
> Most supporters had accepted Leeds were a mediocre Second Division side. But now we had a chance amongst the top teams such as Manchester United, Liverpool, Everton, Tottenham Hotspur and Arsenal. Our title success was something fans thought they might never see, but things were building, and as local lad I noticed it where I lived. Suddenly people were asking me what was developing at the club. It was an exciting time to be associated with Leeds United.

Revie, behind the scenes, had developed his man management skills, helping to create an indomitable team spirit.

> Don was great, and even though it was frustrating not playing, I was still a part of the set up. Everything was so professional, how we trained, how we prepared for a match, and travel arrangements; nothing was left to chance.
>
> Don needed senior pros to be the backbone of his team. Collins had a winning attitude and taught the young lads how to be professional at an early age. Don and Big Jack didn't always see eye-to-eye but he was crucial to the side. Jack was cantankerous and not

the most disciplined of players. At times, he'd join the attack, even if that meant leaving the defence short, but Don made it clear Jack had to be a part of the team. And all credit to Jack, he eventually listened to Don and made his presence felt in attack more selectively, which helped him become a World Cup winner.

We were a close squad with plenty of mickey takers in the group and nobody was exempt, not even the most senior players. In five-a-side games it was like being in the old school playground when captains would shout your name out for a team, and Jack was so easy to wind up. On one memorable occasion the 'captains' decided to pick him last, so as each player was selected you could see Jack getting more and more annoyed. Even lads coming back from injury who could only do light work got selected before him! Jack was livid and had a real rant. "You so and so's, I'm an international player," and stormed off. The lads were killing themselves but it was only a bit of fun and Jack did eventually calm down to see the funny side.

Away from frivolities, for Johnson the role of United's skipper on and off the pitch was crucial.

Bobby Collins was a fantastic player and the main reason Leeds avoided relegation to the Third Division. He led by example and his experience was vital at that time. For me, he is the best signing in the club's history because he changed a team going nowhere to one with a winning mentality. As a young professional making his way in the game, Bobby was the most dedicated footballer I'd seen. His whole persona – the way he dressed smartly, how he approached a game and training, how he helped young lads, and especially his will to win, was incredible.

Without Bobby, Leeds would not have become the team they eventually did under Revie. He pulled everything together; he influenced the lads and made them believe they could be winners. We all know Bobby could rattle opponents, and his tackling was uncompromising, but he also trained like that. He always said that you could not switch off midweek then switch on come Saturday. Bobby trained every day as he played on a match day so it became second nature.

People often say Bremner and Giles were United's best players, and they were brilliant, but in my 600 plus games as a professional footballer, Bobby for me in his size four boots was the best. He was Bremner and Giles wrapped together, that's how highly I rate him. Bobby was a great professional and a great person, he set the standards all the lads followed.

Johnson was determined to stake a claim in the first team when United kicked off the First Division season in 1964/65. It was going to be tough breaking into the side but, with Peacock sidelined through injury for a number of months, opportunities would develop.

United got off to a flyer by winning their opening three league games and soon enjoyed a seven-match winning run to set the early pace with Manchester United and Liverpool. Revie's boys meant business and stunned football reporters with their consistency.

Revie had partnered Storrie with Lawson, Weston and Rod Belfitt. Following his injury woes, Johnson finally returned to first team action for a League Cup tie against Huddersfield Town on September 23rd, 1964.

Revie then gave Johnson his first League outing for two years against West Brom in November when, in his first top-flight appearance, Johnson grabbed the headlines with the only goal of the game.

After 20 matches, Leeds sat in third place, four points adrift of league leaders Manchester United.

Leeds United v West Bromwich Albion, November 28th, 1964

Leeds United: Williamson, Reaney, Bell, Bremner, Charlton, Hunter, Giles, Storrie, Johnson, Collins, Cooper

West Bromwich Albion: Potter, Cram, Williams, Fraser, Jones, Simpson, Foggo, Fenton, Astle, Hope, Clark

Correspondent, Phil Brown, *Green Post*:

> *Collins tried hard to get a penetrating edge on United, and he it was who enabled United's opening goal after 16 minutes. He swept a perfect pass across Albion's penalty area, after accepting one from Bremner, and Johnson had nothing more to do than kick the ball into the net.*

Johnson recalled:

> Scoring in the First Division was obviously special but it was a simple tap-in from close range. Speed was one of my biggest assets and it did take time to get my sharpness back.

Johnson remained in the side during an unbeaten nine-match run that yielded seven League and Cup wins. And during this rich vein of form, Johnson played in a hard fought triumph against title favourites Manchester United at a foggy Old Trafford with a Collins goal on 55 minutes sealing a famous win in early December. Having defeated the defending league champions Liverpool earlier in the season, this result demonstrated Revie's boys were on the march. They were now within touching distance of the league leaders.

Manchester United v Leeds United, December 5th, 1964

Manchester United: Dunne P, Brennan, Dunne A, Crerand, Foulkes, Stiles, Connelly, Charlton B, Herd, Law, Best

Leeds United: Sprake, Reaney, Bell, Bremner, Charlton J, Hunter, Giles, Storrie, Johnson, Collins, Cooper

Phil Brown, *Yorkshire Evening Post*:

"Heartiest congratulations" is a poor brace of words for Saturday's summit victory at Old Trafford by Leeds United, but at least they convey the idea. For this was the present sides "finest hour." Engrave it in gold – Manchester United 0 Leeds United 1.

A shame the struggle was so horribly fogbound, but thank heavens for a referee with the wits to finish it after a halt, and with the character to rule it all through.

Take a bow Mr J Finney of Hereford.

This match could have been torrid. It had, inevitably, a warm moment or two amid its white-hot tension in a stranglehold of a game, but it was very well played throughout, despite nobody holding back an inch or an ounce.

Tactically Manchester swallowed the Leeds bait hook, line and sinker, astonishingly so with the names and the experience in their eleven.

Leeds played the vital first quarter on defence, wingers back, neither wing half going up, with Collins moving relentlessly amid it all, a man of 10 positions to the last.

But Leeds also showed the leaders how it could be done in attack. There was Collins's dagger of a goal after Giles and Cooper had deftly thrust through, and there was some most menacing play by Storrie and Johnson, the latter missed scoring only by inches.

Leeds had no weak link from back to front, and their team discipline in following tactics was positively breathtaking. Even the latest man to enter the side this season, Johnson, was perfectly in step as the regulars.

Johnson recalled:

The conditions were bad because of the fog and near the end you could not see both goals, so we went off which was frustrating because United were getting a good hiding. Matt Busby knew his team were not going to win, so tried to get the game abandoned but the lads were not having it and made their point to the referee. Luckily the Ref was just waiting to see if the fog cleared, which it did, so we could play out the last few minutes and I went close to adding a second goal.

It was a massive win for us and signaled that we were going to be a force, which was great when you think where the club had been. We travelled home in fine spirits and our good form continued.

Johnson then grabbed the headlines when he scored the only goal against Wolves two weeks later.

Wolverhampton Wanderers v Leeds United, December 19th, 1964

Wolverhampton Wanderers: Davies, Thomson, Harris, Flowers, Woodfield, Miller, Wharton, Broadbent, Crawford, Kemp, Buckley

Leeds United: Sprake, Reaney, Cooper, Bremner, Charlton, Hunter, Giles, Storrie, Johnson, Collins, Johanneson

Terry Lofthouse, *Yorkshire Post*:

Leeds United's 11th win in 12 matches, 1-0 at the expense of struggling Wolves at Molineux, completed a second 'double' in successive games and took the team into joint leadership of the First Division with Manchester United.

Now only decimals separate the clubs, Manchester United being 0.6 of a goal better off.

The road to the top has been a hard one. It will be even harder to sustain the Championship bid. But in their present vein, they have the courage, determination, and above all, the 'guts' to beat any team. The defeat of Wolves was another triumph of teamwork and tactics.

With conditions more like a skating rink as a result of a week's heavy frost, United adapted themselves to the situation much better than Wolves, and their policy of banging the ball upfield and chasing everything paid off.

But do not think that the game lacked good football. Indeed the 58th minute goal that gave United victory was a 'peach' coming from a darting run by winger Johanneson and a lovely centre for Storrie to head goalwards. All Davies could do was push the ball out to Johnson, and the young centre forward, who had another promising match, planted the ball in the net.

Leeds sat top of the First Division following a 2-1 victory against Sunderland at the beginning of January. Charlton and Hunter scored the Leeds goals in a clash when only the defiance of Sunderland goalkeeper, Sandy McLaughlan, denied United a more emphatic victory.

Leeds United v Sunderland, January 2nd, 1965

Leeds United: Sprake, Reaney, Madeley, Bremner, Charlton, Hunter, Giles, Storrie, Johnson, Collins, Cooper

Sunderland: Mclaughlan, Parke, Ashurst, Harvey, Rooks, McNab, Usher, Hood, Sharkey, Herd, Mulhall

A correspondent noted:

To the surprise of many people outside of the city, Leeds are at the top of the First Division. In this latest conquest they swept aside a feeble challenge in a match more convincing than the scoreline suggests. Before the season began, the Leeds chariman, Mr H Reynolds, spoke of Leeds participating in the European Cup. The critics were inclined to scoff. But what seemed wishful thinking is now a possibility.

Johnson's third league goal of the campaign, a fortnight after the Sunderland victory, ensured United secured a 2-2 draw at Leicester City after twice coming from behind. But an injury ended his nine-match run.

Leicester City v Leeds United, January 16th, 1965

Leicester City: Banks, Chalmers, Norman, McDermott, Sjoberg, Appleton, Goodfellow, Roberts, Cross, Gibson, Stringfellow

Leeds United: Sprake, Reaney, Bell, Bremner, Charlton, Hunter, Giles, Storrie, Johnson, Collins, Johanneson

Correspondent, George Cranfield:

> *Leeds hit back four minutes after the interval to draw level. And what a goal. Johanneson, who teased right-back Chalmers all afternoon, raced down the wing. His centre was a beauty, neatly pulled away from all the defenders and Johnson cracked a tremendously powerful left foot shot into the net just under the bar.*

Prior to the Leicester clash, Leeds had embarked on an FA Cup run. Johnson made one appearance, scoring United's second goal as they eased past Southport 3-0 in the third round.

With Peacock back from injury, Johnson watched on as a member of the matchday squad as Leeds dispatched Everton after a replay, Shrewsbury Town, Crystal Palace and finally Manchester United in the semifinals, again after a replay, on the road to Wembley.

Johnson recalled:

> When we took on Manchester United at Hillsborough, I really believed we'd win, but it was an extremely tough encounter which ended in a draw, so we had to do it again in a replay at Nottingham Forest's City Ground. Billy got a late goal and the celebrations were fantastic because it meant a first Wembley final.

In the league, following a remarkable campaign, Leeds eventually lost out to Manchester United in the title race on goal average.

The season would end at the Twin Towers and Johnson was in with a chance of playing for the biggest prize in the club's history.

> After completing our league fixtures against Birmingham City on the Monday before the final, we stayed overnight then went straight to our hotel in London. Each day we had a light training session leading up to the big game. On the Thursday, Don pulled me to one side and told me Storrie was struggling for fitness so I'd probably be playing on the Saturday. I was elated because I didn't think that would be happening so rang my parents to tell them.
>
> My girlfriend, Margaret, and mum came down for the Final but dad had been really ill and was having treatment at Leeds General Infirmary. I knew he'd be unable to travel but he was really chuffed for me.
>
> After training on the Friday, Don announced the team on the coach so we would not be left wondering who was in or not. Following our conversation, I expected to be in, but my name was not

mentioned. Don told me later that day that Storrie had told him he'd get through the game. I was so disappointed because my shot at a Wembley final had gone.

Johnson sat in the stands when Collins led United out to face Liverpool at Wembley. The match was not a classic as Leeds went down to a 2-1 defeat in extra time. The Final left a bitter taste for Johnson, but not because of the defeat.

> Don got it wrong when he let Storrie play because he had a knock and you could tell within 10 minutes he was not fit and ended up a passenger. To make matters worse, Albert seemed overawed by the whole occasion, which made it even tougher for the lads. Substitutes did not come in until the next season so we effectively played with nine men for most of the match and you can't do that against a team like Liverpool, and especially at Wembley.
>
> We'll never know if I'd played instead of Storrie whether it would have affected the final score, but I'd have been able to offer more to the team because I was fully fit. I didn't talk about Don's discussion about Storrie with the lads at the time, but it did come up in conversation with Bobby a few years later, and he was really angry. We'd remained friends and Bobby told me if I'd played that day, with my pace against Ron Yeats we'd have had a better chance of winning the cup. Without a doubt, starting with 11 fit players we'd have had a better chance. Missing out on the '65 Cup Final was the biggest disappointment of my career.

The season ended in heartbreaking fashion for Leeds but they would be playing in Europe for the first time in the club's history. On and off the pitch, the club was going places but Johnson's football career was stalling. During the close season, Revie turned down overtures from Birmingham City and Crystal Palace.

> Don kept you informed if a club was interested but when he didn't let you go you'd think to yourself, he must see something in me. After promotion, I'd scored goals in the first team but then been dropped, so I thought to myself, all I need is a run in the team and the goals will come. It's a fact that as a forward if you play you will score goals. But I'd seen Peacock, Jimmy Greenhoff and Rod Belfitt all play so I wondered where I was in the pecking order.

The summers of 1965 and '66 would bring contrasting fortunes for the extended Johnson family following the death of Rod's father, before happier times with his marriage to Margaret.

In what must have been a difficult time emotionally off the field for Rod, at the start of the 1965/66 season, his Leeds career provided a moment of history against Aston Villa at Elland Road on September 1st, 1965 when he became the first substitute for the club to play in a match after replacing Charlton during the game.

> It was only after I finished playing that I discovered my claim to fame as a substitute for Leeds and it is a good quiz question!

Thereafter, Johnson made fleeting appearances, including a League Cup clash against Hartlepools United, when he scored his last goal for the club in a 4-2 win on September 2nd, 1965.

Johnson's final First Division appearance was on September 20th, 1967, as a substitute in a 2-1 victory over Burnley. Three weeks later, he played his final game for Leeds in a League Cup tie against Bury at Elland Road. Every player apart from Charlton had been on the ground staff. And in a twist of fate, Johnson's mentor, Collins, captained Bury on the night. Leeds came into the match having scored a glut of goals after thumping Spora Luxembourg 9-0 then Chelsea 7-0 in their most recent encounters and they duly racked up a 3-0 win against the lower league outfit.

Leeds United v Bury, October 11th, 1967

Leeds United: Sprake, Reaney, Madeley, Gray, Charlton, Hunter, Greenhoff, Lorimer, Belfitt, Johnson, Johanneson. Sub: Hibbitt

Bury: Ramsbottom, Parnell, Tinney, Kerr, Turner, Lindsay, Farrell, Dawson, Jones, Collins, Owen. Sub: Anderson

A correspondent noted:

> Collins returned to Elland Road and saved Bury from becoming the latest chopping-blocks of a Leeds side that has at last discovered goal-scoring flair. The 20,927 crowd applauded the former Leeds idol on and off the field. Once they even cheered him for a midfield success against Hunter (who captained Leeds on the night in Bremner's absence). But Collins and his teammates could not stem the flood of Leeds attacks, even though it was a night of thanksgiving and the

nostalgia must have been worth two extra defenders to Bury.

Johnson recalled:

> Playing against Bobby was strange but we won comfortably. By then
> I knew there was no future for me at Leeds.

Mick Jones' arrival from Sheffield United in a £100,000 transfer in September 1967 ended Johnson's career at Leeds. From a struggling Second Division side, Johnson had witnessed United become one of the most feared clubs in top-flight football though they had yet to win a major honour. Johnson joined Doncaster Rovers for £5,000 as Leeds prepared to face Arsenal in the League Cup Final on March 2nd, 1968. And his Doncaster debut came on the day of the Final.

> The time comes when you have to move on and that day came when
> Jones joined. Revie told me Doncaster wanted to sign me on the
> Monday of Cup Final week. You never know whether you will be
> in a Wembley squad but I didn't think I would be. It was time for a
> new challenge, so I met Doncaster manager George Rayner, who led
> Sweden to the 1958 World Cup Final against Brazil, and signed on
> the Wednesday.
>
> Football often throws up strange situations because I scored on
> my debut against Chester, the same day Cooper won the League
> Cup for Leeds. I was delighted for the lads that they had won a major
> honour but my focus had changed.

Johnson enjoyed two-year spells at Doncaster – winning the Fourth Division Championship in 1968/69 when Lawrie McMenemy was manager – and Rotherham United, prior to a £9,000 move to Fourth Division Bradford City in the final stop on his Football League journey.

During six years at the West Yorkshire club, Bradford survived re-election in 1974/75, when average home attendances of less than 3,000 saw the club consider going part-time. And, whilst City evaluated their financial plight, Johnson enjoyed a loan spell at Chicago Sting in the North American Soccer League during the summer of 1975 before leading the Bantams to the FA Cup quarterfinals for first time in 56 years.

Johnson's dalliance with the NASL was a welcome sojourn towards the end of his playing career. Professional football in America had enjoyed mixed success, but Johnson's arrival came at a pivotal moment with Pele joining New York Cosmos. Pele's appearances guaranteed packed stadia and exposure on prime time television, as soccer searched for a place alongside mainstream American sports. Portuguese legend Eusabio was a hit at Boston Minutemen, whilst British players enjoying summer football included Gordon Hill, Jimmy Johnstone, Peter Bonetti and John Sissons.

The competition saw expansion to 20 teams playing 22 games in Northern, Eastern, Central and Western Divisions followed by playoffs and a Championship 'Super Bowl' game. If a match was level at full time a 15-minute tiebreak then penalty shoot-out guaranteed results. Tampa Bay Rowdies defeated Portland Timbers in the Championship game.

> You always come across old opponents in football, but I did find it ironic that Bill Foulkes was Chicago's manager, because he was centre half when Leeds defeated Manchester United at a foggy Old Trafford in a First Division match which meant a lot to me a decade earlier.
>
> Playing for Chicago, I came up against legendary players and enjoyed the whole experience, playing teams all over America from Denver to Dallas, Los Angeles, Portland, Seattle, St Louis, Miami and Washington. Travelling was certainly different to trekking around the Football League!
>
> Margaret and our children, Simon and Lisa, joined me in Chicago and we loved the lifestyle. I was negotiating another year with Chicago but it fell through when my mother suddenly passed away and I had to return home.

Back at Bradford, Johnson was City captain when supporters dreamt of a Wembley trip in 1976. A memorable cup run saw the Fourth Division outfit defeat Chesterfield, Johnson's former club Rotherham, then Shrewsbury Town in the third round of the competition.

Cup fever gripped the West Yorkshire club after a 3-1 triumph against Tooting & Mitcham in front of 21,152 at Valley Parade which set up a fifth round clash with First Division Norwich City at Carrow Road. When the tie was postponed twice due to a flu epidemic in the Bradford City camp, the Canaries' boss John Bond called for the injury-afflicted club to be thrown out of the competition. But his comments only served to motivate the underdogs when the tie took place. Don Hutchins silenced home supporters with the opening goal for the Bantams and, after Martin Peters equalised, former Leeds United apprentice Billy McGinley intercepted a pass before scoring at the second attempt three minutes from time, sending City fans into raptures.

Valley Parade was packed for the visit of Southampton in the last eight but they went out to a controversial goal when Saints striker, Peter Osgood, flicked a free kick to Jim McCalliog who volleyed past City keeper Peter Downsborough. The Football Association outlawed this type of goal after *Match of the Day* pundits highlighted that the ball had not rolled a 'full circumference' before anyone touched it. Second Division Southampton defeated Manchester United in the final.

> Southampton were a strong side but we went into the game believing we had a genuine chance of making the semifinals. Losing was one thing, but to lose by a controversial goal was heartbreaking and the referee should have spotted it. Despite the disappointment we'd done really well, because when we started out in the first round, no Bradford fan could have realistically thought we'd make the quarterfinals.

The Bantams' endeavours, however, had a silver lining as the cup run provided the funds to boost the squad, resulting in promotion to the Third Division in 1976/77.

> By now I was coaching the team and it was a fantastic experience for the whole squad. To go up is a huge achievement but a new management team came in so it was time to move on.

Johnson ended his career in non-league football at Gainsborough Trinity before retiring from the sport he'd graced for two decades. After working in the insurance industry, he set up a company selling properties abroad before retiring. Rod enjoys following the progress of granddaughters, Poppy and Leah, as they tread the boards in the world of dance, while grandsons, Jack, currently captain of Halifax Town's youth team whilst studying for a sports science degree, and Harry, who is at Manchester United's academy, both have footballing aspirations. Evaluating his own career, Rod experienced the full range of emotions sport offers.

> You need a bit of luck at the right time that can help you cement a place in a first team but, for whatever reason, I never had an extended

run at Leeds United. And I was not the only player who had that experience at Leeds. Lads like Hibbitt, Greenhoff and Belfitt were in and out of the side before enjoying success at other First Division clubs. There were also lads on the fringes who played at lower league teams, however, you don't bear any animosity as its part of professional football.

Although I could have played at a higher level there were highlights, which you do not forget, particularly the banter between the lads. You also remember your first team debut which for me was at Swansea Town, and to this day the win for Leeds against Manchester United in December 1965 was really special. That victory is also one I like to remind my grandson Harry about. Every year the academy team plays at Old Trafford at the end of the season, and I always remind him that when he runs out opposite the Stretford End, that's where Leeds got the winning goal!

5

Barrie Wright

LEEDS United attracted a host of talented youngsters to Elland Road during the early 1960s. Barrie Wright was amongst them having skippered England Schoolboys. An outstanding full back, Wright also played for England Youth, but leading England against Wales at Wembley in 1961 was the highlight of his fledgling career.

Skipper of United's U18 team, Wright was 17 years of age when he played in three Easter fixtures during the 1962/63 season. Wright's 'Easter treble' included his debut against Preston North End, then home and away encounters against Charlton Athletic. Leeds claimed a trio of triumphs and ended the campaign in a creditable fifth place. First Willie Bell, then Terry Cooper's conversion to left back, would ultimately hinder Wright's progress at United but his endeavours are recorded in the club's history.

The third eldest of Vernon and Hannah Wright's eleven children, Barrie was born in Bradford in November 1945, and grew up in a sporting environment.

Wright recalled:

> Dad enjoyed cricket and had a great reputation as a non-league striker with Bradford Rovers. He could have signed for Bradford City but being a footballer was not seen as a profession in his day, so my mother wanted him to get a 'proper' job.
>
> Dad worked for an engineering company in Osset and delivered goods to clients, so in the summer holidays we'd go to seaside resorts in his van every Sunday if he didn't play cricket. We never really spoke about his footballing career but he encouraged us all to play.

Barrie began his footballing journey at Tyersal School, where he won a number of honours locally prior to gaining selection as an U13 player for Bradford Boys U15 team. A number of players from the U15 side enjoyed professional careers including Bruce Bannister, who played for Leeds United juniors before joining Bradford City in 1965. Bannister's links to United would indirectly continue for more than a decade.

A noteworthy striker, Bannister with Alan Warboys spearheaded the Bristol Rovers attack when they won promotion from the Third Division in 1973/74. Dubbed 'Smash 'n' Grab', the deadly duo struck 40 league goals, including seven in an 8-2 triumph at Brighton & Hove Albion televised on ITVs *The Big Match*. Brighton had just appointed Brian Clough as manager after Cloughie had infamously fallen out with the Derby County board. Clough would soon cause mayhem during a shambolic 44-day tenure at Elland Road.

Bannister and Warboys later teamed up at Hull City when their teammates included Billy Bremner and Chris Galvin.

As Tottenham Hotspur and England legend Jimmy Greaves used to famously quip about football: 'It's a funny old game!'

Barrie followed the fortunes of Bradford City and Bradford Park Avenue in the Football League during the 1950s. Occasionally, he also saw Leeds United and Huddersfield Town play. But keen to see topflight football, Barrie supported Burnley when they lifted the First Division Championship in 1959/60.

> I'd play for my school on a Saturday morning before driving over the moors with dad to watch Burnley play, and they had a great team. Jimmy McIlroy was an unbelievable player and seemed to have so much time on the ball. McIlroy was also brave and in one match I recall him dislocating a shoulder, but there were no substitutes allowed so he came back on strapped up and still ran the game. In another match, Jimmy stepped up to take a penalty. Normally a penalty taker would run up, then bang, the ball was in the back of the net. But not on this occasion because this was the first time I'd seen a player run up, shimmy, then wrong-foot the keeper as the ball trickled into the opposite corner.
>
> I was on the ground staff at Leeds when Burnley played Spurs in the 1962 FA Cup Final. Cup Final day was always a massive occasion but I was playing for Laisterdyke Cricket Club, so couldn't watch the match. However, we arranged to get updates and I was devastated when Burnley lost.

Having represented Bradford Boys and then Yorkshire Schoolboys, the next step for Wright was international recognition, which followed when he attended trials for the England Schoolboys XI. And he set a record by captaining England on seven occasions in competitive games in 1961. Wright played left back against Scotland (2), Wales (2), Eire, Ireland and West Germany.

England against Wales at Wembley Stadium in late April was the standout game for English players. A souvenir edition of *The Evening News & The Star* highlighted line-ups and team pictures. Headlined 'Schoolboys' Day', Wright was pictured cleaning his boots for the big game.

England Schoolboys v Wales Schoolboys, April 29th, 1961

England: Ogley, Harcombe, Wright (captain), Parker, Ashcroft, Walker, Bennett, Prosser, Pardoe, Sissons, Kinsey

Wales: Black, Girolami, Griffiths, Edwards, Jones, Coldrick, Humphreys, Lambourne, Roberts, Lloyd (captain), Hughes

Wright recalled:

> It was a huge honour captaining England and at 15 years of age was a hard accolade to grasp. But then to lead the side out against Wales at Wembley was something else. We met up on the day at Lancaster Gate, rested at a hotel, then travelled by coach to Wembley. After getting changed, we had a quick kick-about on the pitch and a stretch. Back in the dressing room our team manager, Mr Roberts, wished us luck then we lined up in the tunnel before walking out on to the pitch which was fantastic but it goes so fast. We met the Chancellor of the Exchequer, the Rt Hon Selwyn Lloyd, then before kick off had another stretch and tried to belt the ball past the goalkeeper when he rolled us a ball. Defeating Wales 7-0 at Wembley was an unbelievable experience, one you never forget, although you can't take it all in at the time.

Of all the fixtures, one clash was guarenteed to be a feisty affair, and that occurred when England took on Scotland. Wright played twice against the Scots at Sunderland's Roker Park then a return north of the border at Hearts' ground, Tynecastle Park. Scotland had claimed the Victory Shield after a 3-2 victory on Wearside, so England came into the Edinburgh clash looking for revenge and earned a creditable 2-2 draw.

Scotland Schoolboys v England Schoolboys, International Match, May 6th, 1961

Scotland: Cargill, Sharp, Totten, Watson (capt), Cattenach, Smoth, Setterington, Quinn, Thomson, Mitchell, Trail

England: Tatham, Harcombe, Wright (capt), Parker, Ashcroft, Walker, Bennett, Prosser, Pardoe, Sissons, Kinsey

Playing Scotland, there was an extra edge and both matches were hard fought. After losing at Sunderland we had to get a better result at Tynecastle and came away with a share of the spoils, which all the lads were pleased about. Every generation of England Schoolboy teams have players who make it. Ogley and Pardoe (Manchester City) and Sissons (West Ham) played in the First Division from that Wales match. Then from other Schoolboy teams, Howard Kendall (Everton) and Peter Storey (Arsenal) went on to win First Division titles. Of course, none of us had any idea who would make it in a big way. You just hope you'll play well on the day to get selected again for England and get spotted by a Football League club.

Wright had the pick of First Division clubs including Wolves, Manchester United and Newcastle United having played representative football at all levels, but chose a different route.

Leeds United had been in touch and my dad was really impressed with Don Revie, who came round to our house a number of times to explain how the club would look after me. Discussing things with my parents, they wanted me to be near home but it was my decision. Weighing everything up, I plumped for Leeds because of Don but also I'd heard a lot of lads couldn't hack moving into digs and I wanted to give myself the best shot at making it.

Joining United's ground staff, Wright took on his duties, enjoyed the banter and embraced a hard-working environment.

We cleaned the stands, washed seats down, in fact all sorts, then trained in the afternoon. All the lads got on; yes, we had our disagreements but helped each other out if someone hadn't finished a duty. It was hard work but there was always time to take the mick. Fans see what happens on a pitch but the best memories for me were the scrapes we got up to behind the scenes.

Wright was soon appointed skipper of an U18 squad packed with talented players. Aside from Wright, United's junior squad included Mick Bates, Rod Belfitt, Nigel Davey, Eddie Gray, Jimmy Greenhoff, David Harvey, Dennis Hawkins, Terry Hibbitt, Peter Lorimer, Jimmy Lumsden, John Price, Derek Ryder, Bobby Sibbald and Graham Smith.

> The gaffer (Don Revie) wanted us to be the best we could be, to look out for each other on and off the park and it helped to develop a fantastic team spirit. Don also found time to treat the ground staff lads, so when Real Madrid played Eintracht Frankfurt at Hampden Park in the European Cup Final in 1961, he took us to the game. Real were the best team around and Don hoped watching legendary players at close quarters, rather than on television, would inspire us. Di Stefano's skills were amazing; how he pulled a ball down then rolled it about the park was unbelievable. Then there was Puskas and Hento who were fantastic to watch.
>
> Real were an incredible team and before I joined, Don had changed the club colours to all-white because he wanted Leeds to be the 'Real Madrid of English football'. When you consider where United were at the time, it's not surprising people questioned Don's ambition, but he aimed to be best and they were the best English team by the late 1960s.
>
> We had a really strong junior team but, for whatever reason, never won any silverware. We did get to the Northern Intermediate Cup semifinals but lost to eventual winners, Sheffield United, who had Len Badger and Mick Jones in their side.
>
> Cyril Partridge, Syd Owen and Les Cocker organised training and toughened us up for the professional game. Les was a feisty chap who believed in standing up for yourself, but at a youth tournament in East Germany he probably went over the top during our long journey. We had to get off our bus at Checkpoint Charlie so guards could look around the coach, which was standard procedure. One guard in particular started going through our kit and medical items, then dipped his hand into a jar of Vaseline to feel for hidden things. Of course there was nothing there, but you could see Les was getting increasingly annoyed. When the guard wiped his hands on our towels, Les totally lost it and yelled at him to stop, then put everything back. The guard looked stunned but let us go. There was a brief moment when I thought Les might get arrested but the situation did calm down.
>
> Les was tough but fair with the lads and put everything into

training sessions. He could also surprise us, and did. I remember when he introduced us to Tommy Younger, a former Scottish international goalkeeper, and wanted a few of the lads to belt some shots at him. Tommy was getting on a bit and might have been a bit chubby but he was diving around and tipping balls over the bar. The gaffer had signed Tommy and he was a really shrewd buy because he worked with Gary Sprake and helped develop him.

Sprakie did lose concentration at times and deservedly got blamed, but there were also games when a defender would dodge out of the way and leave him no time to react, which was not always fair. Gary was a real character and gave us plenty of laughs but he could be a hothead. If one of the lads or coaches had too much of a go, he'd chase them around the training ground, which always had us in stitches.

Wright served his apprenticeship during a turbulent period at Leeds United. In Revie's first season at the helm, United only just survived relegation, and when the 1962/63 season kicked off, the first team made a poor start. With senior players, including close season signing John Charles, injured or struggling for form, following a 2-1 midweek defeat to Bury, Revie decided to give youth a chance.

When Big John came back during the close season the gaffer gave me an unusual role. I was half a boot size smaller than him, so I had to break in his special white boots that he had sent over from Italy. Of course I didn't complain because John had incredible charisma and everyone hoped his move would work out.

I played alongside him against Leicester in a pre-season friendly, and he still had flashes of brilliance, but it was obvious John was past his best. It was no surprise when the move didn't work.

United's reserve team had defeated Liverpool 2-0 at Anfield two days before the Bury debacle. Wright was the second youngest player in the line-up for this landmark fixture that would see seven players from this side make first team debuts during the season. Gary Sprake (17), Paul Reaney (17), Barrie Wright (16), Mike Addy (19), Paul Madeley (17), Norman Hunter (18), Ronnie Blackburn (20), Rod Johnson (17), Peter Lorimer (15), John Hawksby (20) and Terry Cooper (18) played in the Anfield clash.

Five days after the Bury match, Sprake, Reaney, Hunter and Johnson played at Swansea and, by the end of September, Addy had made his senior bow at Luton Town and then played alongside Lorimer in a home fixture against Southampton. The Revie revolution was in full swing and Wright was the next player to taste first team action. He still had his 'duties' to perform but five months after signing a professional contract in November 1962, the teenage full back made his first team debut in a 4-1 win over Preston North End, then retained his place for an Easter double-header against Charlton Athletic inside 24 hours.

Leeds United v Preston North End, April 13th, 1963

Leeds United: Sprake, Reaney, Wright, Bell, Charlton, Hunter, Henderson, Bremner, Storrie, Collins, Johanneson

Preston North End: Kelly, Donnelly, Ross, Davidson, Singleton, Gornall, Wilson, Lawton, Dawson, Spavin, Thompson

Bremner (2), Storrie and Collins scored the Leeds goals against Preston.

> The day before the Preston game, the gaffer told me Granville Hair was injured so I'd be playing in the first team. Naturally, I was delighted but did not know what to say. In those days I was quite shy, so news I'd be making my debut made me more nervous than normal.
>
> I'd played alongside Sprake, Reaney and Hunter in the reserves so felt comfortable at this level, even though I was only 17, but it was still great to get this match under my belt. The game went well and we won comfortably.

The same United XI that defeated Preston enjoyed a 2-1 victory at The Valley two days later when Charlton and Hunter scored for Leeds. With Bremner picking up an injury, Don Weston came in for the return game and opened the scoring at Elland Road. Henderson, Johanneson and Storrie struck the other goals in another 4-1 win for Leeds.

> I really enjoyed being a part of the first team but knew it would only be until Hair was fit again. The main thing was that I'd enjoyed a brief run out and felt I'd get another opportunity soon as the gaffer was bringing in young players. We eventually ended the league campaign in fifth place, which was a massive improvement on the previous season after the lads stayed up on the final day of the season with a win at Newcastle United.

Promotion was the target for Leeds United when the 1963/64 season kicked off. Revie strengthened his team with the purchase of Johnny Giles from Manchester United. Giles' arrival was a statement of intent but Revie also decided to further develop his defence by switching Willie Bell to left back, Wright's natural position.

United's favoured back four of Reaney, Bell, Charlton and Hunter was now a formidable unit, and Bell's inclusion would limit Wright's chances of breaking through. Wright made two appearances during United's promotion campaign, the first a tough looking away trip to Leyton Orient in late November.

Leyton Orient v Leeds United, November 23rd, 1963

Leyton Orient: Bishop, Bolland, Charlton, Elwood, Lea, Lewis, Lucas, Musgrove, Pinner, Ward, White

Leeds United: Sprake, Wright, Bell, Bremner, Goodwin, Hunter, Giles, Lawson, Weston, Collins, Johanneson

Correspondent, Phil Brown, *Yorkshire Evening Post*:

Leeds United took their 2-0 win at Leyton Orient mostly because of an impressive and determined second half display. Collins hallmarked a glorious game with United's first goal from a free kick. Yet, it was one of his 'specials', a 25-yarder with late swing deliberately applied, but this was the 'special' of all specials. The pace on the ball and its late swing away would have done credit to Freddie Trueman at his fieriest … It was also most encouraging to see another youngster, Wright, in the side for the first time this season respond so well to the occasion. He was sharper and sounder than in any of his three previous outings, and that against the fleet and strong Musgrove, and hard-trying inside-forward Elwood.

Wright recalled:

It was pleasing to get a call up, and Bobby scored a wonder goal, but I knew no matter how well I played Don would drop me for the next game if Reaney were fit again. I received good ratings in the Sunday papers and was pleased how I'd played, but it carried no weight. As I anticipated, Reaney was back in the side when Leeds played Swansea Town a week later and he didn't miss another game all season.

When Bell covered for Charlton against Cardiff City later in the season, Don brought me back but again there was little chance of getting another game so I did feel let down. Most of the lads didn't confront Don about not getting many opportunities. There was a sense of waiting to see what developed but it did start to change. Terry Hibbitt was a fiery sort of lad who said his two-penneth. He'd stand his corner and state why he should play and Don respected him for it.

United went on to clinch the Second Division title and Wright was part of the squad that celebrated the success at Leeds Town Hall. Back in top-flight football, as the first team went close to the 'double', Wright made two appearances in weak League Cup line-ups against Huddersfield Town and Aston Villa. Wright then played his eighth and final game for United in a shadow team that did itself proud in a 4-2 defeat against West Brom in a League Cup clash in October 1965.

Leeds United v West Bromwich Albion. October 13th, 1965

Leeds United: Harvey, Davey, Bell, Storrie, Madeley, Wright, Weston, Belfitt, Hawkins, Johnson, Cooper

West Bromwich Albion: Sheppard, Cram, Fairfax, Lovett, Jones, Fraser, Brown, Astle, Kaye, Hope, Clark

Yorkshire Post:

> *After the shakiest of starts when they (Leeds United) found themselves four down after 25 minutes, Mr Don Revie's mostly young side rallied to such purpose that they rubbed off two of the arrears, and in a storming finish, with Leeds fighting like demons, Albion were glad to hang on ... the crowd of 13,455 enjoyed every minute of the game. They gave Leeds a wonderful ovation as they left the field ... Certainly those Leeds youngsters did not disgrace themselves ... but four goals was too much start to give a team like West Bromwich's calibre.*

Although Wright was captain of the reserves, it was clear that his time at United was ending.

As a squad player I knew the score; you bided your time or eventually made a fresh start. Cooper and Madeley were now on the scene when Bell was injured. Both were quicker than me, so I knew I'd struggle to get selected ahead of them. The gaffer also had pace down both flanks because Reaney was lightening quick on the right.

> Don renewed my contract at the end of our 1965/66 season but I was on the same pay. He told me I could leave if a club came in that would develop my career. It was time to consider my future.

With no offers on the table, Wright kicked his heels in the reserves. Then as Christmas 1966 approached, a surprise opportunity surfaced. Professional soccer in America had struggled against traditional mainstream sports such as american football and baseball but now two coast-to-coast competitions, The National Professional Soccer League (NPSL) and United States Association (USA) were in place for the 1967 season.

The New York Generals were one of 10 teams playing in the inaugural NPSL. English players were being recruited and New York boss Freddie Goodwin wanted Wright to join him for the venture starting in April 1967. The New Yorkers would play 32 games in an Eastern Division with the divisional winners playing the 'Western' champions in a two-legged final. Wright was ever present as the Generals finished third behind 'Eastern' champs Baltimore Bays.

Oakland Clippers were crowned NPSL champions after defeating Baltimore in the two-leg finale. In the rival USA tournament, 12 FIFA affiliated teams competed with Los Angeles Wolves defeating the Washington Whips in the Championship game. Wright loved the American way of life.

> I could hardly believe it when the gaffer told me Freddie wanted to sign me. We'd played together in the reserves and always got on so I looked forward to meeting him again.
>
> Freddie told me New York would play games all over America for three months and we'd get paid all year round. I'd just turned 21 and suddenly had a chance to play football professionally in America. I just needed to know if Audrey, who I'd been courting for a few years, would move to America. It did not take us long to make a decision. Travelling abroad was not the norm as it is nowadays; a number of lads had been on a package holiday, as for America, that was for the super rich.
>
> Following our wedding in January 1967, we flew out and arriving in New York was unbelievable; I'd never known anything like it. Our club sponsors, RKO General, flew the players and their families by private jet to a pre-season training base in Hollywood, Maimi, which

had superb facilities. We rented a place on Long Island which had all the mod cons and the lifestyle was amazing.

With the sport just taking off again, only a few thousand spectators watched our home matches at the Yankee Stadium but we were popular on cable television. The standard of football was mixed but I adapted well and loved the razzmatazz.

Wright ran a number of coaching clinics for American youngsters during the close season then returned home for Christmas.

Back in America, a merger of the NPSL and USA saw the formation of the North American Soccer League (NASL), with 17 teams playing across Eastern and Western Conferences. Each conference had two divisions with the 'divisional' winners playing for an overall championship. New York played in the 'Atlantic' Division.

Coaching kids was great but giving public relations talks was not my thing. It was great seeing mates over Christmas and I remember trying to persuade my best man, Nigel Davey, to try out New York life for a summer but he wouldn't and I still have a go at him about not coming out! After a few weeks at home, I couldn't wait to get back for the NASL campaign.

With the demise of a number of clubs, including the New York Skyliners, New York Generals were the only professional soccer team in the 'Big Apple'. Wright was among a quartet of team members to don playing kits for an appearance on the *Johnny Carson Tonight Show* to boost ratings.

Woody Allen was guest host for the night and because soccer was unknown to most sports fans in America, Woody wanted us to show off some skills. TV producers set up five-a-side goals but nothing was planned so we did some keep-me-ups. Woody being Woody, decided to give it a go but was useless, however the studio TV audience lapped it up, and when we did a mock penalty shoot out, Woody smashed the ball over the crossbar in his 'chisel toe' boots. We could not believe the applause. This was entertainment!

Woody was now on a roll so went in goal, and after I side-footed the ball past him, he decided to clip me round the ear. It didn't hurt but I was surprised and was not sure what would happen next. Woody was so unpredictable but totally in control because he burst out laughing and the audience loved it. So that's my claim to fame, being clipped by Woody Allen!

The show was on television a few hours later but when we got home we'd just missed it. All the lads' wives were watching though and apparently the interview came across brilliantly, but to this day I've never seen it.

When the NASL '68 season kicked off, administrators were concerned about its national profile, so arranged for Brazilian giants, Santos, to play exhibition games across America mid-season. With Pele the star attraction, grounds were packed, including the Yankee Stadium when New York Generals defeated the mighty Santos 5-3 to great acclaim on July 12th, 1968.

Pele was a global star and thousands of fans came to see every game Santos played.

For Santos it was a testimonial style game but we were really up for the match, especially as we had a number of South American players in our side including Cesar Menotti who would manage Argentina to a World Cup triumph in 1978. It was a really big deal for the club, so when we were leading at half time, our general manager came in to our dressing room and said he'd double our bonuses if we won.

Pele coasted through the match but it was fantastic to play against him and win!

New York went on to finish third in the Atlantic Division behind Atlanta Chiefs, who defeated San Diego Toros in the NASL Championship Final. One of only three players to feature in all of New York's 32 games, Wright picked up the Player of the Year award for his efforts.

The player award meant a lot to me and I seriously considered making a permanent move to The States for the start of the NASL 1969 campaign.

Whilst Wright pondered a States move, the NASL was in meltdown as attendances again dipped. Despite the success of Santos' visit, Americans did not appear ready for soccer in a big way. Only five teams would now feature in a second NASL season but not New York Generals.

The NASL would eventually expand with Pele joining New York Cosmos in 1975, followed by world stars including Eusabio, Johan Cruyff and George Best across America. But that was all for the future as Wright, who had been at the inception of the NASL journey, rebuilt his career in English football.

> We'd booked return flights to New York but everything was up in the air with the NASL so we rushed around selling our belongings. I put feelers out for a new team but nothing came up which was a huge disappointment.
>
> Back home, Bradford Park Avenue asked me for a trial but I declined. Then out of the blue Freddie rang, he was Brighton & Hove Albion manager and wanted me to see the set up, which seemed great.
>
> After signing, we moved south but I got injured after five league games and missed their Third Division campaign in 1968/69. A possible return to America came up on a semi-pro basis during the close season but Freddie told me I'd be in Brighton's first team so turned it down. In the end, I only played three more matches for Brighton, which was bitterly disappointing.

Disillusioned with the game as a full-time profession, Wright quit football at the age of 25 after a brief loan spell at Hartlepool United and worked in a variety of industries until retirement.

Returning to his home town of Bradford, the Wright's brought up their son Darren. Football though was still a draw for Barrie, albeit on an amateur basis, with non-league sides Bradford Park Avenue, Gainsborough Trinity and Thackley prior to local football teams well into his late 40s.

Looking back on his career, Barrie, who has two grandchildren, has few regrets.

> Captaining England Schools at Wembley, playing with the likes of Billy Bremner and Bobby Collins, then against Pele, they are memories that will always live with me. I played briefly for a great Leeds United side but should have been more vocal with the gaffer. My attitude was not always the best, however, I played with some of the greatest players of my generation and that can't be taken away.
>
> Bobby was the gaffer's best signing because he set standards others followed. Off the field he was a gentleman, and in training was brilliant with the apprentices. Bobby made the lads believe they could be special and compete at the highest level. Playing with Bobby was terrific because he led by example. Even though he was coming towards the end of his career you could see he was still a fantastic

footballer. Also, nobody pushed him around! Throughout a game, Bobby kept an eye out for me and was really encouraging. Even when under pressure, he found time to spread the ball wide, and just when a full back felt he could intercept, the ball would dip and land at one of our lads' feet. In my career, he was the best footballer I played alongside.

When Don teamed up Giles and Bremner, Leeds really started to motor as a team. Johnny was a superb signing and his passing range, with either foot, was fantastic. Billy wanted the ball all the time, was in on everything and always busy. He had this ability to look one way then pass another and was a wonderful footballer. As a midfield pair, they were top draw and at times were unbelievable to watch.

Then there was Madeley, who at 17 years of age was fast, smooth like an antelope, and did the simple things well. Greenhoff was another lad who had it all, and then there was Cooper, Reaney, Lorimer, Sprakie and Hunter. They were just ordinary lads and I was really pleased they had great careers.

As for the gaffer, whilst there was frustration I didn't break through, as a manager I respected him enormously and I've never enjoyed listening to characters like Brian Clough criticising his philosophy. Clough went on about 'Dirty Leeds' yet had some of the dirtiest players around in his Derby team. Every side had players who could dish it out in that era. It was a part of the game. Liverpool had Tommy Smith, there was Dave Mackay at Tottenham, Nobby Stiles at Manchester United and Chelsea had Ron Harris to name but a few. Yes, Leeds had Hunter, Collins, Giles and others who could take care of themselves, but to Clough it was as if Leeds were the only team to have 'hard' players. For whatever reasons Clough had issues with Don, but the gaffer was a top manager and thankfully former players and managers of that era recall his team as one of the best around.

At a Revie reunion dinner a few years ago, it was fantastic catching up with lots of the lads from my playing days. The memories came flooding back from a wonderful time in my life. And not so long ago, I met up with Terry (Cooper) and Nigel (Davey) on a family holiday by chance. We had a few beers and didn't stop talking all night. It was wonderful reminiscing and summed up the spirit of all those young lads at Leeds United.

6

Nigel Davey

A FINE line exists between success and failure in sport. In football, the width of a post, a poor refereeing decision or defensive blunder can scupper a winning goal. A late tackle can also change the course of a career, which was the case for Nigel Davey in April 1972.

There is a saying that 'lightning never strikes twice', but the same afternoon Davey suffered a fractured leg in a Central League fixture at West Bromwich Albion, United's first choice left back, Terry Cooper, sustained a broken leg in a First Division clash at Stoke City. With an FA Cup Final against Arsenal weeks away, United's understudy may have been called up; instead Davey could claim to be one of the unluckiest players of the Revie era.

Paul Madeley stepped into Cooper's boots on the big day at Wembley but one can only wonder whether Revie would have made a different call and played 'Mr Versatile' elsewhere in his team when United lifted the one domestic trophy to elude them.

Davey was a loyal squad member for a decade, illustrating his character, and made one further appearance against Vitoria Setubal in the Fairs Cup. Davey and Cooper have remained friends over the ensuing years and no doubt reminisce about football's vagaries when they get together over a cool beer.

Nigel was born in June 1946 and grew up in Garforth, Leeds. Educated at Great Preston Parochial and Garforth Secondary Modern Schools, Nigel represented his local district team, Rothwell and Stanley, but it was whilst playing for Great Preston Juniors that his footballing journey began. Leeds City Boys were amongst a number of strong teams that Great Preston faced but it was a clash against Leeds United

Juniors when Davey, to his surprise, made a mark and was offered an opportunity to trial for his hometown club.

Davey recalled:

When Leeds City got off their team bus to play us, we knew we'd be in for a tough match. We were aware of a player called 'Madeley' who had a reputation for being a really good player. I'd soon discover Paul was a really nice lad who could play in every outfield position!

Leeds United spotted me when Great Preston played United's junior team one Sunday. Some of our lads shouted, "there's that big bloke," when Madeley warmed up, but there was also Gary Sprake, Paul Reaney, Jimmy Greenhoff and Peter Lorimer in United's line-up. The junior team was brilliant and hammered us 17-1.

Whether they felt sorry for us I'm not sure, but I scored a consolation goal from a corner. And we were lucky to get that because we never got a kick all afternoon.

Shortly afterwards I was invited with Buster Kitson, who also played for Great Preston, to attend a trial at Leeds, which was something of a surprise given how the game went. But Cyril Partridge had been in charge of the juniors when they thumped us and thought we both had potential. Buster was a far better player than me but could not handle pressure when scouts watched us.

In the trial game I must have done okay because Don Revie and Maurice Lindley came over to my house a few days later. Don explained to my parents (Betty and Geoff Davey) how the club would look after me if I joined the ground staff. Of course, I was really excited because I'd watched United play in the 1950s and certain players, like John Charles and Jack Charlton, had stuck in my mind, but also a little feller called Wilbur Cush who in one game dived headlong to score a goal. I thought to myself, I like this bloke.

Leeds were a First Division side, so when teams came to play there were big stars you looked forward to seeing. Amongst them were Tom Finney of Preston and Stanley Matthews; both were brilliant. Everyone remembers the 1953 FA Cup Final when Matthews finally received a winners medal.

We had a little television at home and I loved the Cup Final growing up. It was the big game of the season and live on TV, so you'd get pop and crisps in, settle down then watch the game.

Davey joined the ground staff at Elland Road in February 1964 and played for United's U18 squad in the Northern Intermediate League. Apart from Davey, the squad included Mick Bates, Rod Belfitt, Eddie Gray, Jimmy Greenhoff, David Harvey, Dennis Hawkins, Terry Hibbitt, Peter Lorimer, Jimmy Lumsden, John Price, Derek Ryder, Bobby Sibbald, Graham Smith and Barrie Wright.

United's junior team was a talented group who worked hard on and off the field.

Davey recalled:

> Every Monday we'd sweep the stands after a Saturday match but we also had other duties. If the weather was really bad we cleared snow from the pitch. We just accepted these tasks as part of our apprenticeship.
>
> Cyril Partridge looked after the juniors and was a really nice guy, we were just kids and the young lads all respected him. Syd Owen led training sessions which were organised, hard work and interesting. The gaffer (Don Revie) was really thorough on our passing and set moves. Everyone had to be aware where they should be when it came to marking at any part of a game.

When Leeds United defeated Swansea Town to win Second Division promotion in April 1964, everyone at the club toasted their success at full time, except Davey and his teammates.

> Leeds supporters find this hard to believe but that afternoon we played at Elland Road and no one at the Swansea game let us know the result, so I had no idea we'd gone up until I got home and friends told me! Of course, that would not happen now because of technology, but it was over 50 years ago.

Playing in the Central League, Davey developed his game initially as a left-half. And there was one individual in particular that he looked up to, United skipper Bobby Collins.

> Bobby helped the young lads from day one. He'd sit with us in the dressing room for a chat or on the coach to a game. "How you doing young lad," he'd say, then would tell you what he expected. Bobby wanted you to relax, try things and play your own game. And he wanted to help, especially when you were having a bad time in a game. Returning on the coach after a match, he'd come over and tell you not to worry about it. He'd explain that every player makes

mistakes and the key was how you reacted to put it right.

Bobby was so encouraging and for someone of his stature to make time meant a lot. He was a fatherly figure and for a young player that was comforting. On a Monday at training he'd call you over. "Lad, I want you a minute, I'll show you what you did wrong on Saturday," he'd say. "Have a look, this is what you should be doing and this is where you want to be in terms of positioning." Bobby was a great player at that particular time as he helped the club survive then push on to promotion. But just as important, Bobby helped develop young players breaking through to first team football.

Davey's first pre-season as a professional was a special one as United looked ahead to Division One football in July 1964. There was great anticipation as the playing squad gathered for the pre-season group picture.

Davey not only played for the reserves, but also was still young enough to help the juniors win the Northern Intermediate League Cup for the first time in a two-legged final against Sheffield Wednesday during the build up to the 1965 FA Cup Final against Liverpool. Match reports lambasted both teams after the first leg when Davey and Hawkins scored the Leeds goals in in a 2-2 draw. United's reputation as fierce competitors was growing.

A special correspondent noted:

Don Revie's tough, young teenagers were booed out of Hillsborough last night at the end of this rough and tumble Intermediate League Cup Final first leg.

The trainers were on the field seven times and referee George Martin had to give just as many lectures to two sides that quickly forgot about football and concentrated more on the man.

Leeds go into tomorrow's second leg firm favourites to win the trophy but their strong arm-stuff has lost them old friends that they had in Sheffield.

United won the trophy 3-2 on aggregate with a Hibbitt goal at Elland Road.

Davey was now on the fringes of first team football, and due to injuries and international call-ups, was one of three teenagers alongside Harvey and Hawkins given first team debuts against West Brom in a League Cup third round tie at Elland Road in October 1965. With only two senior players, Willie Bell and Jim Storrie, available, United's youngsters put up a stirring performance that drew plaudits after a 4-2 defeat.

Leeds United v West Bromwich Albion, October 13th, 1965

Leeds United: Harvey, Davey, Bell, Storrie, Madeley, Wright, Weston, Belfitt, Hawkins, Johnson, Cooper

West Bromwich Albion: Sheppard, Cram, Fairfax, Lovett, Jones, Fraser, Brown, Astle, Kaye, Hope, Clark

Yorkshire Post:

> *The crowd of 13,455 enjoyed every minute of the game. They gave Leeds a wonderful ovation as they left the field … Certainly those Leeds youngsters did not disgrace themselves … but four goals was too much start to give a team like West Bromwich's calibre.*

Davey recalled:

> When Don told me I'd be playing I was really nervous but it was a great feeling because, after I signed professional, all I hoped was to get a first team chance. I was also really pleased for my dad who came to all my games and was proud of what I'd achieved.
>
> Dad was always supportive and getting into the first team meant a lot to him. It sounds daft now but on the morning of a match he made me a full English breakfast to get some vitamins in my body. Football dieticians however would raise their eyebrows at that now.
>
> On the night, we had a young team against West Brom so expectations were not that we'd win. I marked Clive Clark, who I'd faced in the reserves, but West Brom were just too strong for us. We quickly found ourselves four goals down but battled back with goals from Madeley and Belfitt. Despite the result, it was great getting that first match under my belt.

Davey would not play another first team game until the end of United's 1967/68 campaign. In the intervening period, Bell had played his final game at left back but Revie was planning ahead and had successfully converted Cooper from left wing to Bell's spot. With Reaney first choice right back, Revie needed cover for both positions. Looking at his options, United's boss had the ever-dependable Madeley to call upon but 'Mr Versatile' might be required elsewhere if other first teamers were unavailable. Revie's solution was for Davey to convert from his midfield berth to both full back positions.

> As a midfield player, getting into the first team was really tough. Bremner, Giles and Gray were regulars, Bates and Hibbitt deputised across midfield, and of course Madeley filled in anywhere outfield. When Don pulled me aside to discuss switching to full back, I had to seriously consider it. Wright was one of the young lads who had come in at full back but had left the club. Barrie captained England Schoolboys and had played a number of first team games but things did not work out for him because competition for places was so tough.
>
> During the summer, a number of lads would travel to Newquay for a month. I enjoyed going because of the swimming and surfing but when Barrie went to play in America he wanted me to visit because, in his view, it was '10 times better' there. Barrie still jokes about me not visiting but I've no regrets as I enjoyed my summers on the coast.
>
> Covering for Reaney and Cooper when Madeley played elsewhere offered a different route to the first team for me, so I jumped at the chance but it didn't happen overnight. Don explained why they wanted to do it in detail. He told me I was pretty quick, a good tackler, had good feet and got crosses over so thought I'd be better playing full back. The coaching staff wanted me to give it a go; they had faith and were really supportive which is what you want as a player. As I was a two-footed player, moving to full back made sense because I could slot in on either flank. It was a natural move for me.

Waiting for a return to first team football, Davey was content being a member of the first team squad where there was daily banter.

> There was a real team spirit among the lads. In the dressing room, you always had your spot to change in (Davey sat between Reaney and Cooper), and the banter was great because there was someone always cracking jokes. Billy was one of the chief culprits taking the mick, but it was always good-natured.
>
> Big Jack was a real character but would get riled about all sorts so the lads liked to wind him up. One day Jack was having a quiet read of his newspaper in the 'reading room' when one of the lads climbed up on a kit box, took a bucket of cold water from Billy then poured it over him. The lads were in stitches but Jack was not happy. Kicking the door open, he yelled at anyone that would listen. "No one

will ever have a peaceful crap at this club again while I'm here!" Jack eventually calmed down but would not admit he'd seen the funny side.

Of course, knowing they could wind up Jack, the mickey taking didn't stop there. During a harsh winter, the lads had to move their cars to the bottom end of the car park when the groundsman arranged for a bulldozer to clear heavy snow off the pitch. Big Jack was not around when we got the message, so a few of the lads got the bulldozer driver to cover Jack's car with a giant mound of snow. When Jack came out after training and saw his car had gone he just assumed he'd parked further down the car park, but when the snow thawed, he went ballistic in the dressing room. He grudgingly saw the funny side, but Jack was not the only one to get the treatment. At one time or other, all the lads were subjected to good-natured mickey taking.

Chasing four trophies in a demanding 1967/68 season, United lifted the League Cup and reached the FA Cup semifinals. Defeat to Liverpool in the final home game ended United's league title challenge but they were still in the midst of a two-legged Fairs Cup semifinal with Dundee.

Needing to rest jaded players, Revie called on his reserves for the last two league fixtures. Davey lined up at left back against Arsenal at Highbury and then in a more inexperienced team at Burnley on a dreadful surface in May. Every Leeds player apart from Johanneson had been on the club's ground staff. Madeley and Gray had come through the ranks and were now first team regulars. United's performance drew praise in the Sunday morning papers.

Burnley v Leeds United, May 11th, 1968

Burnley: Thomson, Angus, Latcham, O'Neill, Merrignton, Todd, Morgan, Lochhead, Dobson, Bellamy, Casper. Sub: Coates

Leeds United: Harvey, Sibbald, Davey, Yorath, Madeley, Gray, Lumsden, Bates, Belfitt, Hibbitt, Johanneson. Sub: Hawkins

A correspondent noted:

There were nine reserves on duty at Turf Moor yesterday for Leeds, the club whose gallant pot hunting has taken such a heavy toll of their playing staff.

And incredibly these gritty youngsters were beaten by the

atrocious, near farcical conditions as much as by Burnley.

In the end Burnley's greater physical strength and know-how, in defence and attack, paid off on a pitch resembling a soggy black pudding. But full marks for Leeds who fought with great bravery and a fair amount of resource from start to finish. Each of them got a pat on the back from a worried-looking Don Revie at the end who had 10 members of his first team squad injured this weekend.

Davey recalled:

Seeing the team sheet for the game with many big name players out was strange but all the lads had played together in the juniors and reserves, so there was familiarity. Don told us to go out and battle away, which we did.

There was no expectation that we'd win; we lost 3-0, which was no disgrace. Gray was incredible that day because some parts of the pitch were unplayable. Eddie had amazing skill on the ball and his close control was something else. In the years to come, Eddie did have injury issues, but when fully fit there was no more dangerous player in the game because he could destroy a team on his own.

Davey did not appear in the first team when Leeds won the First Division Championship 12 months later. But unlike their promotion campaign five years earlier, he was amongst reserve team players at Liverpool's Anfield stadium to witness United achieve the ultimate domestic honour.

One of lads arranged for a minibus to take us to the game. Don sorted tickets for us and there was an amazing atmosphere inside Anfield where we only needed a draw to win the title.

After getting the point required, we were able to celebrate with the lads on the first team coach, which was brilliant. But we left club chairman Percy Woodward behind by accident. Apparently, Percy was having a drink in the director's room but nobody realised until we were half the way down the East Lancs Road!

The journey back to the ground was fantastic and the celebrations went on long into the night.

United attempted to defend their First Division crown in 1969/70 and an unprecedented League, FA Cup and European Cup 'treble' appeared achievable at the turn of the year. The season though was truncated for the World Cup Finals in Mexico and it took a cataclysmic toll on Revie's first team squad who were set to play 10 games in 22 days, including an FA Cup trilogy against Manchester United, during an extraordinary period.

With players mentally and physically fatigued, Revie reluctantly ended United's title challenge 48 hours after a 3-1 home defeat to Southampton by fielding a reserve side at Derby County at the end of March.

When Leeds faced Celtic in a European Cup semifinal clash 48 hours later, it heralded three games in four days!

Derby County v Leeds United, March 30th, 1970

Derby County: Green, Webster, Robson, Durban, McFarland, Carlin, O'Hare, Hector, Hinton, Wignall, Hennessey

Leeds United: Harvey, Davey, Peterson, Lumsden, Kennedy, Yorath, Galvin, Bates, Belfitt, Hibbitt, Johanneson

> The fixture congestion was incredible but Don got on with it and made decisions for the benefit of the team. For the reserve lads, it was a chance to show what we could do against a good Derby side managed by Brian Clough who was never short of having something to say.
>
> When we ran out there was not stunned silence from home fans as our team was not announced in the papers, but I'm sure they would rather have seen the first teamers in action. We got on with the game and lost 4-1 but we were not battered as pundits would have predicted if they'd known such a weakened team was being played.
>
> The Football Association fined Leeds £5,000, which was ridiculous considering how many games the first team lads had played in a matter of days. Nowadays, top clubs don't think twice about making wholesale changes, notably in cup competitions if they are going for the title or battling relegation. Don's decision was frowned upon and he received a lot of bad press when he was actually ahead of his time.

In the final League fixtures, Davey played at West Ham – when Reaney broke a leg – Manchester City and Ipswich Town, but missed Leeds' clash against Burnley through injury when Gray scored two virtuoso goals.

Davey then witnessed the season end in heartache from the sidelines as United lost first to Celtic and then Chelsea in an FA Cup Final replay.

> I was sitting with Paul (Reaney) approaching Upton Park for the West Ham game when Don came over and asked us which side we wanted to play. Paul was not bothered either way so played left back and I played on the right. But that decision demonstrated when lady luck is not on your side, because Paul missed out on the Cup Final and possibly being a part of England's World Cup squad.
>
> If he'd played in his normal position at right back, Paul could have been injured from another tackle or picked up a knock later in the season, but the incident showed how cruel the game could be. Madeley slotted in at right back for the remaining big games when we sadly lost out on winning a trophy.

United were ready to go again by the 1970/71 campaign, but this time around, Revie had a few injuries to contend with when the season kicked off. Davey at last enjoyed a five-match run in the first team as United mounted a title challenge.

To date, Davey had not been on a winning Leeds United side in the League but that statistic ended against Derby County (2-0), Coventry City (2-0), Stoke City (4-1) and Wolves (3-2).

United's strongest line-up came at the end of October against Coventry City when Charlton and Giles scored Leeds' goals.

Leeds United v Coventry City, October 31st, 1970

Leeds United: Sprake, Davey, Cooper, Bremner, Charlton, Hunter, Lorimer, Clarke, Jones, Giles, Madeley

Coventry City: Glazier, Coop, Smith, Carr, Blockley, Strong, Hunt, Martin, O'Rourke, Clements, Mortimer

> Playing in front of small crowds for the reserves was not easy, although you got used to it, but running out in front of a packed house made a massive difference. As a player, you perform better because there seems more to play for psychologically.
>
> The run went well then Reaney got fit and came back in which I accepted. My role was to step in, do a job then step aside. Some people criticised that view but I was happy because I enjoyed being around the lads in the squad.

Playing for the first team, Davey enjoyed the attention to detail when it came to match preparation at team meetings.

> Don took nothing for granted, we'd go through his dossier on opponents then when we were getting changed he'd sit down next to each of us for a last minute chat. It was just a quick word but he'd stress if an opponent was stronger on his left or right foot, whether to jockey him wide or let them come on my inside.
>
> Don knew everything about every player but for some reason was so superstitious, which I never understood, because we could beat any team on our day.

Davey was on the bench for one of the most infamous games in the clubs' history towards the end of the 1970/71 First Division campaign. United had led the way all season, and with four league games remaining were still in pole position to land a second title when they played West Brom at Elland Road. Leeds were clear favourites to win as the visitors had not won an away game all season.

Leeds United v West Bromwich Albion, April 17th, 1971

Leeds United: Sprake, Reaney, Cooper, Bremner, Charlton, Hunter, Bates (Davey), Clarke, Jones, Giles, Gray

West Bromwich Albion: Cumbes, Hughes, Merrick, Lovett, Wile, Kaye, Suggett, Brown, Astle, Hope, Hartford

Richard Ullyatt, *Yorkshire Post*:

> *In the 45 years I have reported on football, I have never seen a worse decision by a referee than the one Mr Ray Tinkler gave at Elland Road on Saturday, which cost Leeds United a goal.*
>
> *It led to Leeds United's defeat at a time when they need every point. It perhaps cost them the League Championship, and it nearly provoked a riot.*
>
> *There were 20 minutes of the match to go when Hunter, rather hurriedly, tried to pass to Gray.*
>
> *Brown in the Albion half of the field intercepted, the ball hitting him on the legs and rebounding into the Leeds half, where Suggett was in an offside position.*
>
> *As Brown chased the ball, Suggett moved smartly away. Brown hesitated as he saw Suggett's position and a linesman's flagged raised.*

Then as the referee lowered his whistle and the linesman dropped his flag, Brown caught up with the ball, took it forward, passed to Astle, himself possibly offside and gave the centre forward a gift goal with Leeds defenders offering belated token resistance.

Nine of out 10 referees would have given offside. Mr Tinkler was the tenth.

Davey replaced Bates during the match and had a bird's eye view of the 'offside' incident that is still debated over four decades on.

I was near the half way line next to our dugout and could not believe what was happening. Don and Les Cocker were going absolutely ballistic. We managed to get a goal back late on but could not force an equaliser.

Back in the dressing room, everyone was so frustrated, which you could understand. We felt so angry and aggrieved. You accept being defeated by a better team but losing to a dreadful refereeing mistake was really tough. Tinkler knew he'd made a mistake but never admitted it, which said everything.

We lost out in the title race to Arsenal by a point, so the West Brom match was key. It was a huge blow missing out on the Championship but you had to credit the lads for their resolve not to end the season without a trophy because they went on to lift the Fairs Cup.

During an eventful European campaign, United overcame Sarpsborg, Dynamo Dresden, Sparta Prague, Vitoria Setubal and Liverpool before defeating Juventus in the final. Davey played his part against Dresden, which were both fiery affairs. Davey's European debut came in the home leg in October.

Leeds United v Dynamo Dresden, October 21st, 1970

Leeds United: Harvey, Davey, Cooper, Bremner, Charlton, Hunter, Lorimer, Clarke, Jones, Belfitt (Galvin), Madeley

Dynamo Dresden: Kallenbach, Ganzera, Dorner, Sammer, Kern, Haustein, Zeigler, Kreische, Hemp, Heidler, Richter

A correspondent noted:

Leeds United's six-year-old tenure near the centre of European soccer power is lurching crazily sideways this morning. Their embarrassment comes from 90 minutes of truly incredible frustration before the massed ranks of the stern-faced defenders of Dynamo Dresden, the shock side of East German football.

Leeds have to thank the sure shooting touch of Peter Lorimer who swept home the goal from a penalty in the 54ᵗʰ minute.

United's preparations were hampered by travel delays for the return leg at the Rudolf Harbig Stadium. However, by kick off they were ready for a night of high drama. On a highly charged evening with Leeds 2-1 behind, following goals by Hemp and Kreishe either side of a Jones strike, a mass brawl ensued after Clarke fouled a Dresden player just outside the Leeds penalty area on 82 minutes. The referee dismissed Bates and Dresden substitute Geyer. Sprake saved the free kick to send Leeds through by the narrowest of margins on away goals. Distraught home fans invaded the pitch at full time with one attempting to strike Charlton.

Dynamo Dresden v Leeds United, November 4ᵗʰ, 1970

Dynamo Dresden: Kallenbach, Ganzera, Dorner, Sammer, Haustein, Zeigler, Hemp, Kreische, Riedel (Geyer), Richter, Sacse (Heidler)

Leeds United: Sprake, Davey, Madeley, Bremner, Charlton, Hunter, Lorimer, Clarke, Jones, Giles, Bates

Playing in Europe there was a different atmosphere. It was electric at times, but it was still a game of football so you had to get on with it. The second leg against Dresden was really intimidating but the lads had seen it all before and knew how to handle the situation. There were a few close calls but we had the advantage of the away goal and saw the game through. Being with the lads after a great win like that was really special because I didn't play that often in a game of such intensity.

Davey went on play in United's 2-1 home win over Vitoria Setubal, then came on as a late replacement for Reaney in the first leg against Liverpool at Anfield on April 14ᵗʰ.

Leeds United and Liverpool enjoyed a special rivalry during this era as managers Revie and Bill Shankly had a high regard for each other. Liverpool supporters also particularly welcomed European nights.

Revie took a gamble when he decided to play Bremner after just 25 minutes action in three months due to injury. And United's skipper, playing as an auxiliary striker, scored the only goal of an absorbing cup tie. Bremner's winner in front of Anfield's Kop after 68 minutes summed up his impact on the team.

Liverpool v Leeds United, April 14th, 1971

Liverpool: Clemence, Lawler, Lindsay, Smith, Lloyd, Hughes, Callaghan (Graham), Evans (Thompson), Heighway, Toshack, Hall

Leeds United: Sprake, Reaney (Davey), Cooper, Bremner, Charlton, Hunter, Bates, Clarke, Jones, Giles, Madeley

A correspondent noted:

It must be the comeback of the season and maybe it was the gamble of the century, but skipper Billy Bremner returned to the Leeds side last night only because of an acute shortage of seasoned troops. And naturally, Bremner scored the goal that gives Leeds a decided advantage in the Fairs Cup semifinal with the second leg to come at home.

Bremner, who played as a forward throughout, was giving Lawler and Hall more than a little trouble until Hall fouled him. Bremner picked himself up, trotted into the goal area and waited for the free kick from Giles. The Liverpool defenders took more notice of the big men like Charlton and Madeley, Giles put his low free kick just into the right spot for Bremner to dive and flick home a header that left Clemence standing and the Kop stunned. And blow me if the cheeky redhead did not offer them a little wave and victory salute full stretch on the goalmouth earth.

When the chips are down, Leeds somehow find that extra to carry them through and it is here where they clinched what is to date their only Championship (April 1969). On that occasion they were cheered off the park. Last night Bremner silenced the Kop.

Davey recalled:

The atmosphere against Liverpool was incredible and Billy returned to nod in the winner late on. The goal was enough to send us into the final as we drew the second leg 0-0 at Elland Road to win on aggregate, which was a great achievement, but we were now desperate to win it. Whenever Billy played it lifted everyone around him and especially in big games. Billy was dynamic and had that special quality which sets top players apart.

Davey was in United's squad for the final against Juventus and flew out to Turin for the first leg clash at the Comunale Stadium in May 1971.

> During the pre-match tactical talk some of the lads suggested to Don that they wanted to play offside, which was not our normal game. This was the first time I'd seen the lads question Don's tactics and he was furious. After making his views clear we played our normal system and I never heard it mentioned again.
>
> The match was actually abandoned because of a waterlogged pitch and replayed a couple of days later when we drew 2-2, which was a terrific result. A 1-1 draw in the return leg gave us the trophy, which was deserved after the effort that season.

Davey's four European appearances took his total in all competitions to 12 games for the season, his highest total during a decade at the club.

Davey didn't receive a replica trophy when United lifted the Fairs Cup at Elland Road, as he was not in the matchday squad. But he did receive a medal and engraved watch when he played in a fixture between the first and last winners of the Fairs Cup, in September.

Leeds faced Barcelona at the Nou Camp Stadium. Barcelona won 2-1 and kept the old Fairs Cup trophy as the competition was to be replaced with the UEFA Cup in the 1971/72 season.

Barcelona v Leeds United, September 22nd, 1971

Barcelona: Sadurni, Rife, Graells, Torres, Gallego, Costas, Rexach, Carlos, Duenas, Morales, Asensi (Fuste)

Leeds United: Sprake, Reaney, Davey, Bremner, Charlton, Hunter, Lorimer, Jordan, Belfitt, Giles, Galvin

A correspondent noted:

> *Injuries robbed Leeds of the services of no fewer than six internationals in Barcelona, yet Don Revie's strange looking side, with several men playing out of position, fought splendidly only to go down to a goal six minutes from time.*
>
> *Revie played Nigel Davey second choice right back on the left flank, moved Peter Lorimer the Scotland winger to midfield and used Billy Bremner, as ever an inspiring captain, as a front-runner alongside the reserve-striker Joe Jordan, 19, and Rod Belfitt.*

The side cost £47,000 ... £32,000 for Johnny Giles and £15,000 for Jordan.

"I was very proud of my team and the way in which they played against what is currently Spain's top club and one of the best we have met in Europe," said Revie.

Davey recalled:

When Don selected me to play it was the most nervous I have ever felt before a game. We had a number of injuries but to be part of this match, even though it was a high profile friendly, was amazing and we really wanted to win. The stadium was not full but there was an electric atmosphere with supporters letting bangers off before the game. After Jordan equalised, we went for it but they scored a late winner.

Davey's watch, which had an engraving of the Fairs Cup on the back, was stolen a few years later following the theft of his car which was set alight.

The watch was in a bag that I kept in my car when I went to a gym, so it was my fault. I didn't think I'd see it again but a few weeks later I heard that a lad was wearing it in a local pub and bragging how he'd got it.

I arranged for some lads to approach him and try get it back but he denied everything and I couldn't prove a thing. It was a nice memento but nothing can take away my memories of playing Barcelona that night which was a highlight in my career.

Davey made one more first team appearance, in the League Cup versus West Ham, prior to his Leeds career effectively being ended in a reserve fixture against West Brom on April 8th, 1972. And in a twist of fate, United's left back, Cooper, broke his leg at Stoke City on the same afternoon.

It's amazing how key moments of my career came against the same club, all at Elland Road. I made my debut against West Brom in the League Cup, played in an infamous match against them that cost a League title then broke my leg against their reserve team. I was caught by a Scottish international and it was a bad tackle – a real leg breaker. He didn't just catch me, he went over the top and I knew straight away my leg was broken.

Don was always concerned when players got injured and immediately visited me at St James' Hospital. He wanted me to go into a private ward but I was happy in a general ward. However, it illustrated what Don thought of the lads, he was always thinking of our welfare.

Injuries are part of the game but when the boss told me about Terry, I could not believe it. We'd been mates for years, in fact Terry was my best man when I married Sandra a few years earlier (the couple have a son, Paul), so was devastated he'd miss the Cup Final against Arsenal.

Fans have debated whether Davey would have played in the FA Cup Final because Madeley had deputised for Eddie Gray and Paul Reaney during the season at different times.

The Final was only a few weeks away, so whether I'd have played if the injury had not happened, who knows, but it's unlikely because Madeley was the natural choice. However, after our semifinal win against Birmingham City, I was part of the build up as a squad member and remained so until the Final.

I was in the Cup Final team brochure and sang on the record 'Leeds Leeds Leeds' written by Ronnie Hilton, which was a lot of fun. Lorimer thought he had a great voice but really we all had terrible voices. Record producers always have singers who can be dubbed in so it sounded great.

On Cup Final day, Don made sure that nobody was left out, so I was on the players' coach and wore the infamous mauve suit. I felt a part of the occasion and of course we beat Arsenal on a wonderful day for the club.

Recuperating alongside Cooper, Davey returned to reserve team action after an eight-month layoff and made one further first team appearance as a substitute against Vitoria Setubal in a UEFA Cup clash in November 1973.

After United claimed a second First Division Championship, Davey signed for Rotherham United during the close season but didn't play a first team match for his new club and retired from the game to carve out a career in the education sector.

Revie demanded loyalty from his players and during a decade of service, Davey exemplified that expectation whilst making a total of 23

Peter McConnell

John Hawksby

Ian Lawson

Rod Johnson

Barrie Wright

Nigel Davey

Dennis Hawkins

Chris Galvin

Sean O'Neill

Roy Ellam

Glan Letheren

Leeds United's players, including Peter McConnell (front, third left), meet new player-manager Don Revie

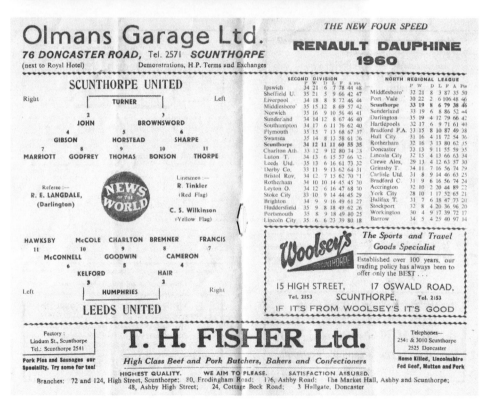

Olmans Garage Ltd.
76 DONCASTER ROAD, Tel. 2571 **SCUNTHORPE**
(next to Royal Hotel) Demonstrations, H.P. Terms and Exchanges

THE NEW FOUR SPEED
RENAULT DAUPHINE
1960

SCUNTHORPE UNITED

Right | TURNER | Left

2 — 3
JOHN   BROWNSWORD

4 — 5 — 6
GIBSON   HORSTEAD   SHARPE

7 — 8 — 9 — 10 — 11
MARRIOTT GODFREY THOMAS BONSON THORPE

Linesmen :—
R. Tinkler
(Red Flag)

Referee :—
R. E. LANGDALE
(Darlington)

C. S. Wilkinson
(Yellow Flag)

HAWKSBY   McCOLE   CHARLTON   BREMNER   FRANCIS
11 — 10 — 9 — 8 — 7

McCONNELL   GOODWIN   CAMERON
6 — 5 — 4

KELFORD   HAIR
3 — 2

Left | HUMPHRIES | Right

LEEDS UNITED

SECOND DIVISION	P	W	D	L	F	A	Pts.
Ipswich	34	21	6	7	78	44	48
Sheffield U.	35	21	5	9	66	42	47
Liverpool	34	18	8	8	72	46	44
Middlesboro'	35	15	12	8	69	57	42
Norwich	35	16	9	10	56	46	41
Sunderland	34	14	12	8	67	46	40
Southampton	34	17	6	11	76	62	40
Plymouth	35	15	7	13	68	67	37
Swansea	35	14	8	13	58	61	36
Scunthorpe	34	12	11	11	60	55	35
Charlton Ath.	33	12	9	12	80	74	33
Luton T.	34	13	6	15	57	66	32
Leeds Utd.	35	13	6	16	61	73	32
Derby Co.	33	11	9	13	62	64	31
Bristol Rov.	34	12	7	15	62	70	31
Rotherham	34	10	10	14	45	45	30
Leyton O.	34	12	6	16	47	68	30
Stoke City	33	10	9	14	44	45	29
Brighton	34	9	9	16	49	61	27
Huddersfield	35	9	8	18	49	62	26
Portsmouth	35	8	9	18	49	80	25
Lincoln City	35	6	6	23	39	80	18

NORTH REGIONAL LEAGUE	P	W	D	L	F	A	Pts
Middlesboro'	32	21	8	3	87	35	50
Port Vale	30	22	2	6	106	48	46
Scunthorpe	33	19	8	6	79	38	46
Sunderland	33	19	6	8	86	52	44
Darlington	35	19	4	12	79	66	42
Hartlepools	32	17	6	9	71	61	40
Bradford P.A.	33	15	8	10	87	49	38
Hull City	31	16	4	11	72	54	36
Rotherham	32	16	3	13	80	62	35
Doncaster	33	13	9	11	55	59	35
Lincoln City	32	15	4	13	66	63	34
Crewe Alex.	29	13	4	12	63	57	30
Grimsby T.	34	11	7	16	56	74	29
Carlisle Utd.	31	8	9	14	46	63	25
Bradford C.	31	9	6	16	56	74	24
Accrington	32	10	2	20	44	89	22
York City	28	10	1	17	52	65	21
Halifax T.	31	7	6	18	47	73	20
Stockport	32	8	4	20	36	96	20
Workington	30	4	9	17	39	72	17
Barrow	34	5	4	25	40	97	14

Peter McConnell and John Hawskby lined up for an away fixture at Scunthorpe United just after Don Revie's appointment. Jack Charlton scored both of the Leeds goals in a 3-2 defeat

Don Revie's Leeds United squad for his first season at the helm, July 1961. Back row: Syd Owen (coach), Les Cocker (trainer), John Hawksby, Alan Humphreys, John Kilford, Jack Charlton, Eric Thompson, Mike Addy, Gary Sprake, Peter Metcalfe, Paul Reaney, Rod Johnson, Bob English (physio), Don Revie (manager). Middle row: Billy Bremner, Gerry Francis, Derek Mayers, Eric Smith, Tom Hallett, Terry Carling, Albert Johanneson, Willie Bell. Front row: Norman Hunter, Terry Casey, Grenville Hair, Alf Jones, Hugh Ryden, Freddie Goodwin, Bobby Cameron, Colin Grainger, Noel Peyton, Peter McConnell, Terry Cooper

Freddie Goodwin, Peter McConnell, Tommy Younger, Derek Mayers, Willie Bell, Billy Bremner and Don Revie are about to depart for a match

Gary Sprake, Paul Reaney, Norman Hunter and Rod Johnson made their first team debut against Swansea Town after impressing for Leeds United's reserves in a 2-0 win at Anfield. A new era had dawned at Elland Road

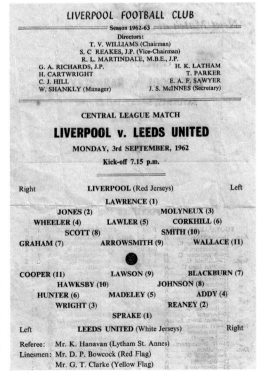

Jim Storrie, John Hawksby, Willie Bell, Grenville Hair and Norman Hunter watch on as Eric Smith shows off his ice skating skills at a frozen Elland Road during the 'big freeze' in the winter of 1962 to 63

Ian Lawson and Huddersfield Town inside-forward Len White battle for possession at Elland Road, May 1963

Leeds United 1963/64. Back row: Don Weston, Norman Hunter, Paul Madeley, Gary Sprake, Willie Bell, Billy Bremner, Barrie Wright. Front row: Albert Johanneson, Paul Reaney, Bobby Collins, Ian Lawson, Johnny Giles

Ian Lawson in action against Manchester City during the 1963/64 campaign. Pictured for City are Alan Oakes and Harry Dowd

Ian Lawson, Barrie White and John Hawksby were among Leeds United's squad at a
civic reception to celebrate the Division Two title triumph

The *Yorkshire Evening Post* celebrates Leeds United's Division Two championship success

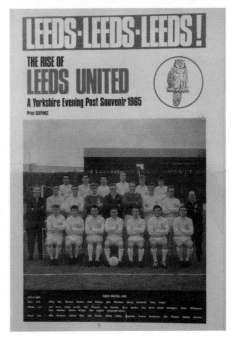

Yorkshire Evening Post's souvenir paper charts the rise of Leeds United, 1965. Back row: Willie Bell, Norman Hunter, Paul Reaney, Jack Charlton, Jimmy Greenhoff, Terry Cooper. Middle: Syd Owen (chief coach), Alan Peacock, Ian Lawson, Gary Sprake, Don Revie (manager), Brian Williamson, Paul Madeley, Barrie Wright, Bob English (physiotherapist). Front: Billy Bremner, Johnny Giles, Jim Storrie, Bobby Collins, Tommy Henderson, Don Weston, Rod Johnson

Rod Johnson fires home the winner against West Bromwich Albion, November 1964

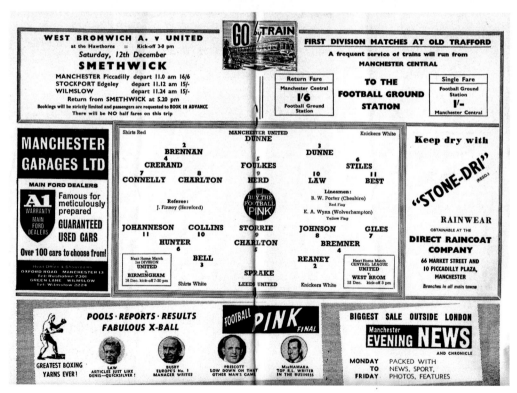

Rod Johnson led the line in Leeds United first victory over Manchester United during the Revie era. Bobby Collins scored the only goal in a famous win, December 1964

Rod Johnson strikes the third goal in an FA Cup third round victory against
Southport, January 1965

Don Weston, Willie Bell, Billy Bremner, Jim Storrie, Alan Peacock, singer Ronnie
Hilton and Ian Lawson promote Leeds United's cup final song in 1965

Leeds United juniors win the Northern Intermediate League Cup for the first time against Sheffield Wednesday, May 1965. Back row: Jimmy Lumsden, Derek Ryder, David Harvey, John Craggs, Eddie Gray, Walter 'Sonny' Sweeney. Front: Stephen Briggs, Dennis Hawkins, Bobby Sibbald, Jack Winspear, Mick Bates, Paul Peterson

Leeds United's roster of players gather for the pre-season group photograph, July 1965. Back row: Mick Bates, Jack Winspear, Rod Johnson, Nigel Davey, Barrie Wright, Graham Smith, Paul Reaney, Norman Hunter, Rod Belfitt, John Price. Centre row: Jimmy Lumsden, Bobby Sibbald, Peter Lorimer, David Harvey, Brian Williamson, Bob Williamson, Gary Sprake, Paul Madeley, Jimmy Greenhoff, Derek Ryder, Terry Cooper. Front row: Dennis Hawkins, Terry Hibbitt, Willie Bell, Bobby Collins, Paul Peterson, John Lawson, Jim Storrie, Jack Charlton, Alan Peacock, Terry Yorath, Walter 'Sonny' Sweeney, Billy Bremner, Johnny Giles, Albert Johanneson. (Absent are Eddie Gray, Don Weston, Maurice Parkin)

Leeds United's juniors line up at the 'Little European Cup' at Lille. Back: Terry Yorath, Jimmy Lumsden, David Harvey, Walter 'Sonny' Sweeney, Jim McKay, Mick Bates, Eddie Gray, John Craggs. Front: Stephen Briggs, Dennis Hawkins, Cyril Partridge (manager), Bobby Sibbald, Terry Hibbitt, Paul Peterson

Leeds United juniors 1965/66: Back row: Terry Yorath, Maurice Parkin, Stephen Briggs, Eddie Gray. Third row: Willie Waddle, John Craggs, David Harvey, Jim McKay, Walter 'Sonny' Sweeney, Brian Mundell. Second row: Eddie Pegrum, Terry Hibbitt, Bobby Sibbald, Mick Bates, Dennis Hawkins, John Lawson. Front row: Derek Montgomery, Ian Kerray, Jimmy Lumsden, Paul Peterson

Dennis Hawkins, right, is ready to pounce as Paul Madeley shoots for goal against West Bromwich Albion in a League Cup tie, October 1965

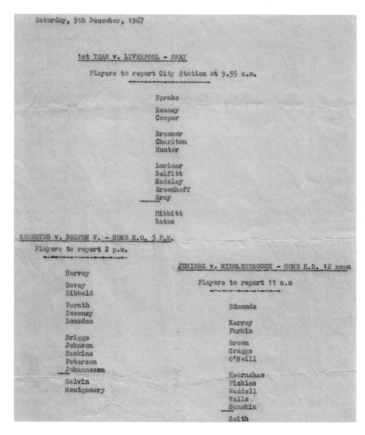

Saturday, 9th December, 1967

1st TEAM v. LIVERPOOL - AWAY

Players to report City Station at 9.55 a.m.

Sprake

Reaney
Cooper

Bremner
Charlton
Hunter

Lorimer
Belfitt
Madeley
Greenhoff
Gray

Hibbitt
Bates

RESERVES v. BOLTON W. - HOME K.O. 3 P.M.

Players to report 2 p.m.

Harvey

Davey
Sibbald

Yorath
Sweeney
Lumsden

Briggs
Johnson
Hawkins
Peterson
Johanneson

Galvin
Montgomery

JUNIORS v. MIDDLESBROUGH - HOME K.O. 12 noon

Players to report 11 a.m

Edmonds

Kerray
Parkin

Brown
Craggs
O'Neill

Hearnshaw
Pickles
Waddell
Walls
Danskin

Smith

On this official team sheet for players Sean O'Neill lines up for Leeds United juniors against Middlesbrough whilst Nigel Davey, Dennis Hawkins, Rod Johnson and Chris Galvin are scheduled to face Bolton Wanderers reserves, December 1967. On the same afternoon, United's first team lost 2-0 to Liverpool when Gary Sprake scored an infamous own goal

Dennis Hawkins, Terry Yorath, Willie Waddle and Bobby Sibbald congratulate Terry Hibbitt following his winner against Sheffield Wednesday, May 1967

Dennis Hawkins, Bobby Sibbald and David Harvey show off the Football League Cup after Leeds United's win in March 1968

Leeds United 1969/70 squad: Back row: Keith Edwards, Sean O'Neill, Chris Galvin, David Kennedy, Norman Hunter, Rod Belfitt, Eddie Gray, Terry Yorath, Brian Mundell. Third row: Don Revie (manager), Bob English (physio), Allan Clarke, Mike O'Grady, Jack Charlton, Gary Sprake, David Harvey, Mick Jones, Paul Madeley, Albert Johanneson, Cyril Partridge (juniors manager), Maurice Lindley (general manager), Syd Owen (coach). Second row: Les Cocker (trainer), David Walls, Paul Reaney, Nigel Davey, Terry Cooper, Terry Hibbitt, Johnny Giles, Billy Bremner, Mick Bates, Jimmy Lumsden, Paul Peterson, Derek Edmunds. Front row: Colin Smith, Robert Malt, Andrew Danskin, Stephen Brown, Seahan Grace, Jimmy Mann, Bobby Rutherford, Brian Stuart, Philip Thrussell, Peter Hearnshaw

Nigel Davey in action against Crystal Palace at Selhurst Park, October 1970

Nigel Davey played in both legs of Leeds United's Fairs Cup clash against Dynamo Dresden during a successful 1970/71 campaign when Billy Bremner lifted the trophy for the second time in the club's history

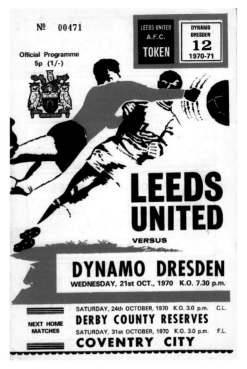

Leeds United's 1972/73 squad gather for the pre-season photograph. Glan Letheren is standing extreme left on the second row from the back. Fifth and sixth from the left are Roy Ellam and Chris Galvin. Sean O'Neill is further along the same row, third from the end

Glan Letheren is named in Leeds United's squad for their clash against Hibernian at Easter Road. United's fourth choice keeper became an overnight hero when he kept goal in a penalty shoot out triumph, November 1973

Official club autograph sheet for supporters, 1972/73 season. Among players featured are Nigel Davey, Chris Galvin and new signing Roy Ellam

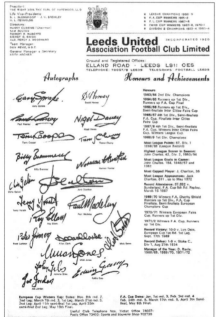

Official player picture holder following Leeds United's second Division One title success in 1973/74. The list of first team squad players are, back: Gordon McQueen, David Stewart, David Harvey, Roy Ellam, Joe Jordan, Allan Clarke, Norman Hunter, Paul Madeley, Mick Jones. Front: Eddie Gray, Peter Lorimer, Terry Yorath, Trevor Cherry, Paul Reaney, Frank Gray, Terry Cooper, Mick Bates, Billy Bremner first team appearances. United's reserve side was packed with talented youngsters, especially in his formative years at the club, and senior players were often coming back from injury.

Although a pillar of the reserves, it is noteworthy that Davey played alongside all the greats of the Revie era in the Football League, Central League, domestic cups or European competitions.

Apparently I was team captain in hundreds of reserve games which at the time you don't think about but is something I'm proud of, even though it's not documented in any record books. Playing with these lads was so easy because they always wanted the ball. At the back, normally I'd knock a ball long looking for a striker but if either Bremner or Giles were playing they'd be screaming for it, so whenever I got the ball I'd just pass it to them and let them do what they did best, which was hurt the opposition. Of all the lads, they were the best players I played with on a football field. Watching close up these two world class players, they had so much time on the ball. There was added pressure though because if you made a mistake you'd know about it.

Big Jack was playing one game when a guy clobbered him after I knocked him a ball a bit short. Jack gave me such a rollicking, telling me what he'd do to me if I did it again. And at half time he was still having a go about me rolling a short ball to him, but after the game he'd calmed down and told me what I should have done in that position. But that was Jack; he was so competitive but he knew I'd not done it on purpose. Moments like that you learn from and it was how you grew as a professional footballer.

I've often been asked down the years what made these lads so good. Quite simply, they were very skillful and natural footballers. I faced them all in training and was delighted not to be playing against them on a Saturday! But I also played alongside them for the first team when my role was to step in when Don needed me. I knew my capabilities and was happy in that role.

Bates stepped in for the midfield lads over the years and played in many top games. In hindsight, I should have stayed at Leeds and not joined Rotherham. Nowadays it would have been easy as there are lots of squad players, but we only had one substitute in those days. Nevertheless, Don made me feel part of everything and I was happy with that situation. Being among the lads season after season was fantastic.

7

Dennis Hawkins

Dennis Hawkins was grabbing headlines as a goal scorer for Swansea and Welsh Schoolboys when Leeds United's scout in Wales, Jack Pickard, first noticed his talent. Pickard, prior to the managerial appointment of Don Revie, had spotted John Charles and Gary Sprake as teenagers in the coastal city of Swansea. Turning his attentions on another Swansea-born teen, Hawkins signed for Leeds then made his debut at 17 years of age against West Bromwich Albion in a League Cup clash in October 1965.

Hawkins gained Welsh U23 honours before playing in a League game for Leeds, but alas, a starring role at United wasn't to be due to fierce competition for places at Elland Road. Making a total of four first team appearances, Hawkins played up front in a memorable League Cup tie at Sunderland as Leeds chased a first major honour. And United's boss tangibly rewarded his attitude over the years when Leeds celebrated Wembley success in 1968.

The eldest of Ron and Edith Hawkins' three sons, Dennis was born in October 1947 and supported his local team, Swansea Town, who played at the Vetch Field. Educated at Penlan Secondary School, Dennis claimed long jump and running titles at the West Counties National Championships but football was his first choice sport.

Hawkins recalled:

Representing Swansea Schools' was fantastic but I almost had to pack in football after one game when it bucketed down with rain. My dad was so upset I'd caught pneumonia he threw my boots in the dustbin and told me it would be the last game, but I was desperate to continue playing as we had a big cup match to play at the Vetch.

My cousin's boots were two sizes bigger than my size seven's, so I wore an extra pair of socks in the cup tie. Those size nine boots then served me well for Swansea and Wales Schools'.

Headline making performances became the norm for Hawkins in Schools' Shield fixtures in 1963. Hawkins hit five goals for Swansea in a 10-0 English Shield win against Pembroke but was on the losing side against rivals Cardiff later in the competition.

A smoother run in the Welsh Shield followed with Hawkins on target as Swansea cruised past Pembroke 5-0 and Aberdare Boys 7-3. Swansea's fiery leader paved the way against Newport then Cardiff in the semifinals.

Hot favourites against Ellesmere Port in a two-legged final, Swansea claimed the Shield for a 25th time, with a 5-0 aggregate win at Ellesmere's York Road ground before 3,000 fans.

A correspondent noted:

Swansea had little difficulty in winning the second leg 2-0 despite a late rally by Ellesmere Port. Territorially, Ellesmere Port had a big share of play, but never showed the same thrust as the Welsh boys who were well led by Hawkins. Swansea scored a fine goal within two minutes, then Hawkins scored their second goal with a lob over Ellsmere's goalkeeper.

During the Schools' International season of 1963, Hawkins played for Wales in Victory Shield matches against Ireland, England and Scotland. He also played international friendly games against Eire and England.

Ireland Schoolboys v Wales Schoolboys, Victory Shield, March 29th, 1963

Ireland: McCallum, McFall, Whalley, Graham, Turkington (capt), Russell, Coulter, Shannon, Walker, Maguire, Gorman

Wales: Davies, Derrett, Yorath, Pearson, Mallard, Thomas, Keetch, Raybould (capt), Hawkins, Murphy, Carvell

A correspondent noted:

Wales gained their 3-0 success because they knew the way to goal. Hawkins played a big part in his side's victory by scoring two opportunist goals. In the 63rd minute, Hawkins scored his first when he rushed onto a left wing pass from Thomas and pushed the ball past Irish goalkeeper McCallum into the net. In the final minutes, after a Raybourne penalty, Hawkins nipped between two Irish defenders to lob the ball into the net from close range.

Wales Schoolboys v Eire Schoolboys, International Friendly, April 6th, 1963

Wales: Davies, Derrett, Yorath, Pearson, Mallard, Thomas, Keetch, Raybould (capt), Hawkins, Murphy, Carvell

Eire: Walsh, Miley, Ryan (capt), O'Connor, Mooney, Rooney, Dixon, Osborne, McEwan, Holmes, Hayes

A correspondent noted:

Wales hammered Eire 9-0 though bizarrely took the lead against the run of play when Hawkins fastened on to a neat back-headed pass from Pearson to fire into the roof of the net from point-blank range. The teen forward got a second when he was left on his own to score easily, then clinched his hat-trick heading in a long cross by Carvell.

Wales Schoolboys v England Schoolboys, Victory Shield, April 20th, 1963

Wales: Davies, Derrett, Yorath, Raybould (capt), Mallard, Thomas, Jones, Pearson, Hawkins, Owen, Carvell

England: Macey, Hinton, Bentley, Langston, Curwen (capt), Boot, Wosahlo, Bradley, Baker, Pearce, Husband

A correspondent noted:

Wales battled hard but went down to a 2-0 defeat. Hawkins of Swansea, the Welsh centre forward, who had notched five goals in two appearances in the red jersey this season, was well held by England centre half and skipper Curwen of Blackpool, although one must give credit to the dark haired leader because he never gave up trying. Late in the game when Curwen made his only mistake, Hawkins was through like a flash only to be robbed at the last moment by full back Hinton of Tottenham.

Leeds United had seen the youngster's potential and set about trying to sign him.

Hawkins recalled:

Jack Pickard wanted me to attend a trial but my dad told him when he came round to our house that we knew nothing about Leeds United.

They were not a top club, not even an up and coming club.

A few days later mum answered the door and had no idea who was standing there. When she asked, Don Revie and Maurice Lindley introduced themselves. They'd driven down from Leeds, which was mighty impressive.

Swansea Town, Cardiff City and Newport County had approached me, and also a number of First Division teams. But Don was the only manager to come round to our house and explain his plans to develop young players. Leeds had watched me and thought I had the potential to become a professional football player. I'd never really heard of Leeds but Don was so persuasive about how he was going to make the team great. It didn't take me long to decide that I would join him at Elland Road.

Whilst Leeds United sorted out their documentation, Hawkins played against England in a friendly game at Wembley before 90,000 spectators.

England Schoolboys v Wales Schoolboys, International Friendly, April 27th, 1963

England: Macey, Hinton, Bentley, Hart, Curwen (capt), Boot, Wosahlo, Bradley, Baker, Pearce, Husband

Wales: Davies, Derrett, Harris, Raybould (capt), Mallard, Thomas, Carvell, Pearson, Hawkins, Murphy, Curten

Wales lost 4-1 and then rounded off their season at Ibrox Stadium against Scotland, who had Edwin Gray (as the programme noted) lining up in a number six jersey.

Scotland Schoolboys v Wales Schoolboys, Victory Shield, May 3rd, 1963

Scotland: Robertson, Stanton, Lynas, Rennie, Callaghan (capt), Gray, Scott, Cumming, Thomson, Dewar, Clunie

Wales: Davies, Derrett, Harris, Morgan, Mallard, Thomas, Carvell, Pearson, Hawkins, Raybould (capt), Curten

Hawkins led the Welsh line with plenty of dash as Wales led twice against the Scots in a 2-2 draw. Suddenly, watching clubs tried to poach Hawkins but the youngster was already Leeds-bound.

Hawkins recalled:

Playing international football was brilliant and gave you the confidence of making it in the game. The Scotland match was the first time I'd come across Eddie and he had incredible skill. I couldn't match Eddie's touch on the ball but Don had seen my potential as a striker.

An Everton scout came round to our house a few days after the Scotland game. He said to my parents, you have something to sell and we are willing to buy it. Poaching of players was not uncommon but I'd already signed for Leeds.

Talent is important but you need to be in the right place at the right time. You also need to find the right club that will look after you in your development. Both my brothers, Pete and Kevin, had talent but neither stayed in the game. Pete was the best left-winger I'd seen as a kid. He captained Welsh Schools' and signed for Northampton Town. Don tried to sign him but could not match Northampton's valuation.

When an offer from Arsenal for £40,000 was turned down, Pete went part-time and drifted out of the game which was terrible because he was a fantastic player.

Kevin was on Swansea Town's books as an apprentice but didn't sign professionally and left the game disillusioned which was really disappointing for him.

With the international season over, Hawkins travelled north to sign for Leeds United.

Don showed us around the area and even arranged a day out to visit Scarborough. Nothing was too much trouble to help me feel settled into my new surroundings. I was delighted to join the club as an apprentice professional.

Correspondent Brian Radford introduced Yorkshire folk to the Welsh sharpshooter during the summer of 1963 in a feature story titled 'Swansea's star schoolboy joins Leeds United'.

Centre forward Dennis 'the menace' Hawkins, chief goal scorer for Wales and Swansea Schoolboys, has joined Leeds United.

He will begin training at Elland Road in a fortnight. So ends a desperate chase by eight clubs.

Representatives of five First Division clubs, including Wolves, Everton and Chelsea, and three Second Division clubs, including Swansea Town, have been in constant touch with Hawkins.

"I settled for Leeds because they have shown much longer interest

in me," he said. "The others only came along after I had played for Wales."

Hawkins' climb to Leeds has involved much scrutiny and considerable discussion. In fact, different representatives of the club checked on him before manager, Mr Don Revie, travelled to Swansea to talk terms.

Hawkins, 15, is the cousin of Roy Vernon, skipper of Everton and Wales's inside-forward.

Several shrewd judges of the game have spoken highly of Hawkins as being another Trevor Ford. His bustling, harassing technique is considered to be greatly similar to that of the one-time fiery centre forward.

Last season Hawkins scored five goals for Wales and 20 for Swansea.

Each day throughout the winter, Hawkins was up long before dawn to help on a milk round.

"I am sure that this keep fit routine helped me a lot to maintain my form," he said.

Hawkins in fact almost missed soccer altogether. He was winning so many awards at long jumping and running that it seemed certain that he would stick to athletics.

But the shrewd eye of a Leeds scout thought otherwise and Hawkins has since graduated superbly at soccer.

Hawkins arrived in Leeds for pre-season training hoping to make the grade in July 1963. Sharing his Harehills digs at 43 Elford Grove were fellow apprentices Eddie Gray, Jimmy Lumsden and Terry Cooper. Norman Hunter, Jimmy Greenhoff and Gary Sprake lived at digs next door.

Hawkins recalled:

There were lads from different apprentice years, we all got on and just mucked in. The club looked after our welfare and there was even a padre called Rev John Jackson we could approach for an informal chat every week.

When I first started training with the lads there was a step up in class. In Swansea it was easy to hold your own but in those early sessions it was tough to shine alongside these lads. I knew about Eddie but there was also Peter Lorimer who had a thunderous shot, as keepers would quickly discover. Terry Hibbitt was a real character on and off the pitch, arguing about everything with anyone. But as a player he had a magical left foot and was a real talent.

If United's coaches didn't think you were right for the club then your stay was cut short. Jeffrey Parry had travelled from Swansea with me but only stayed a few weeks, which did not sit well with me, however, tough decisions on apprentices were made.

Hawkins knuckled down, knew what was expected of him on and off the pitch but also occasionally got into hot water with the boss, Don Revie.

Ground staff lads had to be at Elland Road by 9am every morning. There were fines if you were late for training or a meeting place before a game. A £1 per minute fine may not sound a lot now but when you are on £8 a week it's a big proportion.

Revie was strict in terms of discipline. On a match day we were representing the club, if anyone turned up without a shirt and tie they didn't play. There was no messing about, everyone knew the score.

All the lads had different chores whether it was sweeping the stands, sorting out the boot room or cleaning Bobby Collins' size four boots which I had the pleasure of doing! Bobby was a smashing bloke and a real inspiration to us all. He'd seen it and done it at the highest level and was always available for support.

For some reason early on I seemed to spend half my time with the boss in his office. Some of it was my own doing but also I'd be getting into scrapes with the lads. Don asked me after a few weeks where my wages were going as my clothes looked grubby. I explained that I sent £4 a week to my parents, £2 for digs and had £2 for myself. Don was always interested in our welfare and seemed happy with my explanation. Walking out of his office, he told me to drop into the market to could collect some steak and fruit from a stall that was all paid for by the club to help build me up. I thought to myself, thanks Don, then he told me to get a haircut as it was too long which was a bit annoying but I agreed.

Back at my digs, after telling the lads what happened, Terry (Cooper) told me he was training to be a barber to earn some spare cash so offered to cut my hair. Of course me being gullible I agreed, and after washing my hair, Terry was ready with his towel, scissors and comb laid out neatly on a table. A number of lads had come to watch by now but I still hadn't caught on that Terry was taking the mick. Anyway, Terry started snipping away and suddenly cut off a huge clump across the top of my forehead. The lads were killing themselves because I looked like a monk.

"Chuffing hell Terry, what have you done to my hair?" I yelled.

I'd never seen anything like it, but Terry insisted my hair would be fine after a comb. I knew I'd been done, especially when our landlady kept asking what had happened to my hair, and then on the bus next morning to the ground, passengers were looking at me strangely. The stick I got in the dressing room was unbelievable, and then Maurice Lindley came in and told me the boss wanted to see me. That's all I needed.

Don looked at me, "Who the chuffing heck has cut your hair?"

When I explained Terry was training to be a barber, Don doubled up with laughter. I had a natural Elvis Presley quiff when I joined Leeds but my carefully styled hair was never the same again. My mate Terry apologised but he'd done me good and proper!

Bad haircuts aside, after a season as an apprentice professional, Hawkins signed as a 'pro'. But a practice game against the first team would end in a rollicking after a clash with United's skipper!

All training sessions built to a weekend fixture so the first team would take on the reserves in practice matches to try things out tactically. During the early days I never looked at a teamsheet because there was no way I'd be playing. But one morning I was putting the jerseys out for the first team lads in the dressing room when Terry (Hibbitt) shouts out, "Hawk, you're playing."

You're taking the mick, was my response because Terry liked winding me up. But Terry persisted, "Hawk, I'm serious, you're playing." So I half-heartedly looked at the sheet and thought, blooming heck, Terry's not joking. Bob English ran over and told me to leave the jerseys and get my kit on. Suddenly I was sat with the reserves when Don came in to the dressing room.

"We've got one or two moves we want to try for Saturday's game," he told us. "Let the first team play the ball at free kicks, corners, set pieces. And no tackling, I don't want any injuries."

So I thought, fair enough and did my boots up.

Don walked out and Bob looked at us, "When the ball is in play, bang, chuffing win it."

Now I was thinking, what do I do? Don says no tackling but Bob tells us to win the ball.

Syd Owen was on the whistle as referee when the game kicked off and it was serious stuff. The first team pushed the ball around and no one was tackling as Don stated. The reserve lads kept looking at each other because even Big Jack was looking good on the ball. Suddenly the ball broke to me, and Billy smashed me. The ball hit my shins and I nutmegged Billy. Of course, the senior lads started laughing because Billy had been done by an apprentice, but Billy was fuming; he was calling me every name under the sun.

Later in the game when the ball came my way again, Billy came in from behind straight down the back of my calf. Les Cocker ran over with the 'magic' sponge and told me I'd have to go off but there was no way I was doing that because I now had the red mist. Getting Billy back was the only thing on my mind; I'd completely forgotten what Don had instructed.

When the ball broke again towards Billy, I was straight down the back of his calves and there was a deathly silence on the pitch. Syd blew the whistle, game over.

Billy was helped off and as I took off my boots in the dressing room, Terry said, "You're for it Hawk." And he was right; the boss wanted to see me in his office.

"Chuffing heck Den, what did I tell you about tackling, Billy's out Saturday," he said.

I tried to explain, showing Don my calf but got a rollicking.

Just as I was leaving his office, Don said, "Den, chuffing great tackle but don't do it again."

I felt guilty but vindicated at the same time.

Nothing was said again and even though I'd cost Billy a game, he never held it against me.

Since taking the helm, Revie had bloodied young players. Hawkins had turned professional in October 1964 and United's U18 squad played in the Northern Intermediate League. Apart from Hawkins, the squad included Mick Bates, Rod Belfitt, Nigel Davey, Eddie Gray, Jimmy Greenhoff, David Harvey, Terry Hibbitt, Peter Lorimer, Jimmy Lumsden, John Price, Derek Ryder, Bobby Sibbald, Graham Smith and Barrie Wright.

United's latest crop of youngsters featured in a pre-season team group for the 1964/65 season with the club back in top flight football. And the stars of the future reached the Northern Intermediate League Cup for the first time just before the first team played in the FA Cup Final against Liverpool at Wembley.

Revie's kids were an uncompromising team and in the final took on Sheffield Wednesday. Hawkins scored in a bruising first leg that finished 2-2 at Hillsborough. Match reports including one titled 'Cup final flare up' were not flattering.

A correspondent reported:

Wembley referee Bill Clements can hardly have as much trouble with Leeds and Liverpool on Saturday as George Martin had controlling the youngsters in this first leg at Hillsborough. Fists and feet were raised repeatedly, and referee, George Martin, had to give someone a ticking off every 10 minutes. Trainers were called on seven times before Leeds were finally jeered off. In between, Wednesday centre forward Brian Davies put them ahead, Leeds left-half Nigel Davey equalised, then Brian Woodall put the home side ahead again. But Leeds centre forward Dennis Hawkins gave the Elland Road side a second half equaliser.

Hibbitt scored the only goal in the return leg at Elland Road to win the trophy for United. Gray, Harvey, Davey and Hibbitt starred alongside Hawkins on a memorable night.

Twelve months later, United successfully defended the trophy. This time around, Bates earned a first leg win against Sheffield United at Bramall Lane. A Hawkins double and Sibbald penalty secured a 4-1 aggregate triumph.

Hawkins recalled:

We had a fabulous team with an incredible squad of players. It was a really special occasion winning silverware. Eddie was the first to make the first team and gave us some good-natured stick that he was training with the first team whilst we were sweeping up. But there was never any jealousy because he was not the type to rib you for long. Eddie was a genuinely nice lad who was seriously talented.

European football now was a regular feature at Elland Road. In an inaugural Fairs Cup campaign, United had gone out to Spanish giants Real Zaragoza. But the first team was not the only side to face the elite of Europe. Hawkins was part of the junior team to take part in the 'Little European Cup' at Lille.

United went into the competition having won the Northern Intermidiate League for the first time and Intermediate League Cup against the Blades. The 14-day tour of France, Belgium and Holland was the first major one undertaken by a junior team. Led by assistant team manager Maurice Lindley, Cyril Partridge and assistant secretary Peter Crowther, United's 16-man squad included Maurice Parkin, Stephen Briggs, Eddie Gray, Terry Yorath, Willie Waddle, Walter 'Sonny' Sweeney, David Harvey, Eddie Pegrub, Terry Hibbitt, Bobby Sibbald, Mick Bates, Dennis Hawkins, John Lawson, Jimmy Lawson, John Allot and Peter Peterson.

Participating teams included Anderlecht, Barcelona, Dukla Prague, Feyenoord, Inter Milan, Leeds United, Torino and Ujpest Budapest. In the final, United defeated Barcelona in a penalty shoot out.

Speaking from his holiday centre in Fifeshire, Revie told the *Yorkshire Evening Post*:

> *"This is marvellous. I knew this was a very good team, but to win a tournament like this with all these crack continental teams taking part is magnificent."*

Hawkins made his first team bow against West Brom in a League Cup tie in October 1965 when injuries and international call-ups saw two senior players, Willie Bell and Jim Storrie, line up. The match was a tough baptism not only for Hawkins but also Harvey and Davey making first starts for the club. On the night, United received praise for their fighting spirit.

Leeds United v West Bromwich Albion, October 13th, 1965

Leeds United: Harvey, Davey, Bell, Storrie, Madeley, Wright, Weston, Belfitt, Hawkins, Johnson, Cooper.

West Bromwich Albion: Sheppard, Cram, Fairfax, Lovett, Jones, Fraser, Brown, Astle, Kaye, Hope, Clark

Yorkshire Post:

> *After the shakiest of starts when they found themselves four down after 25 minutes, Mr Don Revie's mostly young side rallied to such purpose that they rubbed off two of the arrears, and in a storming finish, with Leeds fighting like demons, Albion were glad to hang on.*

Hawkins recalled:

> Don pulled me aside at training to tell me I'd be playing and I was

really chuffed but the day before the game I twisted my ankle on a wet surface during a kick around. It wasn't serious so didn't tell anyone because I did not want to miss out on my debut. In any case you generally carried knocks in games but I was taking no chances. I'd worked too hard for this opportunity. There was no way I'd be pulling out.

Bob English on the night asked if anyone needed strappings so I had one. I was nervous but it was fantastic to finally pull on the white jersey for a first team game. Don always gave good advice and just before running out he came over and told me to do what I normally did but slow it down a little.

The big thing for me was playing in front of a larger crowd than normal, even though it would not be a packed house. Through the game I could feel my ankle but it did not restrict me. It was a great experience but we played a weakened team and got a good hiding. West Brom were a strong side and got off to a great start so we just had to battle away. I enjoyed the run out but knew it was a one-off game.

Heady times were developing at Elland Road during the swingin' sixties. And Hawkins was used to a training regime that included rigorous pre-season runs and five-a-sides where all professionals participated. There were also sessions to improve speed and stamina.

The most daunting part of pre-season was circuits around Roundhay Park to build stamina. Being more of a sprinter, I was always at the back for long distance runs with goalkeepers Harvey and Sprake who were also hopeless. And Big Jack used to make me laugh because he seemed to be in the treatment room on a Monday morning when long runs were due!

On the park, the lads had so much skill which you saw close up in five-a-side games. The games were full on, especially when the Scottish and English lads played each other in an 'international' game where tackles would fly in and the boss would have to calm it down. There was great banter though which all the lads were on the end of at different times.

When 'captains' picked teams, I had a standing joke with Yorath because we always seemed to be the last picked. It didn't matter how well we played, we'd be last again next game, although there were occasions when the lads decided to wind up Big Jack, which was not difficult, and he didn't take kindly to being the last pick or awarded a yellow 'bib' to wear for being the worst player. Every time Jack stormed off in a huff it encouraged the lads even more!

The only issue for me was because there were so many international players you could feel intimidated. You'd think to yourself, what am I doing here, but, running out for the Northern Intermediate team on a Saturday, that feeling left because I was scoring lots of goals.

The boss wanted us to have an edge in terms of fitness, so Les ran shuttle drills for a number of lads to improve our speed. This helped enormously as the first few yards were crucial for me and at one point, apart from Albert Johanneson, I was fastest off the mark. Then we'd train with sandbags on our backs to build stamina, or wear heavy jumpers so we felt light as a feather by a Saturday. A lot of thought went into improving our fitness.

Hawkins was part of the senior squad by United's 1966/67 campaign but was frustrated at a lack of first team opportunities. Local reports noted he might be joining Swansea Town but rumours were quashed when he signed a 'first team squad' contract. Yet to make his league debut, Hawkins' first Welsh U23 cap came after Wales made five changes following a record drubbing by England when Fulham striker Allan Clarke scored four goals in an 8-0 win.

Selected to play against Scotland U23 and Ireland U23, Hawkins featured in a local newspaper sports article headlined 'Hawkins Shock Choice'.

A correspondent noted:

Dennis Hawkins walked into Leeds' ground yesterday as third team centre forward and danced out a few hours later as the new leader of the Welsh U23 team!

But sure enough this 18-year-old from Swansea who has never played a game of league football will lead the Welsh attack against Scotland U23's.

This is the shock selection in a 'green' Welsh team that shows a mass defensive shake up from the one that crashed against England earlier this season.

Hawkins played in the Leeds third team last Saturday and has played 13 games in the reserves this season – but a lot of those have been on the wing.

Hawkins made his Welsh U23 debut against Scotland at the Racecourse Ground, Wrexham.

Wales U23 v Scotland U23, November 30th, 1966

Wales: Simpkins (Hartlepools), Thomas (Swindon), Lucas (Wrexham), Summerhayes (Cardiff City), Coldrick (Cardiff City), Page (Birmingham City), Krzywicki (West Brom), Pugh (Newport County), Hawkins (Leeds United), Humphreys (Everton), Lewis (Cardiff City)

Scotland: Clark (Aberdeen), Whyte (Aberdeen), Tinney (Partick Thistle), Stanton (Hibernian), McMillan (Aberdeen), Gray (Leeds United), Edwards (Dunfermline), Hope (West Brom), McCalliog (Sheffield Wednesday), Cormack (Hibernian), Mitchell (Dundee United)

Sadly for Hawkins and the Welsh team, Gray and former United apprentice Jim McCalliog scored twice as a vastly more experienced Scottish XI ran out 6-0 victors.

Hawkins then faced Ireland the following February at Windsor Park, Belfast.

Ireland U23 v Wales U23, February 22nd, 1967

Ireland: McKenzie (Airdrie), Craig (Newcastle United), McKeag (Glentoran), Todd (Burnley), Napier (Bolton), Clements (Coventry City), Campbell (Dundee United), Ross (Glentoran), McMordie (Middlesbrough), Trainer (Crusaders), McKinney (Falkirk)

Wales: Walker (York City), Collins (Tottenham), Thomas R (Swindon), Powell (Wrexham), Roberts (Swansea), Walley (Arsenal), Thomas J (Newport County), Evans (Wrexham), Hawkins (Leeds United), Humphreys (Everton), Mahoney (Crewe)

Ireland led 2-1 after 70 minutes before the match was abandoned due to a waterlogged pitch. Reports noted Hawkins struck the underside of the crossbar with Wales a goal behind. Vic McKinney scored twice for the Irish with Evans replying for the Welsh before extreme cold and atrocious underfoot conditions saw officials call the game off.

Hawkins recalled:

Playing at U23 level was a huge honour and a challenge because England and Scotland had a much bigger pool of players to select from and it showed in results. Of the Scottish side that I played against, Gray, McCalliog, Clark, Cormack, Stanton and Hope gained full caps whereas only Thomas and Krzywicki represented Wales in a full international from our team. Nothing, however, in my football

127

career, gave me more pride than pulling on the Welsh jersey.

Domestically, Leeds earned a top-four finish in the League and in Europe reached the Fairs Cup semifinals where they faced a tricky tie against Kilmarnock.

> The reserves watched home games when the first team played European matches. Extra players would also make up the matchday squad for away games in case of injuries. I was involved on a number of trips including Valencia that season and the atmosphere was very different to domestic games. Some of the grounds were not up to standard and coach trips could take hours. Nothing was left to chance because the club looked after passports and you had to be careful not to say anything at checkpoints. They were great experiences and showed how quickly the club was moving forward.

Revie rested weary players for the Kilmarnock tie and called on United's reserves to complete League fixtures. Every player in United's line-up for the final game against Sheffield Wednesday, apart from Peacock playing out of position at centre half, had been on the ground staff. Only Bremner, making his sole substitute appearance for Leeds, and Reaney were first team regulars while Cooper and Gray had just started to break through. Hawkins and Lumsden made league debuts.

Watching journalists were impressed by United's display after a Hibbitt strike won this derby clash.

Leeds United v Sheffield Wednesday, May 15th, 1967

Leeds United: Harvey, Reaney, Cooper, Lumsden, Peacock, Gray (Bremner), Bates, Hawkins, Johnson, Belfitt, Hibbitt

Sheffield Wednesday: Springett, Branfoot, Ellis, Ford, Megson, Mobley, Quinn, Smith, Symm, Usher, Whitham

Yorkshire Evening Post:

> *Wonders are in grave danger of never ceasing at Elland Road.*
> *Last night Leeds United rounded off a league season in which they had resisted a non-stop torrent of injuries, which would have darned near relegated some clubs, and finished fourth by beating Sheffield Wednesday 1-0 with practically a reserve side.*
> *On an unhelpful, sticky pitch, but a far better one than might have been expected after the weekend's weather, this side ran Wednesday*

nigh dizzy with an astonishing display of spirited well knit football fore and aft.

Don't imagine Wednesday were not at all interested. They played the game hard, and they nearly established themselves in a furious late rally in which only the bar kept their best forward, inside left Ford, from equalising. But this latest collection of Mr Revie's nursery products sailed right into Wednesday from the kick off, passing sharply, running well on and off the ball, chasing everything and everybody, and making winded Wednesday look ponderous in defence and attack.

Mr Revie was so pleased with the result and the form his men showed that he was nearly at a loss for words. Finally he settled for "brilliant" which, by and large, will do for a side of lads who did what they had no right to do.

Hibbitt at outside-left, the scorer of the vital goal after 12 minutes, nipped on to a knock down by Hawkins and snapped a curving shot past Springett, still a fine keeper but completely surprised and beaten this time.

A most remarkable match, with only two flaws to it, the booking of Wednesday's right-back Smith for foul tackling, and the crowd, 23,053, the smallest of the season.

The absentees missed a surprise result.

Hawkins recalled:

When Don told us we'd be playing there was a moment when we looked at each other a bit puzzled but it quickly turned to excitement and on the day was a great occasion. Whilst you always prepare for a game, going through it as the first team, there was more intensity. Yes, it was an end of season match, but still a derby, so we'd have a passionate crowd.

I recall giving Vic Mobley the runaround and for some reason picking a ball up on halfway then half-volleying a crisp ball just above the ground to Hibbitt on the wing which led to Terry's goal. Don was chuffed to bits at the end of the game. He'd got stick for playing a weakened team but we proved the knockers wrong. Our reserve team could hold its own and give teams a run for their money. Terry's goal rightly got the headlines, which I was credited in assisting, and it was great reading the positive publicity for our efforts in the papers next day.

United had a strong first team with a settled defence and among the most feared midfield partnerships around with width on both flanks. Yet, since taking the managerial hot seat, only one centre forward, Storrie, had headed United's scoring charts.

Revie decided to purchase a proven scorer and signed Mick Jones from Sheffield United for a club record £100,000 in September 1968. Jones' arrival impacted on Hawkins' long-term future but his introduction to United's reserve forward took place in bizarre circumstances.

> Mick was having treatment for an injury after signing and above the treatment room was a trap door to the main stand, where the lads would sometimes lark about. On this occasion, one of the lads nudged me, I lost my balance and crashed straight through the ceiling and ended up sprawled on the floor below. Don and Mick were covered in plaster while Les was stood holding his ultrasonic instrument.
>
> After clearing up, I got fined a week's wages and a rollicking, but Don didn't dock my wages. As a man manager, he was superb because I'd learnt my lesson.

Hawkins was regularly knocking in the goals for the reserves, and with Jones cup-tied, after earlier victories over Bury and Luton Town, the young striker was selected to play against Sunderland in a League Cup fourth round clash in mid-November. For Hawkins, there had been little riding on previous first team run outs, but this was a massive game. Chasing a first major honour, United silenced home supporters with a clinical display.

Sunderland v Leeds United, November 15th, 1967

Sunderland: Montgomery, Kinnell, Parke, Todd, Hurley, Baxter, Herd, Suggett, Martin, Heslop, Mulhall. Sub: Gauden

Leeds United: Sprake, Reaney, Cooper, Bremner, Madeley, Hunter, Greenhoff, Belfitt, Hawkins (Bates), Gray, Hibbitt

A correspondent noted:

> *The Leeds United power drill was switched back on last night, outside-right Jimmy Greenhoff, the only 'resident' striker made it work with a great two-goal performance.*
>
> *Between times the drill kept right on running through 90 minutes of a match which could take Leeds right through to Wembley.*
>
> *And the drill is so basically simple: work and cover, cover and run,*

run and hit.

The fact that Leeds reached the quarterfinal without three first teamers piled on the agony for nearly 30,000 Roker Park fans. And if last night's formula holds good when the injured trio get back then the League Cup small fry can look out.

Hawkins recalled:

Don called me into his office a day before the game to tell me I was going to play against Sunderland and I walked out a bit in shock. I was finally involved in a big match in a strong team and I'd be facing Charlie Hurley who had a fearsome reputation.

Hurley was a giant compared to me but I knew that I could beat him in the air. Running out before a packed Roker Park with Billy and the lads for a big cup game was what I'd dreamt about. Greenhoff got both our goals and afterwards Don said I'd given Hurley the runaround, which was pleasing.

Ten days later, Hawkins traveled to Nottingham Forest where he'd play his final game for the club. Forced into changes, Revie's revamped team secured a deserved 2-0 win at The City Ground.

Nottingham Forest v Leeds United, November 25th, 1967

Nottingham Forest: Grummitt, Hindley, Hennessey, McKinlay, Newton, Lyons, Chapman, Baker (Wignall), Barnwell, Taylor, Bridgett

Leeds United: Harvey, Reaney, Cooper, Bremner, Madeley, Hunter, Greenhoff, Belfitt, Hawkins (Lorimer), Bates, Hibbitt

A correspondent noted:

Don Revie's youngsters covered themselves with glory in this fine win. Their two goals exactly doubled the Elland Road club's away goal tally for the season!

This without seven recognised seniors, but Leeds still looked to have the best defence, only 14 goals conceded in 18 games.

Under the inspired leadership of Billy Bremner, they survived a first half hammering to emerge after the break the far superior side.

Hawkins recalled:

Don had to make a few team changes and I played up front with Belfitt. Just before half time the ball came across and I clipped a post with a header. Six inches the other side it would have been a goal. Football is about small margins and whenever Don brought me into the side, I didn't score. If it had gone in maybe Don would not have taken me off. Greenhoff opened the scoring for us then Lorimer smashed home a 30-yard effort for the win.

Following the Sunderland win, United defeated Stoke City then Brian Clough's Derby County to reach the League Cup Final where they would take on Arsenal at Wembley. With Jones returning to fitness, Hawkins was out of the first team spotlight but enjoyed a flirtation with stardom during one of the biggest weeks in the club's history.

Don named me in his Cup Final squad because Belfitt would play if Greenhoff didn't make it and I'd be substitute. I realised it was a long shot but he had to have options. Don always made sure everyone at the club was involved. His attention to detail was amazing. After the FA Cup Final in 1965, I attended the celebration banquet at the Savoy Hotel.

He went out of his way to make sure apprentices, staff and players' partners were part of a big occasion. Despite the defeat to Liverpool, it had been a huge achievement reaching a first Cup Final. This time around, as a member of his squad, my girlfriend joined the party. I'd met Linda (Lin) at the Mecca Ballroom and we'd been courting a while, so Don arranged for her to be with his wife, Elsie, and the other lads' partners for the weekend. The lads knew Lin and a number used to see her parents, Bill and Eileen Gaines, because they lived behind their fish and chip shop on Whitehall Road. Bill and Eileeen were always chuffed to see the lads and have a chat about life at Elland Road.

On Cup Final day, Madeley slotted in for Jones, Greenhoff was passed fit so Belfitt was on the bench. But I was close to playing at Wembley. Seeing Terry (Cooper) get the winning goal and the lads finally win a cup was fantastic. Winning a major trophy was so important for the club, so to be there was really special.

After the match, I joined the lads in the dressing room and they were in great spirits. All of them had collected a tankard when they picked up the Cup but I didn't notice there were some spare ones on a table in the middle of the dressing room when Don came over to me.

"There you go Den, you played at Sunderland so this is your trophy," he said.

Don's gesture made my day but I was stunned at the time. All these years later, I don't have too many mementos from my Leeds career but my League Cup tankard reminds me of a great period of my life and is pride of place at home. Being part of the celebrations at Wembley, the Royal Garden Hotel and then civic reception in Leeds on the Sunday was fantastic.

Hawkins returned to the reserves, then a few weeks into the 1968/69 season joined Third Division side Shrewsbury Town. But it would be a decision he'd quickly regret.

I was dropping down the order of strikers because Jones, Lorimer and Mike O'Grady were playing regularly with Belfitt the backup striker. Greenhoff had joined Birmingham City which puzzled me as he was such a good player and had been in the first team, but I was not looking to move. Then Don told me Shrewsbury Town manager Harry Gregg had seen me play for the reserves at Derby County and had offered £10,000. Don didn't want me to go but understood if I chose to leave.

I was only 20 and unsure what to do but agreed to meet the manager. Lin and I travelled down to Shrewsbury who played at Gay Meadow and we could see ourselves living in the area because it was a lovely part of the country. Harry would match my wages at Leeds; I'd have first team status and get a cut of a transfer fee. The money sounds nothing now but we were about to get married, so I decided to make the move even though Northampton Town had come in with an offer of £15,000.

Don wished me well but after a few games I realised that I'd made a terrible mistake. Facilities and medical care were a world away from Leeds United. Playing wise the move was also the biggest slipup of my career. Tactically, I was an out and out striker but Shrewsbury's style of football was totally different to Leeds' where I made diagonal runs and the midfield lads put the ball on a sixpence. Now, I had to come deeper for the ball, which was not my game. I didn't score many goals and my game went downhill fast. I should have stayed at Leeds like Bates, who enjoyed great times as a squad player.

Whether Don would have kept me long term I don't know, especially when Joe Jordan came on the scene, but I should have taken that chance.

In the midst of a tough time, Hawkins came up against former Leeds

United legend John Charles when he was player-manager of Hereford Town at the end of his career.

> There was thick mud all over the ground, it was pouring down with rain and John ran out wearing plimsolls. I couldn't believe it but before kick off, John winked at me, "Don't worry Den, I won't be doing any running!"
>
> When John scored and jogged back, I gave him a wry smile. He was the complete footballer … physical, clinical and a gentleman on and off the pitch.

Desperate for a new club, when Stockport County offered Shrewsbury £8,000, Hawkins played in a reserve game as County's manager was attending. But it proved a disaster.

> A Stockport defender caught me on my calf with a sliding tackle but I got through to half time. After an assessment, I was given a cortisone injection when I'd actually cracked a fibula, which snapped in the second half.
>
> Shrewsbury did not have the best facilities when it came to rehabilitation and they rushed me back too quickly. I suffered a second break in the same place during a friendly match versus Leicester City and then a third when I went out on loan to Waterford, where Shay Brennan was manager.
>
> I was out a total of 18 months, which was hugely frustrating. It was a tough time but Lin's parents were incredibly supportive, as they had been since I first met them and continued to be in my football career.

Following a three-year spell at the Shropshire club, Hawkins joined Newport County in May 1972.

> I'd started playing midfield because of hamstring problems and felt comfortable, so thought it would be a good move, but the ground was a sight to behold as it sat in the middle of an old speedway track. Even so, I joined but after six games received another knock on my leg. There was no break but I knew that I'd struggle to see out my contract. It was not my style to sit out a deal, so Newport paid half my contract up and I packed in full-time football.

Hawkins was 26 years of age and soon found the desire for a return to football on a part-time basis. Following spells at Telford United and

Nuneaton Borough, after settling near York, where he worked for Rowntrees, an opportunity to play for York City surfaced.

Wilf McGuiness was York's manager and we'd enjoyed some tough battles in the Central League when he played for Manchester United. We'd always got on so I agreed to play in a few reserve games. But Wilf did not have that mean streak a manager needs, so Charlie Wright succeeded him.

Charlie was a former player and a totally different character. After a match at Halifax Town he gave me an envelope on the coach with £1 expenses. As a former professional with Leeds United and Welsh U23, I would not be humiliated and stormed off. Two days later Charlie got the sack, which was no surprise.

York's chairman asked me to manage the side but it was not for me. I looked after Tadcaster Albion and enjoyed it for a period but, like Wilf, I did not have a ruthless side, so resigned.

Now retired and still living in the York area, where Dennis and Lin's son Gary was born, playing for Leeds United was the highpoint of Dennis's career.

Don gave me every chance to succeed as a professional footballer. My natural instinct was to get into the danger area, but to develop my game he played me on the right wing to ping balls in during a couple of matches, however, it was not a success.

The highlight for me was playing in the first team even though it was only for a few games. Being amongst the lads was amazing and Don always appreciated my efforts. Just being part of the squad that won the League Cup was brilliant but I should have stayed on as a squad member and not left for Shrewsbury. It was a mistake but no one can take away my memories of a wonderful time at the club. The lads were brilliant to play alongside but in hindsight I had no chance of breaking through to the team because there were so many great players.

So much has been written about Leeds United but for me Bobby Collins started it off and was a massive inspiration to the young lads. Billy then took over and stands out because he was such a leader of men. A favourite memory was when Leeds played Tottenham Hotspur at White Hart Lane after promotion. Billy and Dave Mackay were fierce competitors, so when Billy put in a crunching tackle and Dave grabbed him by the throat, it became an iconic image. It was a heck of a challenge and Billy needed treatment by half time. He was struggling but carried on as if nothing had happened.

As a partnership, Billy and Johnny Giles were terrific. Both could look after themselves, which you had to do in that era, but they dictated play like no other midfield pairing. When John joined from Manchester United, to improve our skills the young lads took every opportunity to watch him work on set pieces or spreading the ball, which he was renowned for. In terms of technical ability, Eddie was the most skillful footballer I played with or against and, but for injuries, would have gone on to even greater success.

As a striker, I found Big Jack and Norman tough to play against in training games because they gave away nothing. Jack didn't like little speedy players taking him on so gave me a rough time and Norman was far more than just an uncompromising tackler as he had a fantastic left foot. The defence and midfield were so strong and as if facing these lads was not a tough enough challenge, Paul Madeley came in and strolled across the pitch; he was an amazing player. Behind them was Sprakie in goal who made some big mistakes on television. Viewers often didn't see the saves he made that made the team so solid and I felt sorry for him at times.

As a striker, I partnered all the forwards at one time or other, and respected them all.

Leaving Leeds was tough and I missed the banter, but it comes back immediately when you see the lads again. Not so long ago I was on a break in Teneriffe when there was a shout from behind, "Hawk!" Turning around there was Nigel (Davey). Well, you could have knocked me over with a feather, and especially when he arranged for us to meet up with another old friend, Terry (Cooper), for a meal. Together with our wives, we had a fabulous time into the early hours and have met up a few times since.

When you consider what that team achieved, they were just lads trying to make it in the game but they were fantastic.

8

James 'Sean' O'Neill

SEAN O'Neill was on Leeds United's books throughout the most successful period of the Revie era when competition for places was ultra competitive.

O'Neill grew up in Belfast, joined United's ground staff in June 1967 and developed in the Central League. However, he struggled for first team opportunities at left back as he vied for selection with England internationals Terry Cooper, Paul Madeley and later Trevor Cherry. Revie's first team squad was exceptional and O'Neill eventually made three substitute appearances in October 1973.

Timing and luck are intrinsically linked to talent in the world of professional football. O'Neill was a diligent footballer with talent, but the 'luck of the Irish' deserted him when it came to timing, however, he still cites his 'Elland Road years' as a highlight of two decades in the game.

Sean was born in February 1952 and began his footballing journey prior to a much-chronicled period of Irish history.

O'Neill recalled:

Ardoyne was mainly a Catholic and Irish nationalist district of North Belfast. Things did go on and you went into areas you were not meant to, but it never bothered me because my parents (Hugh and Bridie O'Neill) made it clear that you treat everyone with respect.

Coming from Belfast, most kids supported Manchester United, Liverpool, Celtic or Rangers. Manchester United was my team so from that era George Best, Bobby Charlton and Denis Law were my heroes. No one else in my family was sporty but I could hold my own in football matches.

Sean made rapid progress playing for St Gabriel's School and St Patrick's Youth Club and aged 14, had a trial for one of the big clubs in Belfast, Irish League side Distillery FC.

> If you want something badly enough you are focused on getting it but you still need a bit of good fortune to make the grade, and luckily I played for Ireland Schoolboys versus Scotland, Wales and England. Distillery had good players and looked after me but I was not going to sign for an Irish club unless there was no alternative. I wanted a higher standard of football which meant making a living at a Football League club.

When Leeds United scout Mark Willis spotted O'Neill playing for his youth club in January 1967, he immediately arranged a meeting with his parents. O'Neill would be the only schoolboy international from his cohort of players to enjoy a professional careeer.

> Mark wanted me to attend a trial. As a club, Leeds had come to prominence because after promotion from the Second Division, they had finished runners up to Manchester United in the First Division. Leeds had also played Liverpool in an FA Cup Final so had made progress each year. There was a 'dirty Leeds' tag, which I'd read about, but that didn't bother me. When a top club comes in, you think to yourself this is good, and things happened quickly.
>
> During trials we played a match at Middlesborough then watched Leeds at Elland Road on a Saturday afternoon. The crowd and atmosphere was fantastic to experience. Mr Revie explained how the club would look after me later that week and offered me an apprenticeship.

O'Neill arrived for pre-season training in July 1967 and was the sole lodger at digs in Harehills, Leeds.

> Coming over as a 15-year-old was exciting, yet daunting, but to have a chance of becoming a professional footballer and achieve my goal was amazing. The Godridge's looked after me like a son in their home and it never crossed my mind why I wasn't sharing with other lads; it just worked out that way. Living in a 'home away from home' helped me settle and working with a great bunch of lads was all I could ask. But if there were any problems you'd see the boss, Mr Revie, who would sort things out.

O'Neill was listed in United's official club handbook for 1967/68 alongside other first year apprentices Chris Galvin, Robert Malt, Peter Hearnshaw, Andrew Danskin and Colin Smith. Whilst taking up ground staff duties, there was the small matter of what players would call Sean, especially United's first team goalkeeper!

> Everyone made me feel welcome but i had a really broad accent, which some of the lads struggled to understand. The Irish for James, which is what my parents named me, is Séamus or Shaemy, which is what I was known as at home. But Gary Sprake could never remember either so after a few days Sean stuck, and I've been known as that ever since.

A few months into his apprenticeship, Sean's father passed away, and during a difficult time the club offered compassionate support. After returning home for a short period, Sean set about earning his first professional contract.

> I'd heard a lot about our duties but none of them did you any harm. If there was a match on a Saturday we swept the terraces on the Monday. The rest of the week we made sure everything was right for the first team players so we'd put kit out, clean the dressing rooms and so on. There were also occasions in the winter when Don asked me to help roll the pitch after they removed straw from the playing surface. And I was happy to help out because he'd give me a tenner, which was a small fortune when you earned £8 a week.
>
> Dressing room duties on a match day could be interesting because you'd see top players and managers arriving for a game. When Leeds played West Ham, Bobby Moore would walk down the corridor 'ramrod straight' and looking like an Adonis film star. Bobby had so much presence and was a great player but I often wondered why Norman Hunter never seemed to get mentioned in the same light, because domestically he was more consistent.
>
> Les Cocker was England's coach during this period so I asked his opinion but all I got was a rollicking for bringing up the subject. Les wasn't derogatory towards Norman, he could not be more complimentary, but he'd seen Bobby at close quarters and had enormous respect for him.
>
> When Bill Shankly and Matt Busby came to Elland Road, they would always stop for a chat with the young lads. Both were so down to earth and you remember that as a kid. They had so much standing

in the game and Don had enormous respect for both of them.

There were lots of star players around at that time but nobody could top George Best for popularity. Bestie was on a different level to anyone else. I was in the car park chatting to some of the lads after a match against Manchester United when a helicopter landed on the training pitch, which was an unusual sight. We were naturally intrigued, and then suddenly George walks out with Miss World on his arm and flies off. We could not believe it but it summed Bestie up because he was a superstar. The media dubbed George the 'fifth Beatle' and you could see why. Seeing your heroes close up was great.

I never played against Bobby Charlton but if he'd run towards me in a game I'd have probably stepped aside! Joking aside, they were just good blokes who happened to be world-class footballers.

Cyril Partridge managed the youth team and Syd Owen ran our coaching sessions. Syd was knowledgeable, strict and didn't say things behind your back. With Syd, there was no messing about.

The juniors played in the Northern Intermediate League but stepping up to the reserves was important because you played at a higher standard in the Central League against Liverpool, Everton, Manchester United, Manchester City, Newcastle United and other big clubs. Matches were also on the main pitch, so it was an experience playing in front of 50 people at St James' Park with ball boys retrieving the ball when it was hoofed into the stand.

Leeds United's first team was an established side and, after numerous near misses, triumphed in the League Cup Final at Wembley in March 1968. Revie ensured squad players, apprentices and staff witnessed a landmark occasion. Apprentices were also present when United won the biggest prize in domestic football in April 1969.

The League Cup has always been particularly memorable because, apart from watching the lads win at Wembley, I met my wife, Margaret, at The Mecca Ballroom the night before the final. We travelled down on the Saturday for the game and it was a great day out. Winning was really important for the club and, travelling back to Leeds, there was a real sense that more honours would follow.

Just over a year later Leeds went to Anfield knowing a draw against Liverpool would win the league title, so we got a mini bus over in the afternoon. The boss made sure tickets were left at the ground and we watched the game from the corner opposite the Kop. The atmosphere inside the ground was electric and unbelievably tense, but we got the 0-0 draw.

Billy took the lads over to the Kop, which was an amazing scene to witness, and as we got back to the minibus, we saw the team coach was about to pull out of Anfield. The boss must have seen us because he got off the bus and gestured for us to get on. The celebrations were in full swing when someone put a window through, which was a shock, but that was not going to dampen our spirits.

During the journey home, everyone was having a drink and a few of the lads were playing 'pretend poker' with shattered bits of glass pretending they were diamonds! Back in Leeds, the celebrations continued long into the night at the Queens Hotel. To be a part of that experience was incredible. Cyril told the boss in the early hours that we had a game that night but for once Don could not care less. He told Cyril to make sure we were away by 6am!

O'Neill was on Leeds United's roster of full-time professionals for the 1969/70 season. In a memorable campaign, United chased an unprecedented First Division, FA Cup and European Cup treble as a new decade dawned. Fixture congestion ended the title and European challenge, but O'Neill was at Wembley to see Leeds play Chelsea in the FA Cup Final.

The Horse of the Year Show had taken place at Wembley a few days before the final and the state of the surface was dreadful. It looked like a cow patch. On the day we should have won after Big Jack then Mick Jones gave us the lead twice. Chelsea had their chances but we were the better side in a 2-2 draw. Losing the replay was heartbreaking for the lads because they deserved to win something that season.

O'Neill was playing regularly for the reserves and on the fringes of United's first team squad but had little chance of getting a call up because of the strength in depth at the club.

There were around 18 players in the squad and someone was always carrying an injury, so a couple of older lads from the reserves would make up numbers. You became more involved and got to see just how good these lads were in training sessions. When a season got going, the first team was playing twice a week because of their involvement in Europe, so it was a matter of managing knocks to get them out on the pitch. The lads did a lot of set piece work and kept sharp in extremely competitive five-a-sides.

Arriving at Leeds, I thought that I could play a bit, but being on a pitch with Bremner, Giles, Charlton and the other lads, you learnt very quickly that you were not as good as you imagined. There was one-touch stuff in eight, nine and 10-a-side games on a quarter of a pitch with a small goal. It was all about possession football, and you'd get a rollicking if you gave the ball away. It could be brutal so you sank or swam. Bobby Collins had left the club by now but his influence was still there. Bobby instilled a competitive edge in the lads that was awesome, even in five-a-sides.

In one game, Billy went right over the top and straight down my shins. Blood was pouring down my shin as Syd came running over.

"Are you all right Billy," was Syd's first question.

"He's chuffing all right but what about my chuffing leg," was my response

Of course, I knew why Syd checked Billy first and there were no hard feelings. Billy was such a winner and that incident still makes me smile.

United had a wealth of talent to select from, but at various times first team players played in the reserves to get match fit after sustaining injuries. Johnny Giles and Billy Bremner were injured at different stages of the 1970/71 season when Leeds chased a second First Division crown. Giles played for the second string in the early part of the campaign. Playing alongside the 'little general' made a big impression on O'Neill.

You got used to a certain way of playing in the reserves, so when we defended set pieces, I was always at our near post and if a ball came my way I'd hump it clear. That was my job, or so I thought. When the first teamers had a run out it was a real learning curve because their expectations were on a different level. In one game I humped away a goal bound header from a corner thinking I'd done a good job. Running past Johnny on the edge of our penalty box, he gave me the biggest rollicking.

"If you kick a ball away like that again while I'm on a pitch shouting for it, I'll kick you over the stand," or words to that effect, he screamed.

I was taken aback, but after the game Johnny explained that he'd spotted a counterattack so just wanted a short ball. Johnny wasn't having a go at me; it just hadn't crossed my mind to pass him the ball because, when he was not in the side, our midfield lads didn't want the ball in that position. You can't really learn that in a coaching clinic. It's only when a pro points out a certain scenario that it makes sense because it's a live situation.

Leeds had led the title race from the opening games and also enjoyed a Fairs Cup run where they were about to face archrivals Liverpool in the semifinals. Bremner though had endured the longest spell of his playing career away from first team action. Desperate for his inspirational skipper to return, Revie arranged a secret run out against Huddersfield Town reserves 24 hours before United's Anfield clash.

> Don wanted to test Billy's injury but we had no idea until he turned up and it was a surprise. Billy controlled the game throughout and it was fantastic to see him at close quarters. I'd played with and against Billy in training sessions but this was different because it was against opponents. He came through our game and then scored the winner at Anfield with a diving header. Leeds went on to beat Juventus on aggregate in the final.
>
> Playing alongside Billy was brilliant because, like Johnny, he could spot an opening that reserve lads hadn't seen, but he also had the skill to deliver the relevant ball with pinpoint accuracy. As a partnership they were superb, world class players have inherent talent but also understand each other's games inside out. When either received or won a ball, they'd instinctively read each other's movements. There might be a quick glance or shimmy, then they'd execute a pass. And if Billy faced the wrong way, he'd reverse pass a ball to one of the lads and they'd be expecting it.
>
> Playing football with great players is easy because if you are in trouble there is more options. You can coach players all you want however well planned and intentioned, but I learnt far more playing with seasoned pros.

Three days after the Liverpool win, Bremner was in the side when Leeds took on West Brom who had not won an away game all season. In front of *Match of the Day* cameras, The Baggies won 2-1 but the match went down in club folklore because of a controversial 'offside' goal that resulted in a pitch invasion.

Leeds eventually lost out in the title race to Arsenal by a point and faced an FA stadium ban at the start of the season. Playing in the West

Brom midfield on that fateful Saturday afternoon was Asa Hartford. Earlier in the season, his transfer to Leeds United sensationally fell through when he failed a medical due to a heart condition.

> The collapse of Asa's move made headline news but, in football, nothing surprises you. Asa came across as a really nice bloke and for him it was a massive blow. When news of his signing broke, I did wonder where he was going to fit in the team. Asa played in midfield, so was Don going to split up Billy and Johnny? You don't sign a player for £170,000, which was a massive fee then, and not play them. It made you think what might happen, but in the end it was not a decision Don had to make. Losing out to Arsenal was heartbreaking but the lads went on to defeat Juventus in the Fairs Cup Final, which was brilliant.

During a close season, Revie held contract talks with his squad and discussions could be a nerve-wracking experience.

> The boss sat behind a big desk which could be an intimidating sight. I'd been at the club four years but had still to play for the first team, so there was a thought that he might not offer me another contract. During the season one of the lads blurted out to Don that I was getting married to my girlfriend Margaret, so was going to apply for a mortgage. I was on £22 a week at that time which was okay but really I needed a bit more.
>
> Don liked players to be settled so told me at the time to sort out a house as I'd be on £33 a week the following season, and it would be effective from my new contract. But during my contract talks, Don said I'd be on £28, so I quickly thought what's worse, telling the boss he'd offered more or inform Margaret I'd be on less than planned? Plucking up the courage, I reminded Don what he'd said and thankfully he agreed. It's bizarre how you recall little things that now seem insignificant all these years later.

Due to a mini injury crisis, O'Neill joined the first team squad for a prestigious European game against Barcelona at the Nou Camp Stadium on September 22nd, 1971. The winner would keep the Fairs Cup trophy as a new competition, the UEFA Cup, was replacing it.

> I didn't play in the match, which we lost 2-1, but being around the lads on these trips made you more determined to get a first team run out. Often in football timing and a shade of luck can be as important

as talent. Jimmy Greenhoff and Rod Belfitt were on the ground staff before me and led the attack. Both were good strikers but moved on when Don paid big money for Mick Jones and Allan Clarke, who by now were among the best striking partnerships in Europe. Mick did the hard yards, and scored his share of goals, whereas Allan was deadly when 'one on one' with a keeper, which is how he got his nickname 'Sniffer'.

There were other strikers who, for one reason or another, had moved on from Leeds due to a lack of opportunities but that's the nature of sport. Don then found a gem in Joe Jordan when he signed him from Morton for a small fee. During Joe's first reserve game against Derby County he lost his front teeth in a nasty clash with an opponent. Joe scored in the Barcelona game and was as brave as they come. A terrific target man, he had a tremendous career and played in three World Cups for Scotland.

Big Jack also played against Barcelona and was coming to the end of his career. John Faulkner and Roy Ellam tried to succeed him, but Don settled on Gordon McQueen who started out with St Mirren. Gordon was a great combination with Norman Hunter because they complemented each other. Superb in the air and deceptively quick, Gordon was among the best centre backs of his era.

Off the field O'Neill enjoyed the crack at training sessions and in the dressing room.

Lots of the lads took the mick but it was not only the players that got stick. Bob English looked after us if we got injured and was also a real character. Preparing for a match one afternoon, Bob was chatting to the boss along with Les and a few lads while strapping Billy's ankle. When Bob asked Billy how the strapping felt after finishing, Billy says, "the best ever Bob," then after a short pause, "the only problem is it's the wrong ankle!" Bob was apologetic, then after a few seconds Billy winks because he was winding him up. But that was Billy, fiery on the park but a real joker off it.

Leeds United triumphed in the FA Cup at their third attempt in May 1972.

The boss arranged tickets for the big occasion and seeing the lads lift the Cup was fantastic. The next day, we traveled back on a special train put on by the club and the FA Cup was passed down the carriage full of champagne. The atmosphere was fantastic throughout the journey and pulling into Leeds City Station, even stewards were hanging out of the window smoking big cigars.

Winning the trophy for the first time in the club's history meant a great deal to everyone at the club and the thousands of fans that greeted us in. However, the first team was not with us as they had stayed in the Birmingham area because they had to play Wolves in the final league game, hoping to clinch the 'double' two days after the Final.

Playing at Molineux 48 hours after Wembley was ridiculous and would not happen now. A final takes a lot out of you physically and mentally, so the lads had no chance to recover. The Wolves match turned into one of those nights when refereeing decisions cost us dearly and was dreadful because the lads deserved to be known as 'double' winners. The game should have taken place at a later date and we'd have got the result needed.

Later that week, our open top bus parade and civic reception was a great occasion when fans turned out in huge numbers to celebrate.

Before the close season, there was one last game to play and O'Neill was part of the Leeds team that defeated Halifax Town in the West Riding Cup. Lorimer scored a hat-trick in a 4-3 victory.

Leeds United v Halifax Town, May 12th, 1972

Leeds United: Sprake, Reaney, O'Neill, Bremner, Saunders, Yorath, Lorimer, Mann, Jordan, Bates (Hampton), Galvin

Halifax Town: Smith, Burgin, Lee, Wallace, Pickering, Rhodes, Holmes, Kemp, Robertson, Atkins, Waddle

O'Neill recalled:

A few thousand turned up. It was a nice way to end the season and we each received a silver plated tray for our efforts.

The coming season would see Leeds endure heartbreak with an FA Cup Final defeat against Sunderland and controversial European Cup Winners Cup loss to AC Milan. Joining the first team squad for pre-season training in July 1973, O'Neill sought assurances from United's manager about first team opportunities.

It was really frustrating because I had a feeling of not getting anywhere so I asked Don to put me on the transfer list, which he agreed to do. You get to point when there is no other option but to move on.

O'Neill was on the sidelines when United won a record-breaking seven successive league games at the start of the 1973/74 campaign. But he soon gained his long-awaited call up when Revie selected weakened line-ups in UEFA Cup and League Cup opening rounds due to a number of players carrying knocks. Finally, after a seven-year wait, O'Neill made three first team appearances in October 1973.

O'Neill's 10-minute senior debut came against Norwegian part-timers Stromsgodset at Elland Road in early October. United were expected to win the UEFA Cup second leg clash comfortably having drawn the away leg 1-1 in Norway.

Leeds United v Stromsgodset, October 3rd, 1973

Leeds United: Harvey, Reaney (O'Neill), Cherry, Bremner, Ellam, Yorath, Lorimer, Clarke (McGinley), Jones, Bates, Gray F

Stromsgodset: Thun, Wollner (Aarseth), Pedersen, Nostdahl, Anderson S, Amudsen, Olsen, Anderson B, Pressberg, Pettersen S, Pettersen I (Halvorsen)

Stromsgodset gave United a mighty fright early on before Clarke (2), Jones (2), Bates and Frank Gray secured a 6-1 win (7-2 on aggregate).

Correspondent, Derek Wallis:

Leeds won well enough in the end, but there couldn't have been a spectator in the ground who at one stage didn't have doubts about the outcome of this UEFA cup-tie. The Norwegian amateurs challenged the might of Leeds strongly, confidently and despite their status, professionally. It was only when Leeds at last opened a two-goal margin near half-time after the Norwegians had equalised that the Elland Road team could feel secure.

Revie named O'Neill as a substitute for United's League Cup tie against Ipswich Town at Portman Road several days later. Ipswich, managed by Bobby Robson, came into the contest on the back of a UEFA Cup win over Real Madrid. Revie defended his team selection, pointing out to the media that seven international players including Hunter, making his 600th appearance for the club, were in United's line-up.

Ipswich Town v Leeds United, October 8ᵗʰ, 1973

Ipswich Town: Best, Mills, Harper, Collard (Morris), Hunter A, Beattie, Hamilton, Viljeon, Johnson, Wymark, Lambert

Leeds United: Harvey, Reaney (O'Neill), Cherry, Bremner, Ellam, Hunter N, Liddell, Yorath, Jones, Madeley, Gray F

O'Neill's 45-minute second half appearance would be his longest run in a first team jersey. Leeds fought hard but goals by Johnson and Hamilton settled a 2-0 victory. United might have lost out on a chance of cup glory but there were few tears shed in the Leeds dressing room with aspirations focused on the league.

Don Waters, *Yorkshire Evening Post*:

> *The best thing that could have happened to Leeds United. This seems to be the widely held view of Ipswich Town's victory over Billy Bremner and co. Whether you subscribe to the view or regard it as an excuse for defeat, the fact remains that United will now find themselves with more breathing space, something they have not had a great deal of in recent seasons ... Departure from the League Cup will give United more time to pay that little bit more extra attention to training and, not the least of considerations, more time in which injured players can get over any knocks they might receive.*
>
> *Injuries to a number of United's first team men gave Revie another chance to play some of his younger players, and though United were beaten, youngsters like midfield operator Frank Gray, defender Sean O'Neill and winger Gary Liddell all did well.*

Highlighting United's young full back, Waters noted:

> *O'Neill impressed me with his second half display at left back when he came on for Paul Reaney. Belfast born O'Neill, who has been at Elland Road since he left school looked very impressive in defence. Considering his first team experience was limited to a West Riding Senior Cup game and a substitute appearance against the Norwegian amateurs Stromsgodset he displayed a great deal of confidence, tackling bravely and skillfully on more than one occasion.*

O'Neill's final appearance for Leeds United came in a UEFA Cup second round first leg tie against Scottish side, Hibernian, at Elland Road in late October.

Leeds United v Hibernian, October 24ᵗʰ, 1973

Leeds United: Harvey, Cherry, Madeley, Bremner B, Ellam, Yorath, Lorimer, Clarke, Jones (Jordan), Bates, Gray F (O'Neill)

Hibernian: McArthur, Bremner D, Shaedler, Stanton, Black, Blackley, Seith (Hazel), Higgins, Gordon, Cropley, Duncan

Correspondent, Derek Wallis:

> *Leeds United's UEFA Cup hopes took a nosedive at Elland Road last night when a slick Hibs side gave a fine attacking display to fully earn their first leg draw. Hibs lived up to their promise by attacking Leeds at every opportunity without sacrificing the need to be watchful. Leeds, stripped of five players through injury and suspension, were unable to make much headway against a team playing with complete belief in themselves.*

Speaking to the *Yorkshire Evening Post*, Revie credited the Hibernian side for their performance but the tie was far from over:

> *"Considering that we had so many key players on the sidelines we came out of the match fairly well … Of course, we would have liked a goal or two, but we have gone away before in tight situations in European Competitions and succeeded … There's a long way to go."*

And United's boss was right as Leeds defeated Hibernian in a penalty shoot-out during a memorable night of European action at Easter Road. Vitoria Setubal ended United's UEFA Cup run in the third round.

O'Neill recalled:

> It didn't really cross my mind that Don was rotating his squad but, after all the Central League games I'd played, it was a relief to finally get a first team chance. Deep down I knew though that I'd have to move on but if anyone asks me which clubs I played for during my career, Leeds United is the first fans like to talk about. And those three appearances cannot be taken away from me. They meant a lot then and still do to this day.
>
> United's first team squad was packed with international players and lots of reserve players failed to get a first team run out. After all that time, I'd have been really upset if I'd left Leeds without playing a game. For the boss to keep me on and then play me in the first team showed that I was a half-decent player, but I was realistic because I

was competing with international defenders. Reaney had played for England, Madeley was England's current right back at the time and Cherry would go on to captain England, which says it all. The first team was at its peak, so to play alongside Billy and the boys was a big thrill.

Two months after Leeds clinched the First Division title, O'Neill joined Chesterfield on a free transfer. During 12 seasons with the Derbyshire club O'Neill played over 450 games, winning the Anglo-Scottish Cup in 1981 and a Fourth Division Championship in 1984/85.

Don asked me to come off the transfer list after the Ipswich game until the end of the season, which I agreed to do, and I'd probably have stayed on if he had not taken the England job. But it was time to move on, though Chesterfield was a different world to Leeds United. On my first day the kit man issued me with a cotton t-shirt, shorts, a pair of socks, old baseball boots and a towel. When I got home and told Margaret I had to wash them she looked at me as if to say, you're kidding me!

Leeds was one of the biggest clubs in Europe where everything was done for you as a professional. Training gear was issued new pre-season but I left it all behind; I just assumed Chesterfield would have their own but I was wrong. I left behind rugby shirts, shorts, boots, tracksuits and big heavy jumpers for the winter. If I'd know the situation I'd have taken them because it was freezing in the Derbyshire Dales with no tracksuit!

Whilst Chesterfield as a market town became home for the O'Neill children, Emma and Daniel, on the football front for the Spireites, Sean played against a number of his former teammates as Revie's legendary squad broke up over the coming seasons.

Joe Shaw was Chesterfield's manager and one of the nicest blokes you could meet. Bizarrely, I trained harder at Chesterfield than Leeds but it was a different level of football. We played at a much slower pace but always tried to play the ball around.

When I saw Bremner's name on the official teamsheet against Doncaster Rovers, Clarkie at Barnsley then Cooper and Hunter at Bristol City, daft as it may seem, I was still in awe of them but there was no need because they were just ordinary guys. Even now when I see the lads, my respect is there because of what they achieved in the game.

When I get into discussions with fans and ex-players about 'the greats', for me, Billy was the best footballer I played alongside. You hear so-called pundits go on about previous generations of players not having the same fitness levels or skills as modern day superstars like Messi and Ronaldo. Would the likes of Bremner, Giles, Dalglish, Best, Charlton, Bell and other top stars of yesteryear have coped today? Of course they would, and they wouldn't go down if someone blows on them! Yes, it was a more physical game in the 1960s and '70s, but if those lads had the space to play in then as they have now, and on today's pitches, they'd be pinging balls everywhere. Nutrition, medical advancements and pitches have taken the game forward but your Bremner's and co would have been as big a star today as they were then. Great players in any era will always shine.

After hanging up his boots professionally, Sean, who has a grandson called Oliver, ran Chesterfield's social club, worked in the insurance industry then Chamber of Commerce before gaining his coaching badges. Regarding his own footballing journey, O'Neill has few regrets.

In hindsight I could have played a division higher but I was settled at Chesterfield, achieved what I set out to do and enjoyed 20 years as a professional footballer. It doesn't always work out for everyone when you start out as a junior, then play for the reserves and finally in front of a packed house for the first team. But it did for me and I'm thankful for that.

There are things I might have done differently but it could have been much worse. I really enjoyed my time at Leeds United, of course it was tough waiting so long to get a chance, but when I signed as an apprentice, the first team squad was coming to its peak years and quickly won major trophies, so it was always going to be extremely difficult to break into that side. It was the start of a glory period for Leeds and it was an experience being on the periphery with lads such as Nigel Davey, Dennis Hawkins and Chris Galvin.

If I'd waited a couple of seasons after Don left, I might have got a brief run, like Peter Hampton enjoyed when the squad began to split up, but I'd made my mind up to take on a new challenge. Your career moves on and reserve lads from that era enjoyed solid professional careers. Chris played for Hull City whilst Jimmy Mann and John Shaw both went to Bristol City. I played against them for Chesterfield and it was great to catch up. I'm still in touch with a number of my former teammates and the banter is always there.

As for his former manager, O'Neill believes Revie derserves greater recognition.

> Don never seems to get a mention whenever you hear about legendary managers which is crazy because he was a fantastic boss. But I think a lot has to do with the London press who gave Leeds a hard time in that era. As a manager, Don was driven and a big personality but you could only push him so far. The lads knew not to cross a line and his man-management was superb.
>
> People say Don should have rotated the squad more, which may be true, but it was a time when top teams had a core set of players who played every week and Leeds was no different. You only had one substitute, so it was a different scenario to the modern game where coaches continually look at stats and video analysis to tactically change things around. Arguably Don should have let the lads play with more freedom earlier than he did because they would have won even more honours. But he created a formidable team that became one of most feared in European football and deserves more credit for that achievement.

O'Neill was proud to play for Leeds United and a memory from July 1969 remains steadfast.

> Every pre-season there was a team group picture of all the players. The first time that I was in the picture was after they'd won the First Division title in 1969. A double page spread picture with the trophy was published in a *Yorkshire Evening Post* special looking ahead to the 1969/70 season. I had it framed and it's still proudly displayed at home. Leeds United were the champions so to be there at that time was a privilege.

9

Chris Galvin

CHRIS Galvin was the first Leeds United player to make his senior debut in a European Cup match. Galvin could play in attack or on the wing and had just celebrated his 18th birthday when he came on as a substitute against Ferencvaros at The Nep Stadium in November 1969. The Huddersfield-born youngster signed professional forms on his return and was a valuable resource for manager Don Revie as United took on all comers domestically and in Europe.

However, for the 'ground staff class' of '67, and subsequent groups, breaking into a first team packed with international footballers on a regular basis proved an almost impossible task. Nevertheless, Galvin witnessed first hand United's ups and downs during the heady days under Revie before taking up a new challenge in July 1973.

Chris was born in November 1951 and for this football-mad youngster there were plenty of opportunities to hone his footballing skills as his dad, who played locally for Marsden FC, enjoyed many-a-happy hour kicking a ball about in the local park with his two sons. When it came to supporting a team, Chris ventured beyond local side Huddersfield Town.

Galvin recalled:

From my earliest memories I wanted to be a footballer, and my parents (Thomas and Muriel Galvin) were really supportive, but I've no idea why I followed Wolves. In the late 1950s they had a great side captained by Billy Wright but my hero was their midfield general, Peter Broadbent, who for many football writers was the driving force of the team. Wolves won the First Division and FA Cup, and played prestigious friendlies against European teams before the European

Cup began. Looking back, maybe that's what caught my imagination.

Chris played for St Joseph's Primary School U11 football team, but after passing his 11-plus, attended a Catholic grammar school which meant playing rugby union. And he excelled representing Yorkshire at scrum half. A talented sportsman, Chris also played cricket for Yorkshire as an all-rounder.

For all his ability at other sports, football was the favoured game. Naturally left footed, Chris played for Huddersfield Schools' U15 team and attended a trial with Leeds United though it did not go according to plan.

> I was a left-winger for the schoolboy team but developed my right foot by kicking a ball for hours against a wall at home. Loads of scouts watched games so you just hoped to get spotted. When Leeds offered me a trial, they put us up at a little hotel behind Leeds Town Hall and we played a number of games over a few days. Loads of kids took part so you just did your best. On this occasion, both Sean O'Neill and Peter Hearnshaw got apprenticeships but I didn't hear anything so felt nothing was going to happen.

Despondent at being rejected, Chris did not have to wait long for opportunities.

> Bolton Wanderers offered me an apprenticeship, even though I'd not had a trial. I can't recall why they invited me to Burnden Park to watch a game but I was allowed to bring my brother, Tony, and we both really enjoyed the experience.
>
> Bolton did everything to impress me so I was looking forward to joining them but a few days later Don Revie came round to our house and offered me an apprenticeship. For a young kid it was so hard not to be impressed. Leeds United were one of the top teams in the country where a number of players had broken through from their apprentice scheme. Don explained how the club would develop me as a footballer, so I thought I'd be among the next group to get a shot at the big time.
>
> Leeds was a big club but my dad felt I'd be better off at Bolton as I'd get more opportunities of first team football. I did realise it would be harder at Leeds, but what kid wouldn't want to join a top club. The only thing that frightened me was how quick some of the lads were at trials. I'd always lacked natural pace and that would prove to be a

problem throughout my career. At the time though, I blocked pace issues out of my mind. I was headstrong and believed I could make it, but in hindsight dad was right.

My experience is a lesson even now for starry-eyed kids flattered by the attention of the top Premier League clubs where everything is about results. You can be the best youth player around but the big boys generally go for experience. Of course it is tough starting out at a smaller club then moving up the leagues, but it can be done. You need look no further than Jamie Vardy. After starting out at Halifax Town, Vardy played for Fleetwood Town before getting a chance at Leicester City. No one seriously expected Leicester to win the Premier League but they shocked the footballing world and Vardy is now playing for England. Most players won't achieve what Vardy has done but it shows you can go through the leagues.

Galvin was one of Leeds United's first year apprentices in July 1967. Listed in the official club handbook alongside Sean O'Neill, Robert Malt, Peter Hearnshaw, Andrew Danskin and Colin Smith, Galvin took up his duties around the ground. On the pitch he was quick to make an impression in the Northern Intermediate League and at a close season European youth tournament.

Ground staff lads swept the stands top to bottom and cleaned boots or the dressing rooms. During the winter we also had to clear hay to the side of the pitch before a game then put it back after the match. This stopped when under soil heating was installed. We played on a Saturday morning at Fullerton Park and then might have duties for a first team home game. Two lads would be on dressing room duty and another for the match officials.

I remember Jimmy Greaves and Alan Gilzean getting off the Tottenham coach one winter's day looking terrified. That's how intimidating it was to play Leeds at Elland Road. Tottenham knew they'd be beaten and Greaves hardly got a kick. Gilzean lasted a few minutes after he threw a punch at a Leeds player and looked relieved to be sent off.

None of our tasks, however, were difficult; you just got on with it as part of the role. Cyril Partridge ran the junior team and Syd Owen took training. If you trained hard and progressed then you were offered a full-time contract. By that time you should be in the reserves. Syd was like an old fashioned headmaster, he was a fanatic and coaching us seemed to be his life. Every afternoon he'd drive 30 to 40 yard balls to me and I'd have to fire them back. Syd could be intimidating but I never thought of packing in. It was obvious though that some lads were not going to make it, but Leeds was no different to other clubs with a youth set up.

Lots of youngsters took part in trials and if they didn't come up to scratch others were ready to try out. Each season the FA Youth Cup was our big competition but we didn't have a good enough side to win it, although we did get to the quarterfinals. As Leeds was a top European club, they had invites to play in junior tournaments. At the end of my first season we played in France and did well before losing to AC Milan in the final.

In 1969/70, Leeds began their First Division title defence and participated in the European Cup for the first time. Galvin was on dressing room duty when one of his heroes came to town and showed off his footballing skills at Elland Road. The match versus Manchester United marked Jack Charlton's 500th league appearance for the club and took place on September 6th, 1969. Leeds led through a David Sadler own goal when George Best took centre stage.

Paul Reaney had stuck to Best all round the park and it got to a stage when he (Best) didn't seem interested, but George could destroy a team on his own. The gaffer was screaming from the dugout for Reaney to get tight but when he lost concentration for a moment, Bestie was free in the box and scored. George got a second with a great strike from distance when again he had too much room to run at the Leeds defence before Bremner salvaged a 2-2 draw with a brilliant overhead kick. Lorimer almost won us the game when Alex Stepney just managed to save a 35-yard strike but Revie was fuming in the dressing room afterwards because we'd switched off momentarily.

Away from domestic action, United hammered Lyn Oslo 16-0 on aggregate in a European Cup first round match before taking on Hungarian champions Ferencvaros. After the first leg at Elland Road, Leeds took a three-goal advantage to the Nep Stadium in Budapest, where a year earlier they had lifted the Fairs Cup. Leading up to the game, Galvin enjoyed a whirlwind few days when he was selected for international duty, celebrated his 18th birthday, made his senior debut against Ferencvaros and signed his first professional contract for the club.

I was having treatment for an ankle problem when the gaffer told me I'd been called up to England's Youth squad, but I couldn't go, because he'd picked me for the trip to Ferencvaros. Don said he'd informed England's Youth team manager of the situation and was I alright with that. I was young and naive, so just muttered okay.

Don had caught me completely by surpise, and to say I was gobsmacked was an understatement. But then on his way out, Don said he'd also turned down a bid from AC Milan who had seen me play in the youth tournament in France. Again, I was so gobsmacked I just nodded okay.

Looking back it was a crazy but there were no agents like today, you were on your own and I'd not even been offered a full-time contract at the time.

During a historic night for the club in Budapest against a poor Ferencvarous team, Galvin made his first team debut as a substitute for Eddie Gray on 80 minutes. Two goals from Mick Jones and a Peter Lorimer strike resulted in an emphatic 6-0 aggregate win.

Ferencvaros v Leeds United, November 26th, 1969

Ferencvaros: Geczi, Novak, Balint, Megyesi, Juhasz, Scucs, Szoke, Branikovits, Horvath (Vajda), Nemeth, Katona

Leeds United: Sprake, Reaney, Cooper, Bremner, Charlton, Hunter, Lorimer, Madeley, Jones, Giles, Gray (Galvin)

Yorkshire Evening Post:

In years to come, football historians will flick through the annuls of English and European scenes in the 1960s and marvel at the deeds of Leeds United.

They will reflect on glowing chapters relating to performances of a sufficiently high calibre to stamp the Elland Road brigade as the outstanding team of the decade.

United have carved their name with pride in far-reaching corners of the Continent, but nowhere more emphatically than in the rain-drenched Nep Stadium in Budapest.

There was a stunned silence as Leeds, holding a 3-0 lead from the first leg of their European Cup second round tie, ripped into the dispirited Magyars.

This was the destruction of a once-famous Ferencvaros, who were overwhelmingly humiliated by the sheer brilliance of the English champions.

Three more goals without reply could reverberate through Hungarian sport.

National honour was stripped as this huge arena, containing only 5,429 fans, witnessed the setting up of another Leeds record.

Few can be left open to them, but this one will stand as something extra special, for Ferencvaros had not lost previously to a British side in the Nep.

Galvin recalled:

> Making my debut was memorable and is something you don't forget, but I did have a feeling that it was a 'thank you' for missing out on the England Youth game. I didn't get another England call up so that is a regret.
>
> At the time though I was only a kid and didn't have the confidence to say anything to Don, but he should have at least let me think about the possibility of speaking to Inter. My lack of pace would not have been an issue in Italian football, so would have suited my game. I never came close to playing for a massive club again. But you can't change the past and coming on for a game so highly regarded was notable.

The 1969/70 season finished earlier than normal in order for England to acclimatise for the World Cup Finals in Mexico. Though undoubtedly sensible, the decision would impact dramatically on United's audacious bid for an unprecedented First Division, FA Cup and European Cup treble.

With two months of the season remaining, the impossible appeared possible before a hectic fixture schedule took its toll during a farcical run in. Facing 10 games in 22 days, including an FA Cup semifinal trilogy against Manchester United, Revie ended United's title defence with five league games remaining by fielding a reserve team for a trip to Derby County. During a madcap six-day period, Leeds faced Derby, Celtic, West Ham and Burnley.

After Leeds' second string went down 4-1 at Derby's infamous Baseball Ground, Revie's decision to play a weakened side resulted in a £5,000 fine by the Football Association. United's boss was of the belief he had no option with players injured or fatigued, and there was sympathy in sections of the media for United's predicament of in effect being involved in too many competitions. But the varying publicity did the club no favours.

Galvin played against Derby, Burnley, and then in the final league match at Ipswich Town when Revie again rested players between the FA Cup Final and replay.

Derby County v Leeds United, March 30th, 1970

Derby County: Green, Webster, Robson, Durban, McFarland, Carlin, O'Hare, Hector, Hinton, Wignall, Hennessey

Leeds United: Harvey, Davey, Peterson, Lumsden, Kennedy, Yorath, Galvin, Bates, Belfitt, Hibbitt, Johanneson

Galvin recalled:

> The FA fine was harsh but the Derby game was embarrassing because the match was a sell out. People were outside the ground buying black market tickets, but we knew on the morning of the match a reserve side would be playing. No first team players were on the bus, so travelling over I remember thinking we're the second team playing a first team fixture. Home fans in the ground must have been surprised but they still seemed delighted to win.

United's match against Burnley had no impact on the title race but correspondents at the match praised a number of United's young players thrust into first team duty, including Galvin. They also noted two moments of magic from the mecurial Eddie Gray.

Leeds United v Burnley, April 4th, 1970

Leeds United: Harvey, Yorath, Peterson, Madeley, Faulkner, Gray, Lorimer, Bates, Johanneson, Galvin, Hibbitt

Burnley: Mellor, Angus, O'Neill, Waldron, Todd, Thomas, Casper, Docherty, Kindon, Probert (Bellamy), Dobson

Yorkshire Post:

> *Some weeks ago, Leeds United complained that they, like other clubs, were experiencing difficulty in finding young players of high promise.*
> *In the last eight days followers of the club have been given a preview of the Leeds United team of four or five years hence. The*

signs are encouraging.

On Saturday, Galvin looked to be the type of player who may mature into another Clarke, Peterson as though he had taken his cue from Cooper and Faulkner looked to have the temperament of Madeley. Of the other eight reserves in the team that beat Burnley, Harvey and Bates showed again, as many of us know, that Leeds United must have to exercise a deal of charming persuasion to keep them happy in the second team.

These five players are capable of first team football, there is another Gray in the shadows and one or two other youngsters able, I am told, of looking after the club.

Gray scored two superlative goals, sinking Burnley with his own deft feet and fertile imagination. He saw that Mellor had committed himself and was unable to get back into goal and so he floated a lob from 30 yards over the goalkeeper's head when everyone expected a ground shot.

Gray's second half goal was even more spectacular, quite the best I have seen this season. Hemmed in by Burnley players near the touchline, and restricted towards the middle of the field by Johanneson writhing in pain on the ground, he weaved a tight web, the ball glued to his feet and defenders unable to get near it.

He (Gray) feinted to pass this way and that, he bobbed and ducked and finally shot past the helpless Mellor.

What a goal, fully deserving to win the match.

Galvin recalled:

Eddie's goals were superb and he demonstrated his great close control with his second goal, but his first from distance when he chipped the keeper was also outstanding. When fit, Eddie was unplayable, as he showed in the FA Cup Final against Chelsea at Wembley. And we should have won that day but the match went to a replay. We ended up winning no trophies, which was heartbreaking for the lads.

Galvin was making progress and appeared in United's first team squad picture for the 1970/71 season, which must have given him a boost of confidence. But breaking into Revie's all-star team was a different matter altogether as Galvin made just one substitute appearance against Swindon Town in the FA Cup.

The squad that won the league title in my first season was slowly beginning to change. While Allan Clarke and Mick Jones had formed one of the best spearheads around, Jimmy Greenhoff and Mike O'Grady had left to get first team football. Terry Hibbitt and Rod Belfitt would also soon move on and, by my own admission, I felt impatient.

The gaffer picked his strongest team, which was the norm in that era, but that left players hoping for a run disappointed and the gaffer had to manage that situation. I knew a chance would only come if someone were injured so had to push my case and was not the only player to do so. Every other week I'd see Don in his office but he'd say, "Stick it out Chris, you'll get your chance".

Don would sometimes put an extra £5 in my wages as a sweetener, which may not sound a lot, but when you're on £30 a week, the fiver was welcome. However, I did realise that football is a young man's game so you can't just sit back.

United's title bid ended again in heartache when they missed out by a point to Arsenal but they still had a chance of silverware as they took on Juventus in the Fairs Cup Final. Galvin was in the travelling party to Turin for the first leg.

During our pre-match meeting, a few of the lads wanted to play an offside game, which Don was against because we lacked pace in the middle of defence. The discussion got really heated. Don was clearly annoyed and I'd not seen that situation before. Les was left to calm things down. The lads backed down but you could sense Don was beginning to lose some control. The first team had been with him for years but was starting to question his decisions.

Leeds went on to lift the Fairs Cup but then made an indifferent start to the 1971/72 season. A Football Association ban from playing their opening three home fixtures at Elland Road (following a pitch invasion in the penultimate home game of the previous season against West Brom) didn't help, but Revie was also juggling his side because of injuries to various players. United's attacking options in particular were being stretched with Clarke and Jones sidelined.

Galvin was selected to play in a six-game run in the side during September 1971. In his first start since April 1970 against Ipswich Town, Galvin faced Lierse SK in a UEFA Cup first round tie in mid-September. The UEFA Cup had succeeded the Fairs Cup and was in its first season of competition. Lierse SK had lost 8-0 on aggregate to Manchester City two years earlier in the European Cup Winners Cup, so Leeds, even with a weakened side, were expected to win comfortably.

Lierse SK v Leeds United, September 15th, 1971

Lierse SK: Engelen, Dierckx, Krivitz, Michielsen, Golen, Vermeyen, De Ceulaer, Davidovic (Mertens), Janssens, Denul, Ressel

Leeds United: Sprake, Reaney, Yorath, Bremner, Faulkner, Hunter, Lorimer, Galvin, Belfitt, Giles, Bates

Correspondent, Ronald Crowther, was full of praise for Galvin after United's 2-0 triumph in his match report under the headline GALVANISED!

Chris Galvin, a teenage forward who thought he had gone to Belgium just for the ride, shot Leeds United into the lead last night against UEFA Cup rivals Lierse SK.

Galvin, an 11th hour choice when Allan Clarke became the sixth international to drop out of the Leeds side, struck in the 25th minute for his first goal in Europe.

And what a valuable goal it was, for it took a lot of pressure off his side after a bright and aggressive start by the Belgians ...

Things had looked ominous for the English side when young Galvin, with only a few league appearances behind him, covered himself with glory by changing the course of the game.

Apart from the occasional flurry and long-range shots by Peter Lorimer, little had been seen of the Leeds attack up to that point.

Then Lorimer made his persistence pay off when, in an electrifying burst on the right, he rounded the sturdy Hungarian, Krivitz, and banged a low ball hard into the goalmouth.

There was Galvin who had read the situation so well, and even though he had to fight off a frantic effort by right back Dierckx to impede him, he slotted the ball into the net from six yards. Immediately, the deflated Belgians lost much of their early bounce and assurance.

United had injury woes for the return leg a fortnight later, but with a two-goal advantage, were overwhelming favourites to advance against the Belgium minnows at Elland Road. However, Lierse sent shockwaves around Europe with a 4-2 aggregate triumph.

Leeds United v Lierse SK, September 29th, 1971

Leeds United: Shaw (Sprake), Reaney, Cooper, Yorath, Faulkner, Madeley, Lorimer, Mann (Hunter), Belfitt, Bates, Galvin

Lierse SK: Engelen, Dierckx, Krivitz, Michielsen, Golen, Vermeyen, De Ceulaer, Davidovic, Janssens, Denul, Ressel

The Guardian:

> *Mr Don Revie calculated that a largely inexperienced side, who were bound to take time to capture any rhythm or method, could protect a two-goal lead. He must regret not starting with his strongest side and calling off his more valued players when the match was won. Theories, however, are all very well but they tend to fall apart in practice when the human element is involved, and no one could have leglislated for the unfortunate error by Shaw, the third choice goalkeeper, which cost the third goal and not only dealt Leeds a severe blow but convinced the Belgians that their mission was far from impossible.*

Galvin recalled:

> The away leg at Lierse was comfortable after taking the lead. It was a bonus to get my first goal for Leeds but it counted for nothing after our 4-0 defeat in the second leg. Don made changes but we should have had enough to beat Lierse. John Shaw and Jimmy Mann made European debuts but were replaced after we shipped three goals by half time. We went for it in the second half but they caught us out on a break and the papers slammed us the next day. The result was a real shock.

In between these two fixtures, Galvin was a late call up against Liverpool when a Lorimer strike secured a fine win.

> I was aware Clarke had a knock but didn't expect him to miss the game, so when Don told me he'd failed a fitness test on the morning of the match it came totally out of the blue. But it was great to be playing in such a big game. Liverpool were a formidable team under Bill Shankly but we played well on the day for the win.

After United's win against the Merseysiders, there was little time to reflect as Leeds took on Barcelona in a Fairs Cup play off match at the Nou Camp Stadium, with the winner retaining the trophy. Shorn of six starters, Leeds went down gallantly to a 2-1 defeat.

Barcelona v Leeds United, September 22nd, 1971

Barcelona: Sadurni, Rife, Graells, Torres, Gallego, Costas, Rexach, Carlos, Duenas, Morales, Asensi (Fuste)

Leeds United: Sprake, Reaney, Davey, Bremner, Charlton, Hunter, Lorimer, Jordan, Belfitt, Giles, Galvin

The Guardian:

> It says much for Leeds' reserve strength that they were able to match Barcelona in initiative and tenacity for long periods, but as the match went on, the Spaniards gained a measure of control through their experience.

Correspondent, Denis Lowe:

> Injuries robbed Leeds of the services of no fewer than six internationals in Barcelona, yet Don Revie's strange looking side, with several men playing out of position, fought splendidly, only to go down to a goal six minutes from time.
>
> Revie played Nigel Davey, second choice right back on the left flank, moved Peter Lorimer, the Scotland winger to midfield, and used Billy Bremner, as ever an inspiring captain, as a front-runner alongside the reserve-striker Joe Jordan and Rod Belfitt.
>
> The side cost £47,000, £32,000 for Johnny Giles and £15,000 for Jordan.
>
> "I was very proud of my team and the way in which they played against what is currently Spain's top club and one of the best we have met in Europe," said Revie.
>
> "You can assess our performance by imagining what Leeds would be expected to do if the Spaniards came to Elland Road without six top men."

Galvin recalled:

> Playing against Barcelona was a huge boost but I struggled with the pace of the game and it was a big disappointment to lose, however, it was a great experience.

Galvin's mini-run ended with a derby against hometown club, Huddersfield Town, who recorded a surprising 2-1 win at Leeds Road, then a goalless draw against West Ham at Elland Road.

When Don Revie strengthened his squad by signing West Brom midfielder Asa Hartford for £177,000 in November 1971, the transfer made headline news. Since promotion in 1964, Revie had brought through a host of young players alongside two major signings – Jones and Clarke. Where would Hartford slot in? The 21-year-old Scot joined the first team for training before a proposed home debut against Leicester City on the Saturday. But the transfer collapsed three hours before kick off when medical tests detected a heart abnormality.

> When Asa arrived at the club, I really thought this was the start of Don switching things around. He could not spend that much money on Asa and not play him. Before the Leicester game, Don pulled me aside and said, you've nagged and nagged, well things are now changing. I was down to play in a practice match alongside Asa for the first team, so realised this was a big opportunity.
>
> Don told us in these games to hold back on challenges to avoid injuries, but they were competitive, and I took a swing at Giles when he caught me with a late challenge. Don dragged me off before I totally lost it and told me he'd see me after training. I got a rollicking but Don told me I was in the side against Leicester as Eddie Gray was carrying a knock, and Asa would partner Billy in midfield. I left Don's office really fired up.
>
> On the Saturday, when I went into the dressing room, Asa was sat on a bench clearly upset. He would not tell me what had happened but said I'd find out. I never saw him again. After the lads drifted in, Don told us Asa had failed his medical but wouldn't go into details. When he announced the team, it was same as the last match against Manchester United. Eddie played, I was substitute, and at that point I realised Don would not build another team.

The 1971/72 season saw United lift the FA Cup but miss out on the double in the final league game against Wolves when dubious decisions against Leeds made headline news.

Galvin was increasingly frustrated at his lack of opportunities and those feelings intensified after making only three appearances in 1972/73. United's penultimate league match at Birmingham City would be his last for the club.

Galvin was a non-playing substitute when AC Milan controversially defeated Leeds in the European Cup Winners' Cup Final in Salonika.

In what was a black day for European football, UEFA and the Greek Federation suspended referee, Christos Michas, after the worst officiating of a match during the Revie era.

Galvin recalled:

> My match fitness was suffering as I was only playing occasionally in the Central League. The only way you could get a game was if a player had a bad injury or there was nothing to play for at the end of a season, which happened with the Birmingham game. Nobody wants a fellow professional to get injured but that's the harsh side of the game. As a door shuts for someone then you get a chance, and that's how Joe Jordan got in when Jones started getting injuries that saw him eventually retire.
>
> Most Leeds fans only saw home games, and did get on a players' back if they weren't performing, but the major issue for me was that no one seemed in danger of being dropped, even if they had a run of bad games. Come what may, the gaffer was fiercely loyal to his first teamers. If there were a criticism of Don, he was a bit blinkered. Don had his first team and they played.
>
> Against AC Milan there were a few injuries and suspensions, so I thought I might have a shout of playing. But Bates, Yorath and Frank Gray came in for Bremner, Giles and Eddie Gray. I was on the bench and hugely disappointed. In the second half I was stripped to go on when Don called one of the lads over but they wouldn't come off so he told me to sit down. It would have been great to help the lads out but was a farcical moment.
>
> Throughout the match I've never seen a more biased referee, who was later banned from officiating, and on the night everyone was so frustrated. There were rumours we might have issues with the referee but you never really believe such blatant bias could happen in a final, however it did.
>
> Around the final there were strong rumours that Everton wanted Don, but the board persuaded him to stay on for another season. I doubted though that I'd be at the club much longer.

Galvin returned for pre-season training in July 1973 but a new challenge soon emerged.

> We'd just had our squad picture for the 1973/74 season taken when Don called me into his office to tell me Hull City and Wolves had put in bids for me. It was up to me what I wanted to do. At the time Susan

and I had decided to get married and had agreed to buy a house in Huddersfield. Hull and Wolves coming in for me changed everything, so we pulled out.

I had to move on because none of the lads I'd been apprentices with had broken through on a regular basis. Wolves were in the First Division but Don advised me to join Hull who played in the Second Division as I'd get straight into their first team. In hindsight I should have spoken to both clubs but Don's advice seemed to make sense. So I joined Hull, who were managed by Terry Neil, and played in their pre-season friendlies in Ireland.

The Tigers ended the 1973/74 campaign six points off the promotion places. Middlesborough, managed by Galvin's former teammate Jack Charlton, cantered to the title 15 points clear of Luton Town and Carlisle United.

Bobby Murdoch was Jack's first signing and 'Boro's equivalent to Bobby Collins when he came to Leeds in the early 1960s. As footballers they had the same attitude; both were experienced, very aggressive and led by example. Big Jack had learnt from Don but was his own man and built the side around Murdoch and a young Graeme Souness. Leeds had partnered Collins and Bremner, then Bremner and Giles and 'Boro linked up Murdoch and Souness. Like Billy, Souness was always involved and could handle himself on a football field.

Middlesborough, like Leeds, were organised, could mix it and competed against any team. 'Boro ran away with the title and Jack won the Manager of the Year Award. Of all the Leeds lads who went into management, Jack was the most successful. After 'Boro, he enjoyed spells with Sheffield Wednesday and Newcastle United then thrived with the Republic of Ireland. My brother, Tony, played for Tottenham Hotspur and Ireland when Jack was manager and he always seemed impressed with his man-management skills.

John Kaye succeeded Neil as manager after an inconsistent start to Hull's 1974/75 season. For Hull fans, the campaign was memorable for two feisty affairs against Second Division champions-elect Manchester United. Galvin played in both matches and infamously had a dust up with United boss, Tommy Docherty.

Stuart Pearson had joined Manchester United from Hull during the close season, so we went out determined to get stuck into them and won 2-0 in front of our biggest gate of the season when the ground was rocking. Both teams were really fired up in the return fixture when all sorts went on off the ball at Old Trafford. I had a do with Docherty in the tunnel after one of United's players had a go at me about an incident in the first half. There was a lot of pushing and shoving but things did calm down. And despite the incident, it was great playing in front of a full house though we lost 2-0.

Our form dipped after the defeat but there were more big games against Aston Villa and Sunderland. In the FA Cup, we played Fulham who had Bobby Moore and Alan Mullery in their side. Fulham knocked us out in a third round replay and eventually lost to West Ham at Wembley.

During this period the 'Galvin shuffle' entered Hull City folklore.

I had to keep possession because of my lack of pace, but that only helped for so long. Luckily, I had an old-fashioned body swerve in my locker although it didn't take me away from players, so I worked out a trick in training that sent players the wrong way and gave me an extra yard to get past a player then put a cross in. It worked a treat and it's great that Hull fans remember that I had the shuffle before Ronaldo!

When Hull ended the 1975/76 season six points off relegation, Hull manager Kaye persuaded Billy Bremner to make a £25,000 move to Boothferry Road in September 1976. Bremner added a wealth of experience to Hull's young team.

When John told me he had a chance of getting Billy, I told him to snap him up. It was a real coup for Hull, even though he was at the end of his career. Lots of fans wondered why Billy joined Hull but the answer was simple. Top professional footballers, if they remained fit, carried on playing down the Leagues. Although they'd earned big money at their peak, it was not enough to make them secure for life.

Billy was still a great player but he didn't have star players around him now. On his debut against Nottingham Forest, he tried to play a ball blind across his body, as he'd done at Leeds, but no one read it, so the crowd went beserk. 'You're not at Leeds now Bremner, watch where you are passing,' was the message from fans, and they were right because the Hull lads were not on the same level technically as the Leeds boys. But credit to Billy, he adapted and was the best player in our team by far on top of being a great influence off the park.

Being part of the first team, I felt more an equal now with Billy and I'd like to think he thought I was a better player than he saw at Leeds.

Either side of Galvin having a brief loan spell at Third Division York City, there was managerial chaos at Hull City during the 1977/78 season. Bobby Collins had been appointed Kaye's assistant manager, but when Hull sacked Kaye after a poor run of form, Collins took over after Bremner had applied for the post. But Collins' fiery nature and appointment of Syd Owen as assistant manager affected team morale badly.

After four months of mayhem, Collins was sacked and Wilf McGuiness accepted a caretaker post. Bremner then announced his intention to retire when his contract expired at the end of the season. Youth coach Ken Houghton took up the managerial hotseat but it was too late to save the beleaguered club, who finished well adrift at the bottom of the Second Division table.

> Billy and Bobby did not see eye to eye after Bobby became manager, which was a real problem. The atmosphere in the dressing room was shocking and I ended up in the middle as I was friendly with both. At one point Bobby wanted a scrap with Billy and told me to tell Billy he'd see him outside. But while Bobby was clattering around in his studs, Billy sensibly was away before things got ugly.
>
> Bobby was a legend as a player but as a manager was out of his depth. The board should have appointed Billy manager; he went on to enjoy promotion at Doncaster and almost did the same as Leeds United's boss. When it comes to their managerial careers, however, most fans don't recall them, and why should they because Billy and Bobby were both world class footballers.

Galvin considered retirement following relegation mainly due to a persistent knee injury after 143 appearances for Hull. But he went on to play on another continent.

> Hull offered me a pay off through the clubs' insurance because I'd developed a limp which looked comical in games, but then out of the blue, Australian side Melbourne came in for me even with my injury. However, within a few days of Hull releasing me, Melbourne sacked their manager before my flight, so I was a free agent.
>
> Football is a small world because when I got home, there was a message from Mike Summerbee who was player-manager at Fourth

Division Stockport County. After chatting to Mike I met the chairman, a real character called Freddie Pye, and signed a two-year contract, but after each game it would take me two days to get going again.

I'd now played throughout the Football League pyramid and Stockport as a club illustrated how football has changed down the years because Summerbee, a League Championship winner at Manchester City, and George Armstrong, a double winner at Arsenal, played on opposite wings. During one game at half time, Armstrong asked me what I thought of his performance, but when I told him it was shocking he was almost crying. I couldn't believe it but his legs had gone. Armstrong in his day was a top player but he was now embarrassing to watch. The crazy thing is Summerbee had played worse yet was full of it!

Players don't like thinking about retirement but lots of First Division players played for lower League clubs, including the Leeds lads, apart from Big Jack, Madeley and Jones (who retired through injury).

I was resigned to packing it in when suddenly a team from Hong Kong called Tsuen Wan offered me a two-year deal where I'd be earning more than double my best salary in England. The club was aware I was nowhere near fully fit but wanted me to go out for a month to see how it went. Chatting to Susan, we decided to go with our two daughters at the time, Laura and Leanne, and loved the lifestyle. Our third daughter, Sara, was born the following year. Playing for Tsuen Wan, the standard of football was much lower than the English game which meant I could hold my own with a dodgy knee, and I even represented Hong Kong in friendly matches!

During Galvin's Hong Kong adventure he faced one of his footballing heroes but it didn't live up to expectations.

George Best had short spells for a number of clubs after he left Manchester United. I'd come across George and Rodney Marsh during my time at Hull when they played for Fulham, and Bestie still had touches of brilliance but he had a drink problem which everyone knew about. George flew out to Hong Kong for an exhibition game but it was embarrassing. He was so drunk they had to take him off at half time and put him on the first plane home. It's dreadful how things turned out for George but, thankfully, he never lost his status as a legend.

Retiring from the game, Galvin was a players' agent in Hong Kong prior to working in a number of businesses. Chris has four grandchildren and, looking back on his Leeds United career, there were frustrating but memorable times.

Over the years football fans have asked me about my time at Leeds United and without fail they always recite Don's great team ... Sprake, Reaney, Cooper, Bremner, Charlton, Hunter, Lorimer, Clarke, Jones, Giles, Gray. Most, however, don't believe me when I tell them this line-up only played one match (against Mansfield Town in 1970) because Paul Madeley was always in the side! Paul was an exceptional footballer and so unassuming as a person. But for lads queuing up hoping to get a first team chance, you only got a run out if more than one change was needed. I was among those players and it was frustrating, but you couldn't argue with the gaffer's thinking as we won trophies.

The only time I genuinely thought I'd be more involved was when Asa Hartford signed. Don told me he was going to switch things around but that changed overnight when Asa's transfer collapsed. He went back to his trusted line-up as Paul could play across defence and midfield effortlessly. It was demotivating but the lads won more trophies, so Don's decision made sense. Maybe I should have stayed on when Hull came in for me to see how things developed, but you make a decision based on what you think is right at the time.

Don was a tremendous manager but he did have an exceptional crop of players from the ground staff in the early 1960s that all came through together. Eventually, Harvey replaced Sprake and Yorath came in during Don's final seasons but from my apprentice group onwards, no one broke through on a regular basis. And Leeds had the pick of kids from around the country.

I've always believed that with a decent run of games I'd have had a chance of retaining my place, but playing an odd game here and there was no way to show what you can do. Don had a set of lads that knew each other's game inside out. Because they played so often together, they anticipated where they'd be on the pitch and never overcomplicated things.

When Mick Bates came in for Bremner and Giles for long periods of the 1970/71 season, it was a huge disappointment from my perspective because I felt I could offer more to the team. I'd have wanted to make things happen, whereas Mick didn't interfere with the pattern of play but I understood Don's decision and every week

Leeds mostly won. Good luck to Mick, he liked being a squad member but I couldn't sit on the bench every week.

Don built one of the best club sides in Europe, and I was a part of it, which supporters still appreciate all these years later. Being in the matchday squad for a number of seasons, I saw the lad's play week in and week out, and for an 18-month period they were the best club team around. Billy and the boys had an inner strength, skill and a cutting edge that was brilliant to watch.

10

Roy Ellam

CENTRE-HALF Roy Ellam was seen as the natural successor to Jack Charlton when he joined Leeds United in a £35,000 transfer from Huddersfield Town in the summer of 1972. Big Jack was coming to the end of a remarkable career spanning two decades where he had been a stalwart in the heart of United's defence. But finding a replacement for the veteran stopper had floundered due to Charlton's consistency over the years.

Ellam was a seasoned pro. However, after making his first team debut against Chelsea at Stamford Bridge in the opening league match of the 1972/73 season, Ellam would ultimately be a valued squad member due to the surprise progression of Gordon McQueen to the side. During a two-year spell at the club, Ellam played in notable European and domestic matches culminating in United's second First Division title.

Roy was born in Hemsworth in January 1943, one of five children. Tragically his parents, Elise and Arnold Ellam, lost a son called Joseph shortly after his birth. Growing up in West Yorkshire with siblings Maureen, Avril and Ray, Roy loved all sports and quickly demonstrated his prowess across a range of disciplines. An opening batsman and bowler, he was also a keen runner, winning certificates at sprint, middle distance and cross country. But football was Roy's great passion.

Ellam recalled:

I was sport daft as a schoolboy and participated in everything that I could. In the last term at school we had to see a careers advisor who wanted to know what we'd do with our lives in terms of a job. They didn't have much advice to offer because I wanted to be a footballer.

I'd played for South Emsall boys and was crazy about football, followed Barnsley and even watched Barnsley reserves play in the Central League. Tom Finney of Preston North End was my footballing hero because he was an incredible player. Finney played down the right, the left and through the middle. Together with Stanley Matthews of Blackpool, those guys were incredible players. Their skill and ability would have shone in any era.

Roy left school aged 15 and started an apprenticeship at Vickers-Armstrongs in Wakefield who manufactured steering gear for ships. His footballing journey began at West Yorkshire League side Robin Hood Athletic, then hometown club Hemsworth Town FC where he impressed scouts as an open age player.

Travelling to the bright lights of London, Roy played for Queens Park Rangers U18s but returned north to Bradford City, initially on an amateur basis then as a professional in May 1960.

I travelled to Valley Parade on three buses each day for training and within no time at all was in the reserve side, probably because I was a big guy for my age. Peter Jackson was manager and its strange how things pan out because one of my first games was against Leeds United. It was a big match because of the local rivalry but I was just making my way and trying to impress. Billy Bremner played as an orthodox outside-right that day and was electrifying on the ball. You could tell he'd make it in the game.

I'd just turned 18 when I made my first team debut away to Gillingham. We lost but I was over the moon to have played; I could not believe it. City paid me £18 a week with a bonus structure for winning or drawing a game. It's crazy thinking back, because we went out like gladiators, kicking lumps out of each other, all for a £4 win bonus! But that's what it was like and I enjoyed the physical battle.

The Bantams suffered relegation to the Fourth Division in Ellam's debut season and, after missing out on promotion twice, City suffered the ignominy of applying for re-election to the Football League in the summer of 1965.

Throughout an inconsistent period in the club's history, Ellam was learning his trade and one rivalry stood out.

Playing Bradford Park Avenue in our local derby was the big game of the season. Attendances would push 20,000 and as a player it gave you a lift to perform. We always had a fantastic battle and tackles would fly in but I loved the challenge. I always looked forward to the matches but nearly missed a derby as it was on my wedding day! When Margaret heard City were playing Park Avenue on February 22nd, 1964, she was not happy, but I was a professional so had to play.

After a registry office service in the morning, both families came to the match and we won 1-0. Rodney Green scored the all important goal and it was a fantastic day all round. City enjoyed some exciting derby games and cup encounters, but I had to move on to develop my career.

Norwich City was the first club to express an interest in City's talented centre back. But needing a striker, Bradford agreed a swap deal with Huddersfield Town for their forward, Derek Stokes, on New Year's Day, 1966. After 169 appearances for City, Ellam made the short journey to Leeds Road.

Someone in our village was Town daft so I knew a fair bit about their recent history, especially what a great player Denis Law had been when he played for the club. Tom Johnston was manager and there was a step up in class with the players around me but I quickly adapted.

My debut was against Bolton Wanderers, who had Wyn Davies playing centre forward. Big Wyn went on to play for Newcastle United and was a Welsh international. He could be a real handful but I got stuck in and relished the challenge. Bolton also had Francis Lee playing on the right wing. Frannie was a mouthy so and so but went on to be some player for Manchester City and England. Another tough opponent was Andy Lochead who played for Burnley then Leicester City. Andy was a strong lad and one of the toughest to mark. You certainly knew you'd been in a game with him!

Huddersfield Town celebrated winning the Second Division Championship in 1969/70. Ian Greaves was manager as top-flight football returned to the area. The Terriers used 15 players and finished seven points clear of runners up Blackpool. Ellam, Dennis Clarke, Geoff Hutt, Jimmy McGill, Jimmy Nicholson, Terry Poole and top scorer Frank Worthington were all ever-present. Trevor Cherry and Jimmy Lawson missed only two games.

We played a 4-4-2 system which was flexible and Greaves gave us belief we could succeed throughout the season. He went ballistic if anyone started getting carried away with promotion talk but told us when Queens Park Rangers came to Leeds Road (January 20th, 1970) that if we won then we'd go up. There was still a third of the season to go, but Rangers were a big test because they'd been relegated from the First Division, so it was a benchmark where we stood.

Rodney Marsh was Rangers' best player, but we had McGill who would stick to anyone if asked. Before the game in the dressing room, Greaves told Jimmy to sit on Rodney's shorts, and he did just that all that afternoon. Rodney never had a kick.

Worthington was the star player of our side and a real maverick. Frank got both goals in a 2-0 win against Rangers and it boosted our confidence.

The celebrations after clinching promotion at Middlesbrough then the title at Blackburn Rovers were really memorable, but the main feeling was one of relief that we'd done it after 42 matches. There was a civic reception at the Town Hall which was a wonderful occasion but our focus was taking on the big boys. Everton were the reigning champions but we'd also face the likes of Leeds United, Liverpool, Manchester United, Tottenham Hotspur, Chelsea, Arsenal and Manchester City.

Back in top-flight football for the first time in 15 years, Town opened up with wins against Blackpool and Southampton, and then surprised many pundits by finishing comfortably above the relegation zone. And The Terriers were one of a few teams to defeat champions Arsenal.

Town ended the campaign by defeating West Ham at Upton Park in the final game of the season. Ellam was the only ever present for Town and scored twice, including the winner against Coventry City and Town's second goal in a 3-2 defeat of Brian Clough's Derby County.

We had the makings of a good team but didn't sign a single player, which must be unprecedented. It was tough but we had some great wins, including a 2-1 victory over Arsenal who went on to win the double. Worthington scored the winner with a penalty. We also defeated a strong Manchester City side when Cherry scored the only goal of a tight game.

We did well to avoid relegation but needed to strengthen the squad. Money was tight but new players freshen up a side, competition for places increases and there is a feel-good factor that you are moving forward as a club. Worthington scored a few goals but I knew we faced an uphill challenge the following season.

Ellam's fears were justified when Town made a calamitous start to the 1971/72 league campaign before a short run of form when they enjoyed four wins in five games, including a 2-1 victory against Leeds United. The derby clash attracted an attendance of 26,340 at Leeds Road.

Huddersfield Town v Leeds United, September 25th, 1971

Huddersfield Town: Lawson D, Clarke, McGill, Hutt, Ellam, Cherry, Smith, Chapman, Hoy, Worthington, Lawson J

Leeds United: Sprake, Reaney (Edwards), Cooper, Bremner, Charlton, Hunter, Lorimer, Galvin, Belfitt, Giles, Madeley

Leeds, playing in red, had just played Barcelona in a Fairs Cup play off match. With Allan Clarke and Mick Jones unavailable, Rod Belfitt and Chris Galvin led the attack. Town struck early with a scissor kick from Lawson on 17 minutes. Charlton leveled for Leeds before half time but Ellam grabbed the headlines following a corner kick when he lashed home a rebound after Gary Sprake saved from Lawson just before the hour.

Correspondent, Keith Macklin:

Like the pugnatious terrier who likes nothing better than to bait the alsation, Town's terriers made light of form and reputation ... Defensive vulnerability must take much of the blame (for the winner), Chapman put the ball into the penalty area. It seemed to bob about for an eternity before centre half Ellam took deliberate aim and blasted the ball into the roof of the net.

Ellam recalled:

Playing Leeds was the big game and not just because it was a local derby. Leeds were the team everyone wanted to beat; they were at the height of their powers and a real force in the game. You looked out for the Leeds matches when the fixture list was announced.

Town's win was the only time I came out on top against them in a top flight encounter, and it was a memorable occasion in front of a packed house. After I scored, Big Jack played up front so I ended up marking him, and he was constantly in my ear trying to put me off but he wasn't going to get one over on me. Scoring was special because I only got a few in my career. I went up for set pieces to cause a bit of disruption in the penalty area and hoped one of the lads may pick up a knock down. On this occasion, the ball dropped in front of me so I just hit it with my left foot and it flew in. Sprakie had no chance!

Winning just six games throughout the League campaign, Town finished bottom of the table. Ellam was the only Town player to play in every match during both First Division seasons.

Town struggled in the League because opponents nullified Worthington. We had nowhere to go. How can you not sign a player?

Nowadays when a team gets promotion, squad members all want a chance to play but don't always get the opportunity, and that's how it should be. That second season we really struggled and getting relegated was dreadful. I found the step up fine and it never concerned me who I was marking because I was so revved up to play every game. There were great partnerships right through the League and we generally faced two forwards but I didn't need motivating.

When we played against Astle-Brown (West Brom), Clarke-Jones (Leeds United), Toshack-Keegan (Liverpool), Greaves-Gilzean (Tottenham Hotspur) and Radford-Kennedy (Arsenal), I took the big man and Cherry took his partner, which worked well for us. It's hard to select a toughest pair but Dougan and Richards at Wolves maybe edged it. Dougan was gangly, awkward and a real handful but Richards was also a great striker who scored a stack of goals.

Manchester City bucked the trend by playing Lee-Young-Summerbee up top, with Bell pulling the strings in midfield. Summerbee roamed from the wing a bit with Frannie playing as the front man. And if all these lads were not enough, there was Law-Charlton-Best at Manchester United. They naturally swapped positions so were really dangerous as a three. Bestie would cut you to shreds, Charlton had a rasping strike and Denis was such a clinical finisher. Facing these guys was a tremendous challenge and one I revelled in but we also played against some of the best strikers of a ball. Charlton had a cannonball shot in both feet but Peter Lorimer had a more powerful strike and hit the target more often. Peter was so dangerous outside the penalty area and when it came to a penalty he frightened the life out of keepers. He'd either put his foot through the ball or place it so accurately in the corner that a goalkeeper never had a chance. Nowadays, some penalty shootouts really annoy me and it's incredible how many shots are wide or high. I'm fine if a player works a goalkeeper but I cannot get my head round some fancy dan run up to psyche a keeper out. Players should just put their foot through the ball.

Relegation was the lowest point of my career because, after sampling top-flight football, you don't want to leave it. And that was the case for all the lads.

Ellam had made 225 appearances for Town but his days at the club were ending.

A local newspaper reported that senior players had demanded money to stay up, which was nonsense. Yorkshire Television wanted me to put the record straight, which I was happy to do, as I had nothing to hide. But within an hour, Town banned me from speaking to reporters. My contract had a clause where I could not speak to the media without permission from the club, so I said fair enough but insisted on seeing Greaves. During the season a few of the senior lads had discussed issues with the manager and did ask if we avoided relegation would there be a bonus, which we didn't think was unreasonable. Nothing else was said on the matter so we soldiered on and went down, which was really deflating. To then read about private discussions being blown out of proportion was really upsetting so I wanted to know how the story got out and why players were named. Greaves agreed to see me then spoke with the chairman but came back with a nonplussed response.

I was uncomfortable with things behind the scenes so put in a transfer request. Cherry had already joined Leeds for £100,000 but a deal taking Worthington to Liverpool collapsed on medical grounds. When I returned with Frank for pre-season training, we had to train with the youth team as we'd requested moves. I was now determined to leave because I'd done nothing wrong.

Ellam returned home to ponder his future but did not have to wait long for a surprise opportunity.

When the phone rang, Margaret said Don Revie was on the line. At first I thought it was joke, but she was not joking. Don was aware of the issues going on at Town, asked how I was doing and then told me he'd agreed a transfer fee with the club. Did I fancy joining Leeds United? I could barely believe what I was hearing, replied I'd welcome the challenge, and that was it.

Don told me to be at Elland Road for a medical the next day. Also, if any journalists telephoned, deny links with the club because of Asa Hartford's transfer the previous season which collapsed on medical grounds. I appreciated his request so agreed.

Don wanted me to succeed Big Jack who was coming to the end of his playing career. They were massive boots to fill but I was ready for the challenge. Doc Adams took me to see a number of specialists and I'd never been so rigorously tested. I met up with Don in his office late in the afternoon and chatted about how it had been an intense day. Doc Adams then joined us to tell me I was A1. Negotiations were quick and I signed my contract. I'd enjoyed playing for Town but joining the FA Cup winners was a wonderful feeling.

Whilst I moved to Leeds, other senior players soon left Town. David Lawson joined Everton for a British record fee of £80,000 and it was not long before Worthington went to Leicester City for a similar amount.

Signing for Leeds United was the biggest step of Ellam's career.

Leeds had a bigger training ground than Town and, of course, the administration was more complex because of larger attendances, media interest and European travel. But the major difference was the ability of the first team squad. The Leeds lads were virtually all internationals and had played at the highest level.

I'd played against Leeds for City then Town in reserve, West Riding Cup and League games, so knew most of the lads and they were a great bunch. Billy went out of his way to help. If I were put to task, he'd have a quiet word and was an incredible person. The training intensity was terrific and I never felt out of my depth.

In terms of fitness, the boss thought Trevor and myself were coasting through sessions so wanted to know what Town did differently to Leeds. All I could think was that Town had to be super fit to compete against top club's who had more technically gifted players.

Due to suspensions and injuries, Revie selected his summer purchases in the centre of defence against Chelsea for the opening league fixture of the season. When Leeds arrived at Stamford Bridge, the ground was going through redevelopment so they had to change in a portacabin.

Chelsea v Leeds United, August 12th, 1972

Chelsea: Bonetti, Harris, McCreadie, Hollins, Dempsey, Webb, Garland, Kember, Osgood, Hudson, Cooke

Leeds United: Harvey, Reaney, Cherry, Bremner, Ellam, Madeley, Lorimer, Bates, Jones (Yorath), Giles, Gray

Leeds made a promising start in front of a capacity crowd but the match took an unexpected twist after 25 minutes when Harvey and Jones were carried off following separate incidents. Lorimer went in goal and gallantly held Chelsea at bay before the Londoners recorded a 4-0 win.
Yorkshire Evening Post:

> Although one could have only the highest possible praise for the brave way the depleted side fought on there was only one conceivable outcome.
> In the circumstances, it was difficult to judge the value of United's two new signings, £100,000 defender Trevor Cherry and £35,000 centre-half Roy Ellam from Huddersfield Town.
> Both performed reasonably well in new surroundings and under the inevitable extra strain, which was placed on the whole side.

Ellam recalled:
> Don realised that I had a great understanding with Trevor as we'd played at Town together for a long period so we intuitively reacted to situations. I handled the big fellers and Trevor picked up the pieces. Players used to tell me they hated facing us at Leeds Road because we were dirty so and so's. I'd like to think we were hard but fair!
> Before the Chelsea match, of course I was nervous, but once the game started it was just another match. I had confidence in my ability to play alongside these guys but losing Harvey and Jones was disorientating. It was a mess. We lost and I took a lot of flak but the defeat was not down to me. To say I was disappointed when Don dropped me and played Jack in the next match at Sheffield United, which we won 2-0, was an understatement.
> Don brought me back for a couple of games at Wolves and then at home against Manchester City. Lorimer scored in both, which we won, and his dipping volley against City was brilliant. But with Jack struggling with an injury, he decided to partner Madeley and Hunter

for the remainder of the season in central defence which was really frustrating.

Away from League action, Ellam played against Liverpool in a high profile League Cup tie.

Liverpool v Leeds United, October 31st, 1972

Liverpool: Clemence, Lawler, Lindsay, Smith, Lloyd, Hughes, Keegan, Cormack, Heighway, Toshack, Callaghan. Sub: Boersma

Leeds United: Harvey, Madeley, Cherry, Bremner, Ellam, Hunter, Lorimer, Clarke, Jones, Bates, Gray. Sub: Yorath

Anfield was my favourite ground because of the atmosphere and I've never known a better bunch of supporters in football, especially in the Kop. Billy told me about the night Leeds won the League in 1969 and Don told him to take the lads over to the Kop. He was not sure at all but Don insisted and the Koppites were unbelievable. The Leeds lads really appreciated the applause they received and a special bond was formed. I played at Anfield for Town and came away with nothing, but this time Leeds got a 2-2 draw. Jones and Lorimer scored but we lost the replay 1-0 which was a disappointment.

Away from domestic matters, Ellam played in Europe for the first time against Turkish side Ankaragucu in the European Cup Winners Cup.

Ankaragucu v Leeds United, September 13th, 1972

Ankaragucu: Tohumcu, Hotlar (Aktan), Dilber, Toroglu, Yalman, Gonculer, Yilmaz, Yalcintas, Atakan, Coscun, Mesci

Leeds United: Harvey, Reaney, Cherry, Bremner, Ellam, Hunter, Lorimer, Galvin (Yorath), Jordan, Giles, Madeley

Following the first leg in Ankara, which ended in a 1-1 draw, Revie brought Clarke and Jones back into the side for the return fixture at Elland Road two weeks later, Galvin and Jordan dropping out, whilst Bates replaced the injured Madeley. For Ankaragucu, Aktan and Behzat replaced Gonculer and Atakan respectively.

Playing in Europe was a big target for me when I moved to Leeds and the atmosphere against Ankaragucu in the first leg was intimidating. Jordan scored an important away goal which gave us the advantage

for the home leg which we kept tight and then Jones scored the only
goal to send us into the next round.

United's 1972/73 season saw the emergence of centre half McQueen,
after he joined from St Mirren a month after Ellam arrived at Elland
Road. And the youngster quickly pushed for a first team spot.

Revie brought Ellam back into the first team for the last few games
of the League season with FA Cup and European Cup Winners Cup
Finals coming up. Following a defeat at champions-elect Liverpool,
which ended lingering title hopes, Ellam was named substitute for
United's next clash at Southampton and replaced Charlton in his final
game as a professional. Saints won the match 3-1. But Ellam's season
ended prematurely when he sustained a broken elbow in United's
penultimate League match against Birmingham City at St Andrews.

> No one at the club, not even Don, expected Gordon to make such
> rapid progress, but having been Big Jack's successor, I was becoming
> a squad player. To compound matters, my injury at Birmingham put
> me out of the Cup Final squads which was a massive disappointment.
> Sunderland of course caused a major shock at Wembley and the
> club dinner at the Café Royal was not the celebratory event we'd all
> hoped to enjoy. We went into the AC Milan match with injuries and
> suspensions, however, I've no idea if I'd have played. But Frank Gray
> and McQueen both came in so I might have been in with a shout.
>
> Leeds finished third in the League but playing reserve games was
> not why I joined the club. As much as I enjoyed being with the lads,
> I'd not been given a run in the team and at this stage of my career I
> wasn't going to warm a bench hoping for an occasional game. During
> the close season I told the gaffer that it might be best for me to find
> a new club. Don understood my feelings but hoped I'd change my
> mind.

When United's first team squad returned for pre-season training, Revie
pulled Ellam aside for a chat.

> Don did not want me to leave but Coventry City had made an offer
> and I'd be guaranteed first team football. I was tempted but we'd
> have to move home and that was a sticking point as Margaret was
> a home bird. A few weeks later, Leeds turned down an offer from
> Manchester United because of the rivalry between the teams, which
> I reluctantly had to accept. After chatting things through with Don, I

decided to stay till the end of the season.

Whilst Leeds made a record breaking start to the 1973/74 League campaign, winning their first seven fixtures, Ellam played in a League Cup defeat against Ipswich Town. Ellam then helped United progress in the UEFA Cup.

> Don had been criticised for always selecting his first pick of players over the years, but this season he seemed to take a conscious decision to prioritise the League and rotate players in Cup games. Don was experienced in European competition, so after our first round away leg against Norwegian side Stromsgodset, he was a firm believer in giving you a day off to recuperate.
>
> Playing weakened teams was a gamble but it gave Don an opportunity to experiment and test the strength of his squad. In hindsight, the gaffer was forward thinking because, in the modern game, top players are often rested in lesser competitions until the later stages.

There was a buzz both sides of the border when United drew Hibernian in the UEFA Cup second round. Revie had called up Ellam, Gary Liddell, Frank Gray, Sean O'Neill and Billy McGinley for the first leg at Elland Road that ended in a 0-0 draw on October 24th. But when the return fixture at Easter Road came around, Harvey, Hunter, McQueen, Giles, Jones and Madeley were all unavailable. To compound United's problems, David Stewart, who had recently replaced Gary Sprake as reserve goalkeeper, was ineligible for European games.

Lining up against Hibs at Easter Road, Ellam partnered Yorath in the centre of United's strange-looking defence that included 19-year-old third choice goalkeeper John Shaw making his second first team appearance as Revie grappled with a goalkeeping crisis. Youth keeper Glan Letheren was two years younger than Shaw and among United's substitutes.

Hibernian v Leeds United, November 7th, 1973

Hibernian: Arthur, Bremner D, Shaedler, Stanton, Black, Blackley, Edwards, Higgins (Hazel), Gordon, Cropley, Duncan

Leeds United: Shaw (Letheren), Reaney, Cherry, Bremner B, Ellam, Yorath, Lorimer, Clarke, Jones, Bates, Gray F

On the night, both teams went close to breaking the deadlock. Cropley hit United's crossbar, as did Ellam from a Gray corner. Leeds were also indebted to Cherry, Lorimer and Bremner for clearing goalbound efforts off the line. But this clash is best remembered for Bremner's performance and the contrasting fortunes of United's teenage goalkeepers.

The Guardian:

A bizarre evening at Easter Road last night ended with Leeds United, against all odds and against the pattern of play, eliminating Hibernian in their UEFA Cup second round second leg tie by 5-4 on penalties after the teams had remained locked in a goalless struggle after extra time.

Appropriately, the final word was left with Bremner whose penalty it was that sent Leeds through.

Leeds were pinned back on defence for most of the match, yet escaped, helped by four goal line clearances and actually struck the crossbar themselves, and the final impression was that Hibernian, for all their huffing and puffing, were not good enough to overwhelm opponents who were missing seven familiar faces.

Ellam recalled:

Billy protected Shaw until he went off with two broken fingers, then our 17-year-old youth keeper Letheren came on. Billy loved the challenge and was smiling throughout the game; it was so easy for him.

I'm sure the boss would not have been that upset if we'd lost, but as the game wore on, Billy grew more and more into the role and then his competitive nature kicked in when the match went to a penalty shoot out, which was a first for the club. We lined up on the half way line and Lorimer stepped up to smash home the first. Stanton missed Hibs' first spot kick and we held our nerve as Gray, Bates and Clarke kept us in front before Billy hammered in the winner for a 5-4 win. There was sheer delight in the dressing room afterwards.

Vitoria Setubal ended United's UEFA Cup run in round three but the main target was a League title. And by Ellam's return to first team action 10 months after his last league game, they were in pole position ahead of nearest rivals Liverpool.

Following a substitute appearance against Everton at Goodison

Park, Ellam played in United's afternoon midweek clash against Arsenal at Elland Road in February. The match took place during the miners' strike, when a three-day week was one of the measures introduced by the Conservative government to save electricity consumption. Despite the inconvenient kick off time against the Gunners, almost 27,000 fans saw the game.

Leeds United v Arsenal, February 5th, 1974

Leeds United: Harvey, Reaney, Cherry, Bremner, Ellam, Hunter, Lorimer, Clarke, Jordan, Yorath, Madeley. Sub: Cooper

Arsenal: Wilson, Rice, Nelson, Brady, Storey, Simpson, Armstrong, Ball, Radford, Kennedy, George. Sub: Powling

Correspondent, Frank Clough:

Although Leeds were dominating all the action, it looked like being one of those afternoons when they would never score.

But even as the fans were beginning to groan and jeer with disappointment, Leeds burst back into the game with a sensational three-goal blitz, which sent Arsenal home empty handed.

Ball played well in midfield, but Arsenal too often lacked penetration up front, where Radford and Kennedy were rarely able to escape Hunter and Ellam.

Ellam recalled:

Before the game the gaffer had a quiet word with every player in the dressing room. With McQueen injured, there was pressure on me but Don told me to play my normal game. Don was aware I'd grown up near Arsenal centre forward John Radford and played against him many times. "Big man, I understand you know Radford," he said. "Make sure you mark him for everything ... corner kicks, free kicks, whatever happens you mark him. Radford has pace but you can match him."

The boss filled me with so much confidence, there was no way Raddy would get anything in the game. Don also told me not to leave Hunter isolated. "Let Norman take the slow coach, Ray Kennedy, and we'll be fine," he said.

Don had also spoken to Norman who had a word with me before kick off. "If Radford and Kennedy swap, go with Raddy, don't leave him with me as I can't flippin' run like you," he said.

People have often asked me about Norman and that 'Bite yer Legs' nickname. Norman might not have been a sprinter but what a great player he was to play alongside. He'd mark opponents close, stop them from turning and that was his great strength.

Don had done his homework because, although Arsenal led at half time, they hardly had a sniff in the second half and we ran out comfortable 3-1 winners. Jordan scored a couple of goals and Simpson put through his own goal.

Leeds held a seven-point lead over Liverpool after their success against The Gunners and consolidated their position with a 2-0 away win at Manchester United.

In the FA Cup, United had progressed to the fifth round, having overcome Wolves after a replay, then comfortably beat Peterborough United 4-1 when Ellam enjoyed a solid display in defence. Bremner earned the runaway League leaders a draw against Bristol City at Ashton Gate with a late strike before the underdogs knocked the Cup favourites out with a Don Gillies goal. Ellam had played in the replay and with Leeds now able to concentrate on the League, retained his place as United looked to equal Burnley's 53 year-old record unbeaten run of 30 matches at Stoke City.

Stoke City v Leeds United, February 23rd, 1974

Stoke City: Farmer, Marsh, Pejic, Mahoney, Smith, Dodd, Hudson, Greenhoff, Ritchie, Hurst, Robertson. Sub: Skeels

Leeds United: Harvey, Yorath, Cherry, Bremner, Ellam, Hunter, Lorimer, Clarke, Jordan, Giles (Cooper), Madeley

In a remarkable game, after Bremner and Clarke gave Leeds a 2-0 lead by the 18th minute, Stoke produced a stunning comeback for a 3-2 triumph. In spite of the reverse, United were still favorites to win the First Division title.

Yorkshire Evening Post:

Despite the fact that United's brilliant run of 29 games without a defeat has ended, Billy Bremner and his men are still the side to beat as the season reaches its climax. They are still eight points clear of Liverpool and, even though the Anfield side have a game in hand, I cannot see United letting the title slip from their grasp.

Ellam recalled:

> Mike Pejic and Alan Hudson scored, then Denis Smith came up for a set piece for the winner which was a real blow. We ploughed forward looking for an equaliser but couldn't find a way through their defence. Back in the changing room the lads were shell shocked after shipping those goals. They took their boots off and threw them against the wall in frustration.
>
> Losing a match from a 2-0 lead didn't happen to Leeds. But it's when things are not going well a manager comes to the fore. "Pack it in, we've lost one game. We'll win the league, don't worry about it," the gaffer said.

Ellam made his final appearance for the club in the next game, a rearranged fixture against against Leicester City at Elland Road. After Lorimer gave Leeds a first half lead from a penalty, Leicester equalised late on with a goal from Keith Weller.

Despite another dropped point, Leeds went on to regain their form and clinch the First Division title a few days after their penultimate match, a tense 3-2 home win against Ipswich Town when Arsenal defeated Liverpool at Anfield in a midweek fixture. United eventually finished five points clear of Liverpool after defeating Queens Park Rangers in the final game at Loftus Road.

> I made four League appearances during the 1973/74 season, which was not enough for a medal, but I'm in the record books having been in a title winning team squad. Playing in the First Division was the epitome of my career and meant everything. Being involved in a memorable season in the club's history cannot be taken away from me and was an incredible experience but my days at the club were numbered.

Ellam returned to former club Huddersfield Town during the close season and stayed a season.

> Don had not yet taken the England job when he told me Town wanted me back. Bobby Collins was manager, I spoke to him and re-signed for Town. I'd played against Bobby in his Leeds days and he could be a nasty so and so on a pitch. But Bobby was a great player and decent coach, however, he was lacking in terms of managerial skills.
>
> There were no rumours Brian Clough was going to become Leeds manager. But after Cloughie took over, Bobby told me he gave him

a rollicking for pinching me because I'd impressed him when he was Derby County manager. If there had been an inkling Clough would turn up a week after I left Leeds, I'd have stayed on to see what would happen because a new boss generally gives players a chance. And I'm sure I'd have got a run as I was not one of Don's long serving players he'd been so outspoken about. Cloughie had his critics but was a great manager because none of the clubs he succeeded at was colossal. Derby County won the league the year Town were relegated in 1971/72 and then Nottingham Forest picked up consecutive European Cups.

I joined Town with the best of intentions but the rot had set in and Bobby was out of his depth. Tom Johnston returned for a second spell as manager but also didn't last long. After Town slipped into the Third Division they paid my contract up.

Ellam was not ready to retire from the game. Having served three West Yorkshire teams he crossed the Pennines to play for Northern Premier League side Mossley FC. He then crossed the Atlantic Ocean to play for the Philadelphia Atoms in the North American Soccer League.

Professional football had experienced mixed success since its inception in America but Ellam's timing was perfect as the NASL welcomed its biggest star during the summer of 1975. Pele's arrival at New York Cosmos guaranteed packed stadia and prime time exposure as soccer searched for a spot alongside American football, basketball and baseball. Twenty teams played in four 'Divisions' across the country followed by playoffs and a Championship 'Super Bowl' game. Philadelphia played in the Eastern Division but failed to qualify for the playoffs. Tampa Bay Rowdies defeated Portland Timbers in the Championship game.

Twelve months on, Ellam was ever-present for the Washington Diplomats when they made the playoffs and travelled to the Big Apple to take on Pele's Cosmos team. Both sides had enjoyed a victory apiece in divisional games, but in their third clash of the season Pele opened the scoring in a 2-0 playoff victory for the New Yorkers at Giants Stadium. Toronto Metros-Croatia defeated Minnesota Kicks in the Championship game.

During his two-year sojourn, Ellam faced an eclectic mix of players. Aside from Pele, other stars included Giorgio Chinaglia (New York

Cosmos), Eusabio (Toronto Metros-Croatia), Bobby Moore (San Antonio Thunder) and Rodney Marsh (Tampa Bay Rowdies). One player Ellam didn't come up against was George Best (Los Angeles Aztecs) as 'El Beatle' entertained fans in the Western Division.

Ellam recalled:

> I was at the tail end of my career, so playing for Philadelphia Atoms then Washington Diplomats was an incredible experience. Both teams gave me the same contract I'd been on at Town and Leeds which was amazing. The NASL was growing and Pele joining New York Cosmos ensured a number of stars followed.
>
> Philadelphia, however, did not have star names but was organised and could compete. It was surreal that I was coming up against the likes of Pele, Eusabio and Moore but it just became the norm. Marking Pele was an experience and the crowds loved him. Overall, playing in the NASL was a fabulous experience and I enjoyed every game.

Ellam kept fit by turning out for Mossley FC during the NASL close season and then had a spell as player-manager at Gainsborough Trinity, but when a seven-a-side indoor American league folded, he decided to hang up his boots.

> After football an opportunity came up to sell to garden centers and I loved it, because once I'd given my card in I had my foot in the door. We'd chat for 30 minutes about football, business for two minutes then I'd walk out with an order. However, as a national sales manager, I was often away from home, which Margaret didn't like, so like many former players I decided to buy a pub.
>
> Over a 20-year period we ran The Nelson in Dewsbury, The Red Lion in Silkstone and then The Gate, also in Dewsbury. It was a wonderful time, especially in the 1990s because sportsman's dinners became really popular and punters loved hearing tales from iconic footballers in my playing days. Seeing lads that I played with and against was brilliant. Billy Bremner, Allan Clarke, Johnny Giles, Nobby Stiles, Roger Hunt, Gordon Banks, Tommy Smith, Steve Kindon and Duncan McKenzie were among many who entertained the punters. They were fantastic nights, the lads had great stories and fans still worshipped them.

Family and fitness has always been a big part of Roy's life, so it is apt that apart from spending time with his grandchildren, Bethany, Raull and Giovanna, after briefly retiring he now helps out his fitness fanatic daughter, Jeannie, run Roy Ellam's Premier Health Club in Mirfield and Fitness Connection in Ravensthorpe. Chatting with customers, his ventures on the football field often crop up. And he still keeps tabs on former clubs.

Whenever Leeds and Town play there is extra spice, but I can't lose because I'll always have a foot in both camps. Its disappointing that Town have not played top-flight football since my era, but I'm still involved and kick every ball when I attend matches with my grandson. As for United, my son Graham has always been Leeds daft which I'm delighted about and, hopefully like Town, they will return to top-flight football soon.

Being a professional footballer was majestic. It never bothered me if I was playing against Leeds United, Manchester United, Liverpool, Blackpool, Coventry City or Hull City. I was never overawed taking on any opponent. I was always confident and upbeat. Leeds United was the club to play for at that time. Don Revie was one of the top managers around so it was an awesome feeling to play for his team but I was caught between Big Jack not quite being finished and McQueen coming through. I was also unfortunate to make my debut against Chelsea when we lost two players and got thumped. Don decided to stick with what he knew and Leeds went on to win the League for a second time so his decision worked out.

They were a great bunch of lads at Leeds and the atmosphere was terrific but I had to move on. Looking back, I should have asked Don why he left me out after the Chelsea game because the boss was a first class motivator and not difficult to approach. He'd always encouraged you. "Strengthen your strengths and work on your weaknesses," he'd say to me.

At team meetings he spoke to us collectively but on a match day he'd give you a final message about what was important. Don was not a shouter if things were going badly at half time. He kept his counsel because there were lads at Leeds who knew how to turn things around. I played against them all, and good grief, Don had an incredible team in its pomp. There was Bremner and Giles in the middle of the park, Reaney and Cooper rampaging forward, Hunter and Charlton in front of Sprake or Harvey in goal, Madeley capable of playing anywhere, Gray and Lorimer available to strike, and then one of the best forward partnerships in Clarke and Jones.

191

Supporters will tell you Jones did all Clarkie's running, which is true to a degree, but Sniffer put in a shift and was one of the most clinical finishers of his day. I first played against Clarke when Town drew at Fulham in a League Cup quarterfinal. We beat them in a replay and Clarkie was not pleased. He was a real character but also cockey, which all great strikers tend to be.

Bremner was the best footballer I played alongside and Giles was not far behind. But there was also my roommate Madeley, and boy oh boy could he play. To have a player in your side capable of playing anywhere, Paul was a solid gold nugget, never complained, rarely said anything and just got on with his job. I shudder to think what he'd cost nowadays. That team had so much experience. I've still not seen a better squad than United's from that era and in the modern game they would be priceless. Though I'd have liked more game time, being around those lads was a highlight in my career.

11

Glan Letheren

GLAN Letheren grabbed the headlines on his first team debut against Hibernian during a sparkling night of UEFA Cup action two nights after bonfire night in 1973. Leeds United's 17-year-old youth team keeper made one substitute appearance during the Revie era and kept a clean sheet before skipper Billy Bremner fired home the winning spot kick in the club's first ever penalty shoot out.

When Revie took the reigns at Leeds, a major aim was European success and his charges reached four finals during nine campaigns, winning the Fairs Cup on two occasions. European nights had a special atmosphere, and the Hibs tie was memorable as it catapulted United's fourth choice keeper into the spotlight due to a goalkeeping crisis. Letheren became an overnight hero but would only make one further first team appearance. A Welsh U21 and U23 international, Letheren was on the bench for the 1975 European Cup Final but it is his Edinburgh endeavours that ensured him a unique place in United's history.

Born in Briton Ferry in May 1956, Glan moved to Dafen near Llanelli at the age of eight. The second youngest of Arnold and Enid Letheren's five children, Glan was a talented sportsman and represented Wales Schoolboys at cricket. His football journey began fortuitously at secondary school.

Letheren recalled:

Llanelli was a rugby town by tradition but football was as popular in every other sense. Watching *Match of the Day* was among my earliest memories, so as a Manchester United supporter it was brilliant seeing my heroes Denis Law, George Best and Bobby Charlton play.

I played cricket and rugby at school but when one of my teachers started a football team he chose me initially at centre forward, then in goal. Being tall certainly helped but I also read the game well and had good reflexes. To develop my skills I watched goalkeepers on television, and in an era when there were a number of great British keepers for me Pat Jennings of Tottenham Hotspur was the best. Jennings, apart from being a great shot stopper, commanded his penalty area with authority and had no fear when saving at an opponents feet.

Llanelli FC manager Gwyn Grant invited Glan to play for his hometown club at 15 years of age and he was soon keeping goal for the senior team in the Welsh Premier League.

Leeds United's Welsh scout, Jack Pickard, had spotted John Charles, Gary Sprake, Terry Yorath and Byron Stevenson as teenagers. Pickard's next target for the Elland Road club was Llanelli's young keeper.

Jack was chatting to my parents in our lounge when I got home from school one day. I'd no idea Jack had been watching me at a game but he wanted me to attend a trial at Leeds and I could not wait to travel over.

Leeds United was one of the biggest clubs in British football and had a massive following in Llanelli because of the Welsh players associated with the club. I stayed at the Faversham Hotel during the trials which lasted five days. Leeds wanted a goalkeeper to follow John Shaw who was in his last year as an apprentice. Obviously I hoped that might be me and was delighted when told I'd have that chance.

United's coaching staff were clearly impressed with the teen trialist because when Shaw was selected to represent Scotland U18s in a post season game, Letheren lined up for Leeds in an international youth tournament in Cannes during the close season in June 1973. Teams from Brazil, France, Argentina, Russia, Portugal and Yugoslavia participated. United's 14-man squad, managed by Cyril Partridge, included Peter Hampton, Frank Gray, David McNiven, Neil Davids and Billy McGinley. Voted the best goalkeeper at the tournament, Letheren signed apprentice forms on his return.

The Cannes tournament was shortly after Leeds played against Sunderland in the FA Cup Final. I travelled with my parents to Wembley and attended the club's Café Royal dinner in the evening. Sadly it was not the joyous occasion we all hoped it would be because Sunderland created a massive shock by winning with an Ian Porterfield goal. Being a part of the occasion was special though and I recall Byron's name being in the printed menu as he'd already signed apprentice forms. The youth competition was a great experience although we didn't win it.

Letheren moved to Leeds in time for pre-season training but took time to settle in his new environment.

Joining Leeds United was fantastic but the reality of how to cope was enormous. Coming from a quiet village, it was daunting arriving at a bustling Leeds City station. Nobody from the club met me, I was told to take a taxi to my digs in Chapletown, which was not in the best of areas.

I did get homesick so travelled home on occasions but I was determined to stick it out. It helped having Welsh lads around me like Byron, who I'd played against as a kid, and eventually I moved to Beeston which was a far nicer area of Leeds.

Letheren worked hard alongside United's latest crop of apprentices in training but had to toughen up if he was to succeed.

I'd had continual praise throughout my early career, but becoming a professional footballer was different to what I expected because immediately I had to prove myself again. Cyril managed the junior team and Syd Owen was responsible for training. Unfortunately Syd had a critical nature, which was really demotivating. Syd's attitude was 'you've come from schoolboy football but now you'll have the crowds calling you every name under the sun'. He wanted to know whether we could cope.

Looking back, Syd's viewpoint made sense but it wasn't easy to deal with as a kid. A number of lads could not handle his negativity and really struggled. But once you proved yourself, Syd's attitude shifted and you could not do anything wrong.

Since retiring from the game, I've coached around the world and I couldn't get away with the way Syd dealt with youngsters. But were Leeds any different to other clubs back then? Probably not.

It was a different era and we'll never know if a less critical approach would have achieved better results, but hardly any apprentices from my group made it at Leeds so it does make you wonder.

The junior team played in the Northern Intermediate League so it was a long way for my family to travel but Don always looked after them if they came. Don's man-management was fantastic because he made you feel a part of the club.

Leeds United had an experienced 18-man first team squad packed with international players when they kicked off the 1973/74 season. Determined to erase the heartbreak of losing FA Cup and European Cup Winners Cup Finals the previous campaign, Bremner and co got off to a record-breaking start in the First Division. Subtle differences in priorities had seen Revie rest players carrying knocks in Cup competitions when in the past they might have played.

Playing free flowing football, an assault on a second title seemed clear, though there was no official line from Revie that United were prioritising the Championship. On the goalkeeping front, there was a change as Gary Sprake, after more than 500 appearances, had joined Birmingham City for a £100,000 fee in October 1973. Revie signed Ayr United and Scotland U23 keeper David Stewart as back up to first choice David Harvey but no one at the club could have predicted how Stewart's arrival would impact on United's UEFA Cup second round clash against Hibernian on November 7th, 1973.

United had disposed of Norwegian side Stromsgodset in the opening round and Letheren was on the substitute bench when Leeds, fortuitously, drew 0-0 with Hibs in the first leg at Elland Road. Revie had called upon fringe players for the match including Roy Ellam, Gary Liddell, Frank Gray, Sean O'Neill and Billy McGinley. When the return fixture at Easter Road came around Harvey, Norman Hunter, Gordon McQueen, Johnny Giles, Mick Jones and Paul Madeley were unavailable.

With Stewart ineligible for Europe, Revie had no alternative but to call up his teenage goalkeepers, John Shaw, 19, and Letheren, 17, to the matchday squad. Shaw would keep goal but it was to be a major test of his character having been substituted in his only other first team appearance, an embarrassing 4-0 defeat to part timers Lierse, in a Fairs Cup clash two years earlier. Letheren was named amongst the substitutes.

Yorkshire Post correspondent, Terry Brindle, was unconcerned on the eve of this clash about United's weakened side:

Revie is no longer obliged to risk players with minor injuries; he can blend established players with experienced reserves and talented newcomers and still come up with a formidable side.

The team which Revie fields tomorrow will not be his strongest but it will nevertheless be an appreciable force, a team which properly motivated could put Leeds through to the next round.

Hibernian v Leeds United, November 7ᵗʰ, 1973

Hibernian: Arthur, Bremner D, Shaedler, Stanton, Black, Blackley, Edwards, Higgins (Hazel), Gordon, Cropley, Duncan

Leeds United: Shaw (Letheren), Reaney, Cherry, Bremner B, Ellam, Yorath, Lorimer, Clarke, Jones, Bates, Gray F

The Times:

> Somehow it was appropriate that Bremner, Scotland's captain, should settle the affair. This has been a golden night for him with a performance of deadly skill, spiced with arrogance, which, as it were, thumbed a nose at all his brothers north of the border.
>
> It was whispered before the start that Leeds did not particularly want to win, keeping their energies primarily for the League title; they certainly disguised it pretty well …
>
> Letheren, he was the second hero of the night behind Bremner, with at least four dazzling saves as Hibernian threw everything into attack.

Letheren, told the *Yorkshire Evening Post* that he had an attack of nerves when he ran out for the second half. He added:

> The first 10 minutes were nerve-wreaking but when I got over that I became confident and as the game went on really enjoyed it.

Hibernian protested after the game that Leeds had infringed UEFA rules because Revie and Cocker were both in the centre circle with the players during the penalty shoot out. But their appeal to UEFA for a change of result was dismissed. Revie did, however, receive a one-match touchline ban for the breach. Hibernian's behaviour was lambasted in the media.

Don Waters, *Yorkshire Evening Post*:

> It was a pity United's fine performace against the odds should be marred by a childish complaint from Hibs born out of the bitter disappointment of defeat.
>
> As Revie said at the time, Hibs were beaten fairly and squarely. They could not manage a goal in 120 minutes against a seriously-

depleted side whose first line of defence for the first 45 minutes was a 19-year-old, making only his second first team appearance, and for the rest of the game a 17-year old thrown in at the deep end for his first team debut.

Letheren recalled:

Don told me on the morning of the match I was flying to Scotland with the squad because Harvey had not recovered from a knee injury. It was a huge surprise but at that age you don't feel fear, you're just excited to be involved. It didn't cross my mind we had a goalkeeping crisis because Shaw was set to play. John was a confident, bubbly character and looked up for the challenge. I was going along for the experience and would be on the bench.

After our flight landed we went to a hotel for our pre-match meal then got a coach to the ground. The UEFA Cup may not have been a top priority but the lads wanted to win this game, and especially the Scottish lads. Bremner, Lorimer and Gray were all in the side and there was no way they were leaving town with a defeat.

As for the match itself, Letheren has clear recollections:

When the match kicked off, there was a fantastic atmosphere in the ground. Hibs went close when Cropley clipped the crossbar and Lorimer had to save a shot on the line, but we also had chances, the best when Ellam hit the crossbar from a corner.

Shaw came out for a 50-50 ball around 10 minutes from half time and I remember him checking his fingers before carrying on, but it did not cross my mind he might be in trouble. And it still didn't when Les Cocker told me to stay out and warm up when the half time whistle went. I just thought keeping loose was standard practice. I'd been doing some stretching exercises for a few minutes when Les ran over and told me to get stripped in the dressing room because I was going on.

Everything happened so quickly that there was not much time to take everything in, but I must have been in a state of shock because my legs had gone. Back in the changing rooms, Don came over, told me to relax and enjoy the occasion. All the lads wished me well and I always recall Clarke's comment. "Good luck son, when you come out, it'll be like picking cherries off a tree," he said.

I'm not sure whether that helped, but I'd played with the lads in five-a-sides and kept goal in shooting sessions, though obviously not in a full-blown match. Running out for the first time before a packed crowd, there was a massive roar then I tried to stay focussed when I got between the sticks. I knew Hibs were going to test me but the lads were great because they shielded the ball away at every opportunity, although I was thankful when Reaney headed the ball off the line twice.

After a while the nerves went, I grew into the game and did enjoy the experience. I remember stopping a couple of strikes from Cropley but, because of injuries, Bremner played sweeper that night and it proved a masterstroke by Don because Billy was so in control. He was taking the mick with back heels and flicks, and at one point stopped the ball on our goal line then did a back flick across goal for Frank Gray to clear! I thought to myself, roll it to me and I'll pick it up or hoof it upfield. But there was no need to worry because Billy put in a magnificent display.

We were pretty comfortable and the lads wished me luck for the penalty shoot out. When Hibs captain Stanton put their first penalty wide we were in control. Lorimer was first up and made no mistake, then Gray, Bates and Clarke all scored. Billy stepped up to take our fifth penalty, and sure enough he fired in the winner.

Back in the changing rooms spirits were high and Don warned me I'd get a lot of media attention. He said that if any reporters asked for a quote, to just say I'd enjoyed it. Don wanted me to take in the moment but also keep my feet on the ground, which didn't take long as we played Sheffield United in front of two men and a dog a few days later on the Saturday!

Letheren had demonstrated he could handle the big occasion and continued his development away from the limelight as United lifted the First Division title for a second time.

When Revie departed to become England manager during the close season, news of his successor was keenly awaited, but it would be a tough challenge because of the success he'd brought to the club. The appointment of former Derby County manager, Brian Clough, shortly after United's squad returned for pre-season training as defending champions made headline news.

Clough was an outspoken character and one of United's biggest critics over the years, even calling for the club to be demoted for its disciplinary record. Clough's 44-day tenure as manager would rock the club to its core.

Letheren recalled:

I'd signed as a pro and was devastated when Don left because he knew my game and gave me my debut. As one of his boys, I wanted to play for him. Clough's appointment was a huge surprise and I had little to do with him. My main recollection was his arrival at the first training session when he took a quick look at a practice game then went to a five-a-side pitch for a kick-a-bout with his son, Nigel. It was bizarre behavior.

After that, the only other time I came across him was the odd afternoon when he wanted to do some shooting practice. "Come here young man, hit some crosses over," he'd say. I'd smash balls across goal and he'd try finishing them off into an empty net.

I didn't know what to make of Cloughie, he might have been the right manager to appoint because of what he'd achieved at Derby, but he was offered the Leeds job at the wrong time as he had so much disrespect for the club.

Jimmy Armfield's appointment by the Leeds board provided stability but any chance of a title defence had gone. United's senior players though were able to embark on a final crack at the European Cup. After comfortable wins against FZ Zurich and Ujpest Dosza in the opening rounds, Stewart slotted into the side when Harvey picked up a season ending injury. Letheren was on the bench as back up goalkeeper for the remainder of the Cup run.

Armfield was a calming influence from the madness of the opening weeks. Billy and the lads knew they'd be going their separate ways because it was an ageing team. This was their last shot at the 'big one' so they gathered themselves for a real push at the European Cup and put in some great performances.

I was on the bench from the quarterfinals against Anderlecht, which was a great experience. After our 3-0 first leg victory at a fog-bound Elland Road, we flew out for the return and the weather was atrocious. Anderlecht organised a brass band that had to walk across a muddy pitch, which was crazy. Then on the night, Billy scored the only goal so we now faced Barcelona in the semifinals.

Johann Cruyff was Barcelona's captain and arguably the best player in the world at the time. It was going to be a really tough test but being around the lads at this particular time was special because most of them had seen it all before. They could handle the biggest of occasions and over 50,000 roared us on in the first leg at Elland Road. The atmosphere was cracking and goals from Bremner and Clarke gave us a 2-1 win.

Barcelona did have an away goal but we fancied our chances to nick a goal at the Nou Camp because they'd be under enormous pressure from home fans to attack us. It was a massive game and a few of the lads popped into a little church inside the ground. I've no idea if any of them said a silent prayer but jogging out in front of 110,000 fans was incredible. The noise was deafening. We needed to silence the crowd, and Lorimer did just that when he gave us an early lead with a terrific strike that gave the keeper no chance, and it settled any nerves. When it came to striking a ball, Peter was incredible. I'd faced him many times in practice sessions and his strikes had been timed at 90 miles an hour. For any keeper to see him line up a shot was daunting. Striking a ball is about timing and connection, and Peter was a master at getting his head over the ball then striking it like a rocket.

Barcelona needed three goals and tried to intimidate us, but we had lads with experience who were not going to be denied, despite McQueen being sent off late on. The lads deservedly celebrated our 3-2 aggregate win after our 1-1 draw because it was a massive achievement knocking out Barcelona, however, Gordon was inconsolable because he'd miss the final.

Armfield rested players carrying injuries in the build up to the European Cup Final against Bayern Munich. With Stewart nursing a groin strain, United's boss handed Letheren a first start against high-flying Ipswich Town in the final home League match of the season. Bobby Robson was building an exciting team at Portman Road. Led by Mick Mills, Ipswich had knocked Leeds out of the FA Cup after a marathon quarterfinal that went to a third replay and would finish third in the League.

Leeds United v Ipswich Town, April 19th, 1975

Leeds United: Letheren, Reaney, Cherry, Bremner, McQueen, Hunter, Lorimer, Madeley, Yorath, Giles (Harris), Gray

Ipswich Town: Sivell, Burley, Mills, Talbot, Hunter, Beattie, Hamiton, Osborne, Johnson, Wymark, Lambert. Sub: Woods

It was great to get a first team outing, and after Wark tucked the ball past me early on, I had a good game, saving a couple of long-range efforts from Beattie. We got back into the game before half time when Cherry equalised, then Harris came on for his league debut and scored a late winner in front of the Kop. I still remind Carl he took the headlines from me and joked with Yorath afterwards that I'd never lost in a Leeds shirt, which must be a record! Whenever anyone asks me about my time at the club, I still pull out that statistic.

Leeds United's squad flew to Paris for the biggest game in their history when they hoped to become Champions of Europe for the first time.

Bayern Munich v Leeds United, May 28th, 1975

Bayern Munich: Maier, Andersson, Durnberger, Schwarzenbeck, Beckenbauer, Roth, Torstensson, Zobel, Muller, Hoeness, Kapellmann. Subs: Wunder, Weiss S, Rummenigge, Weiss G, Robl

Leeds United: Stewart, Reaney, Gray F, Bremner, Madeley, Hunter, Lorimer, Clarke, Jordan, Giles, Yorath. Subs: Gray E, Hampton, McKenzie, Cherry, Letheren

Letheren recalled:

Winning the European Cup had been Don's great ambition, and the lads really felt they had a shot going into the game at the Parc des Princes Stadium. My parents had tickets but I later found out they could not collect them at the stadium as police had cordoned off streets around the ground, so they watched the match in a nearby bar.

After our final preparations we had a police escort to the stadium. The atmosphere was tense but also exciting and the lads were ready. On the night we controlled the game for long spells and should have had a first half penalty when Beckenbaur clearly chopped down Clarke in the area.

After half time Lorimer had a goal disallowed when Bremner was harshly adjudged to be offside. At that moment I did think maybe it was not going to be our night. Bayern scored on the break twice but we didn't give up, and then there were horrendous scenes of hooliganism which was dreadful to witness on a heartbreaking night for the club.

The lads were devastated and our glitzy reception we had to attend was really flat. McQueen was a huge loss and I'm sure we'd have won if he had not been suspended because Gordon was commanding in the air and would have reveled in the big game atmosphere.

Over the years you cannot help but wonder how things would have turned out if refereeing decisions had gone our way, however, football is often a case of ifs, buts and maybes.

Letheren's remaining two seasons at Leeds were a frustrating period of his career as he didn't play again for the first team. He did come close to facing Manchester United at Elland Road in October 1975 when Harvey was sidelined, but it was not to be.

The lads used to joke that 'Jimmy's indecision was final' and my experience of this viewpoint came in the build up to the United match which left me feeling hugely disappointed. Billy told me the day before the game that Harvey was injured, so I was playing. Every player hopes for opportunities and often it comes because of an injury. That is the nature of sport, so I genuinely believed I'd play.

I rang my parents, who arranged to travel up, but when the team sheet went up my name was not on. Obviously I was gutted. It hadn't crossed my mind to check with Jimmy about the line-up, but someone must have told Billy or he would not have said anything to me.

When I spoke to Jimmy in his office and explained what Billy had said, his response was simply, "Bremner does not pick the team", that was it. Jimmy was a nice enough guy but I lost a lot of respect for him that day.

Fortunately there were brighter times behind the scenes for United's young keeper.

I'd played and followed rugby union from being a kid, so was well aware of the Welsh greats. Throughout the 1970s, Wales had legendary players including Gareth Edwards, Phil Bennett, JPR Williams and Gerald Davies who all played for the British Lions. During the Five Nations Championships, as it was then, the Leeds lads would bet on the Wales versus England match.

Wales were in their pomp and defeated England on a regular basis, yet the boys wanted to bet against me on England winning. I could not believe my luck because I'd give them six to nine points start and still win. It was like taking candy off a baby! I'd come in on a Monday morning, collect my winnings and earn a small fortune. In fact, I was making more money on Wales winning than playing football for Leeds.

Away from rugby bets there were personalities at the club. And one in particular had a novel way of earning extra cash.

> Duncan McKenzie was a hell of a boy and a real character. Although slightly built, Duncan bet the lads that he could jump over a mini. Well, Lorimer was straight in and soon there were wagers from loads of lads. When we put the secretary's mini in front of reception it was chucking down with rain. With the lads watching on, Duncan jogged towards the mini, flipped his legs up then straddled clean over the car. We could not believe what we had just witnessed. Duncan had a hell of a spring in him, but that was not the end of his talents because he also claimed to be able to throw a golf ball the length of a football pitch. Now I was a bit of a cricketer and could throw a cricket ball far but a golf ball was far harder. I was not convinced. Again lots of lads put down cash. Taking a short run up from behind a goal, Duncan sent the golf ball clear out of the ground. As with the mini, all we could do was look on in amazement. Duncan had cleaned up again!
>
> Away from party tricks, he was a terrific footballer and one of the game's entertainers alongside Rodney Marsh, Frank Worthington and Stan Bowles from that era. Whenever Duncan played, fans loved to watch him.

Revie's legendary squad had begun to break up as the 1976/77 season unfolded. Charlton was manager of Middlesborough, Giles player-manager at West Brom whilst Cooper, Bremner and Hunter were seeing their careers out away from Elland Road and Jones had retired through injury.

Armfield meanwhile had started to build his own team around new signings Tony Currie and Arthur Graham. Harvey and Stewart still shared the goalkeeping duties leaving Letheren no alternative but to move on. The coming seasons would see Letheren play for Chesterfield and Swansea City.

> Not getting a look in at Leeds affected my confidence but I'd also suffered with a couple of injuries. My muscles were still developing as an apprentice, so I struggled with goalkicking distances. It would take time to hit my peak strength. Syd's way of remedying this was to stand on the half way line at the Fullerton Park pitch while I fired goal kicks at him repeatedly. There was no proper warming up and I simply overdid it, so ended up damaging knee ligaments and was out for a

few months. Later I picked up a hairline fracture of a toe, but it was not picked up so I experienced shooting pains when kicking a ball, which took months to diagnose. But even allowing for these injuries, I was not close to breaking through to the first team so went out on loan, initially to Scunthorpe United for a month, which was extended to six months.

One of my earliest 'learning' encounters came against Crewe Alexandra when I came up against a wily old-fashioned centre forward called Wyn Davies, who made his name at Bolton Wanderers then Newcastle United. Wyn was a Welsh legend in his heyday and made life really tough for goalkeepers. During the match, he caught me with his studs then turned away when I came for a cross. I didn't want to show I'd been hurt but that incident taught me a big lesson because I learnt to stand my ground.

Further loan spells at Chelsea and Notts County made me a better pro and toughened me up, which I needed, but John Lukic, who had been an apprentice, was now ahead of me in Armfield's thoughts. It was obvious that I needed a fresh start and after a reserve match against Stoke City, Jimmy told me Chesterfield had made an acceptable offer to the club. I'd be guaranteed first team football, so it was an easy decision to join them in December 1977. Chesterfield paid £10,000, with a further payment of £10,000 if I was transferred on. Manager Arthur Cox was a taskmaster and taught me a lot in terms of my discipline.

Playing for Chesterfield turned out to be a good move before Swansea City signed me for £50,000 in September 1979. I enjoyed my spell at Swansea. I was part of their promotion team to the First Division but playing for John Toshack was not easy, especially when you had a lean spell. When Swansea signed Stewart from Leeds to replace me in goal it was time for another challenge.

On the international front, during Letheren's final season at Elland Road he represented Wales at U21 and U23 level. Bizarrley, Glan won his sole U23 cap, against Scotland, before playing for the U21s. The U23 clash at the Racecourse Ground, Wrexham on February 4th, 1976 also saw United's rising star, Carl Harris, make his Welsh debut in a 3-2 defeat.

Letheren played twice for the U21s, firstly in a goalless draw against England at Molineux, Wolverhampton before a 3-2 defeat to Scotland at Easter Road, Edinburgh on February 9th 1977. Like Letheren, United youngsters Byron Stevenson and Gwyn Thomas made U21 debuts against England. Stevenson also played against Scotland.

During the post-Leeds years, Glan was a member of the Welsh national squad for 13 international matches, including the last time Wales defeated England at Wembley in 1977.

England U21 v Wales U21, December 15th, 1976

Wales: Letheren (Leeds United), Bater (Bristol Rovers), Tibbott (Ipswich Town), Stevenson (Leeds United), Roberts (Wrexham, capt), Hughes (West Bromwich Albion), Sayer (Cardiff City), James (Swansea City), Thomas (Leeds United), Curtis (Swansea City), Evans (Bristol Rovers). Subs: Norman (Burnley), Evans (Norwich City)

England: Bradshaw (Blackburn Rovers), Keegan (Manchester City), Jones (Everton), Wilkins (Chelsea, capt), Sims (Leicester City), Futcher (Luton Town), King (Everton), Sunderland (Wolverhampton Wanderers), Swindlehurst (Crystal Palace), Talbot (Ipswich Town), Fairclough (Liverpool). Subs: Hoddle (Tottenham Hotspur), Barnes (Manchester City)

Mike Smith managed me in the U21s and U23s so knew my strengths. Playing against England and Scotland we came up against lots of top players including Glen Hoddle, Ray 'Butch' Wilkins, Willie Pettigrew and Paul Sturrock. I was at Chesterfield when Mike called me into the full squad as back up to Everton keeper Dai Davies. We had a number of First Division players including Toshack, John Mahoney, Leighton James, Brian Flynn, Alan Curtis and Terry Yorath.

During the Home Internationals I was on the bench when James scored a penalty in a 1-0 win against England at Wembley, which was a massive occasion for the squad, and no Welsh team has achieved that since. It would have been wonderful to get on for a few minutes in one of the European Championship qualifying campaign games when I was among the subs but it was not to be. At the time I was disappointed and it's still something I reflect on to this day. However, I travelled everywhere and was a part of it all.

After Swansea, Letheren continued his career at Oxford City, Scarborough and Bangor City, with whom he played against Northwich Victoria in the 1984 FA Trophy Final at Wembley. Bangor lost the replay at Stoke City's Victoria Ground.

Following a 20-year career, Letheren ended his playing days at the club where everything started, Llanelli FC, in the Welsh Premier League.

Retiring from the game in 1985, Glan and his wife Ann, from Rothwell, Leeds, brought up their sons, Callum and Kyle, in Llanelli. Now doting grandparents to grandson Mason, dad Kyle has continued the Letheren goalkeeping legacy.

> Kyle played cricket at schoolboy level before serving his football apprenticeship with Swansea City. He made an appearance for Barnsley and was a substitute at Plymouth then had two great seasons with Kilmarnock and Dundee. He's also played for the Welsh U21 team and been in the Welsh squad. Watching Kyle play is far worse than playing because I know what he has to deal with and there is no hiding place for a goalkeeper and no second chances.

After two decades as a player, Glan gained his UEFA pro-licence and has stayed in the game. The Football Association of Wales, Swansea City, Leicester City and Exeter City have all benefited from his coaching skills. He has also worked with Leeds United and Manchester United as Chief Scout for Wales. Glan's most recent venture was setting up Top Catch Goalkeeping in 2010. Apart from running coaching clinics in Australia, Haiti, St Kitts & Nevis, St Lucia and St Vincent, Glan has covered various tournaments to spot potential players, including the U20 World Cup in New Zealand and he also travels to America every year searching for future stars.

> If lads are good enough we arrange for them to come over for trials, and seeing them make it is the closest you get to that feeling of playing. I'm not tied to any club now, which is the way I like it, and presently we have players on trial at Manchester United and Fulham.

Away from coaching commitments, an annual 'Glan Letheren dinner' helps young sports stars in Llanelli reach their potential. Glan started the fundraising initiative 21 years ago.

> There are lots of kids aged eight to 14 whose parents can't provide the funds required for them to reach their sporting goals. The local press puts in nominations and we select the best one. We offer funding for coaching, transport, travel and so on. Billy Bremner spoke at our first dinner and was absolutely brilliant. Since then we've had lots of great speakers including Jack Charlton, Kevin Keegan, Paul Merson, Bryan Robson, Barry Fry, Duncan McKenzie and Ray Parlour.
> Terry Yorath is great at question and answer sessions because,

apart from his time at Leeds, Tottenham, Coventry and Wales, he can chat about Ryan Giggs, Gareth Bale, Gary Speed and other Welsh stars he managed, so it's a great mix of topics.

Sponsors always help make it a good night but the main thing is we raise a lot of funds. Last year we booked Keegan and it sold out in 10 days. Kevin's drawing power is incredible. We had over 300 people and the venue was choc-a-block. We are not a big town but the gala event always sells out. So far we have raised over £50,000 and it's been a big hit.

In terms of Leeds United's history, the 1973/74 campaign was the first time five goalkeepers played in competitive games. And the European venture is still the only time four Leeds keepers played in a campaign. Sprake, Harvey and Shaw saw action but the youngest, Letheren, won the main plaudits.

Playing for one of the biggest clubs around cannot be taken away from me, although I'd have liked more games than the ones against Hibernian and Ipswich Town. But circumstances play a massive part in football; one moment you can feel on top of the world then everything can suddenly change. If Don had stayed, I'm sure he'd have handed me opportunities and got the best out of me. Don looked for signs of improvement, which I showed, but then the upheaval started. His departure was disastrous because I had to start again. Everything turned on its head and there was so much upheaval.

Things were not the same again when Don left. Training was not as enjoyable and I began to feel that I could not hack it. Although I got on with the lads, there was very little support on the goalkeeping front. The keepers rarely spoke about techniques and there was certainly no 'keepers union'. Harvey, in particular, was a difficult character to fathom. I'd often go in goal for shooting practice, and I remember before I'd played in the first team saving everything fired at me in one session. I joked to him that he'd better watch out but Harvey thought I was trying to make him look foolish. I thought to myself, are you serious, I was having a laugh? Overall though I have great memories.

I was a good trainer and had the ability but, for whatever reason, never fulfilled my potential at Leeds. Should I have left when Chesterfield came in? There were no agents then, so when everything was happening off the field, I had to make my own decisions and accept the direction that took me.

Glan might have only played a couple of matches, but still has a memento from his time at the club.

Each season we used to be in squad pictures at the start of a new campaign, which was great for the young lads because you thought you'd made it. The Leeds squad lining up before the European Cup Final is on a wall at home and rekindles great memories. It was an important time in my life and both my sons follow the club, which I'm pleased about. I still look out for Leeds' results and hopefully they will soon be back in the Premier League.

Leeds United Roll of Honour 1961 to 1974

Football League First Division - 1968/69, 1973/74

Football League Second Division - 1963/64

FA Cup - 1971/72

League Cup - 1967/68

Inter-Cities Fairs Cup - 1967/68

Charity Shield - 1969/70

Football League First Division runners up - 1964/65, 1965/66, 1969/70, 1970/71, 1971/72

FA Cup runners up - 1964/65, 1969/70, 1972/73

European Cup Winners Cup runners up - 1972/73

Inter-Cities Fairs Cup runners up - 1966/67

Football League First Division: Top 4 - 1964/65 to 1973/74

FA Cup semifinalists - 1966/67, 1967/68

European Cup semifinalists - 1969/70

Inter-Cities Fairs Cup semifinalists - 1965/66

Player Records

A = Appearances

S = Substitute Appearances

G = Goals

Peter McConnell

	League			FA Cup			League Cup			Europe			Other		
	A	S	G	A	S	G	A	S	G	A	S	G	A	S	G
60/61	9		1												
61/62	23		3	2			3		1						
Total	32	0	4	2	0	0	3	0	1	0	0	0	0	0	0

McConnell other clubs: Carlisle United, Bradford City

John Hawksby

	League			FA Cup			League Cup			Europe			Other		
	A	S	G	A	S	G	A	S	G	A	S	G	A	S	G
60/61	7														
61/62	25						4								
62/63	5						2								
63/64				1			1								
Total	37	0	0	1	0	0	7	0	0	0	0	0	0	0	0

Hawksby other clubs: Lincoln City, York City, Kings Lynn, Bedford Town, Kettering Town, Dunstable Town, Stevenage Borough, Rushden Town, Desborough Town

Ian Lawson

	League			FA Cup			League Cup			Europe			Other		
	A	S	G	A	S	G	A	S	G	A	S	G	A	S	G
61/62	11		1												
62/63	6		5				2								
63/64	24		11	3		1	2		3						
64/65	3														
Total	44	0	17	3	0	1	4	0	3	0	0	0	0	0	0

Lawson other clubs: Burnley, Crystal Palace, Port Vale, Barnsley

Rod Johnson

	League			FA Cup			League Cup			Europe			Other		
	A	S	G	A	S	G	A	S	G	A	S	G	A	S	G
62/63	4		1				2								
63/64															
64/65	9		3	1		1	1								
65/66	2	3					2		1						
66/67	3														
67/68		1					1	1							
Total	18	4	4	1	0	1	6	1	1	0	0	0	0	0	0

Johnson other clubs: Doncaster Rovers, Rotherham United, Bradford City, Chicago Sting (USA), Gainsborough Trinity

Barrie Wright

	League			FA Cup			League Cup			Europe			Other		
	A	S	G	A	S	G	A	S	G	A	S	G	A	S	G
62/63	3														
63/64	2														
64/65							2								
65/66							1								
Total	5	0	0	0	0	0	3	0	0	0	0	0	0	0	0

Wright other clubs: New York Generals (USA), Brighton & Hove Albion, Hartlepool United (loan), Bradford Park Avenue, Gainsborough Trinity, Thackley FC

Nigel Davey

	League			FA Cup			League Cup			Europe			Other		
	A	S	G	A	S	G	A	S	G	A	S	G	A	S	G
65/66							1								
66/67															
67/68	2														
68/69															
69/70	5														
70/71	6	1		1						3	1				
71/72							1						1		
72/73															
73/74											1				
Total	13	1	0	1	0	0	2	0	0	3	2	0	1	0	0

Davey other clubs: Rotherham United

Dennis Hawkins

	League			FA Cup			League Cup			Europe			Other		
	A	S	G	A	S	G	A	S	G	A	S	G	A	S	G
65/66							1								
66/67	1														
67/68	1						1								
Total	2	0	0	0	0	0	2	0	0	0	0	0	0	0	0

Hawkins other clubs: Shrewsbury Town, Chester (loan), Workington Town (loan), Waterford (loan), Newport County, Telford United, Nuneaton Borough, York City

Sean O'Neill

	League			FA Cup			League Cup			Europe			Other		
	A	S	G	A	S	G	A	S	G	A	S	G	A	S	G
73/74							1			2					
Total	0	0	0	0	0	0	0	1	0	0	2	0	0	0	0

O'Neil other clubs: Chesterfield

Chris Galvin

	League			FA Cup			League Cup			Europe			Other		
	A	S	G	A	S	G	A	S	G	A	S	G	A	S	G
69/70	3										1				
70/71					1						1				
71/72	2	1			1					2		1	1		
72/73	1						1			1					
Total	6	1	0	0	2	0	1	0	0	3	2	1	1	0	0

Galvin other clubs: Hull City, York City (loan), Stockport County, Tsuen Wan (Hong Kong)

Roy Ellam

	League			FA Cup			League Cup			Europe			Other		
	A	S	G	A	S	G	A	S	G	A	S	G	A	S	G
72/73	6	1					1			2					
73/74	3	1		2			1			4					
Total	9	2	0	2	0	0	2	0	0	6	0	0	0	0	0

Ellam other clubs: Bradford City, Huddersfield Town, Philadelphia Atoms (USA), Mossley FC, Washington Diplomats (USA), Gainsborough Trinity

Glan Letheren

	League			FA Cup			League Cup			Europe			Other		
	A	S	G	A	S	G	A	S	G	A	S	G	A	S	G
73/74											1				
Total	0	0	0	0	0	0	0	0	0	0	1	0	0	0	0

Letheren other clubs: Llanelli, Scunthorpe United (loan), Chelsea (loan), Notts County (loan), Chesterfield, Swansea City, Oxford City, Scarborough, Bangor City

Bibliography

Revie's Boys: The 75 Players under Don Revie at Leeds United by David Saffer (Vertical)

'and we've had our ups and downs' 100 Years: Leeds United and Leeds City 1905-2005 by David Saffer & Gary Shepherd (Vertical)

Bobby Collins: The Wee Barra by David Saffer (Tempus)

Leeds Legends by David Saffer (Tempus)

Leeds United: The Complete Record by Martin Jarred & Malcolm Macdonald (Breedon)

Leeds United Cup Book 1920-1991 by Martin Jarred & Malcolm Macdonald (Breedon)

Leeds United: The European Record by Martin Jarred & Malcolm Macdonald (Breedon)

The Who's Who of Leeds United by Martin Jarred & Malcolm Macdonald (Breedon)

Leeds United: Player By Player by Andrew Mourant (Guiness)

Leeds United: The Official History of the Club, Don Warters (Wensum Books)

Don Revie: Portrait of a Footballing Enigma by Andrew Mourant (Mainstream)

Revie: Revered And Reviled by Richard Sutcliffe (Great Northern Books)

You Get Nowt for Being Second by Billy Bremner (Souvenir Press)

Nice One Skip: From Elland Road to Brunton Park by Peter McConnell (Print Graphic)

NASL: A Complete Record of the North American Soccer League by Colin Jose (Breedon)

Pele: My Life and the Beautiful Game by Pele with Robert L. Fish

About the Author

David Saffer left a career in the computer industry to become a full time author and journalist in 2002. His writing exploits began five years earlier when impulsively he penned a book on Leeds United winning the FA Cup for the only time in the Centenary Final of 1972. And two decades later he has now written 24 sports-related books, *Revie's unsung Heroes* being his latest offering. Among his other publications are authorised biographies of Allan 'Sniffer' Clarke, Bobby Collins and Duncan McKenzie, a number of club histories, and an account through player memories of FA Cup Finals (1953-69).

Married to Deborah, with three children and a grandson, life is never dull for the Leeds-born writer. Now based in a sleepy Hertfordshire village, his freelance work includes creative writing courses whilst teaching English as a foreign language is an imminent project. But sport is David's great passion with nowadays rugby union and rugby league an on-going feature of his endeavours in 'The Smoke'.